PICTURES OF THE EARLY CHURCH

Welcome to the New Testament

NICHOLAS KING

**kevin
mayhew**

kevin
mayhew

First published in Great Britain in 2016 by Kevin Mayhew Ltd
Buxhall, Stowmarket, Suffolk IP14 3BW
Tel: +44 (0) 1449 737978 Fax: +44 (0) 1449 737834
E-mail: info@kevinmayhewltd.com

www.kevinmayhew.com

9 8 7 6 5 4 3 2 1 0

ISBN 978 1 84867 845 3
Catalogue No. 1501521

Cover design by Rob Mortonson
© Image used under licence from Shutterstock Inc.
Edited by Nicki Copeland
Typeset by Angela Selfe

Printed and bound in Great Britain

Contents

For my Jesuit brethren
at Xavier House, in Brighton MA,
with gratitude.

About the author

Nicholas King SJ is a Jesuit Priest who taught for many years in South Africa, and then at Oxford University. After a sabbatical year as a Visiting Professor at the School of Theology and Ministry at Boston College, he is now Academic Director of Theology at St Mary's University, Twickenham.

In 2014 Kevin Mayhew published his translation of the entire Greek Bible; and in the same year Nicholas also produced *The Helplessness of God* (1501439), on how governance is done in the Bible. He is currently working on *The Scandal of Christian Disunion – a biblical approach.*

Introduction

This book has its origin in a request from Now You Know Media, in the spring of 2015, to record 36 talks on the New Testament. It also springs from the increasing awareness that there are people 'out there' who show a real thirst for reading Scripture and who know almost nothing about the New Testament. It seemed good therefore to combine these two facts and offer a good reason why you (the person who has just picked up this book) should read it. What can we offer you?

One thing we can offer is a series of pictures of the early Church (hence the title of the book). The New Testament represents 27 very different attempts to put on paper the mystery of Jesus, which allow us a number of glimpses into the way Christians in that first century tried to live out that mystery. As you read, try to see the very different pictures of the Church that emerge from the New Testament.

That, of course, raises an important question:

What is the New Testament?

Well, it sounds and looks like a book, but you will do better to think of it as a library containing just 27 texts. Just in case it has slipped your mind, we shall do well to rehearse what those texts are. To start with, there are 13 letters apparently written by Paul (though, as you will see, these are not letters in the sense in which we normally understand the term).

Then there are five Gospels. What is a Gospel? To that question there is a simple answer: it is a narrative of the life and ministry, death and resurrection of the Galilean rabbi, Jesus of Nazareth. But you thought, I imagine, that there were only four. And of course you are right: in the order in which they were probably written we have Mark, Matthew, Luke and John. But there is another narrative, which in many ways parallels these four Gospels: the story of how the life of Jesus continued in the group of followers he left behind. We call it 'Acts of the Apostles', though only two of these apostles, Peter and Paul, really seize our attention. It is the Gospel of the early Church.

Then there are some more 'letters'; the ones we call 2 John and 3 John are probably the ones that people in the ancient world would most readily have recognised as 'letters'. 1 John, which comes before them in your New Testament, is not really a letter but a beautiful meditation on the place of love in the Christian life. (At this point you may find yourself saying, 'Oh! Not that old guff about love!' If that is your reaction, please sit down and read slowly and reflectively through that extraordinary text.) There are two letters attributed to Peter, the leader of the early Church; there is one attributed to James, Jesus' brother, and one to Jude, which hardly anyone ever reads (and, again, perhaps none of these four are really 'letters' in the sense in which you and I understand the word).

There is also one extraordinary piece of theological thinking, which endeavours to help its hearers work their way through the question of how to talk about Jesus: that is the letter to the Hebrews.

Finally, there is the Book of Revelation, as it is called from the Latin, or Apocalypse, as they know it in Greek. (Both of these terms refer to a 'lifting of the veil' or an 'uncovering' of the mystery of what God is doing.) This is a book that terrifies the wits out of some people, and towards the end of this book I shall be talking about it in more detail and inviting you to read it.

Why do we have just these 27 documents? The chances are that you have heard of other 'Gospels': the Gospel of Thomas, for example, or the Gospel of Mary, or of Peter or Jude, and the Protevangelium of James. Very often you will read the overheated outpourings of excited journalists suggesting that the Church has concealed these texts from ordinary people in order to keep our darkest secrets carefully hidden. Well, writing such allegations is great fun, and they probably make their authors a great deal of money, but they are not to be taken seriously. You can find all these apocryphal gospels translated into English and readily available for you to read. I suggest you spend some time with them, and I'm prepared to bet that you will find them a little tedious, though in places they show a rather overdone imagination, which relieves the boredom. But I guarantee that you will not find yourself clapping your hands to your brow and saying, 'Of course! The Church has been keeping this from me, all these years.' Indeed, I suspect that if you move from these texts to the four Gospels in your New Testament and read them through, you will find yourself admiring the Church's sobriety in selecting just these four.

One thing we need to know is that the Church did not immediately get down to the business of writing; Jesus himself does not seem to have written anything, though he clearly said a great deal. The only evidence of him actually writing is the story that you will find at the beginning of chapter 8 of John's Gospel, though it does not belong there – the lovely anecdote of the 'Woman Caught in Adultery'. When this unfortunate lady is brought before Jesus, just to check that it is all right for them to stone her as the Law says, we are told that he (twice) 'stooped down and wrote on the earth', but that was a delaying tactic, and tells us nothing about his levels of literacy.

By and large, those first Christians followed Jesus' example. It is a safe guess that not many of them could read and write, and for the most part, as they rushed around that Mediterranean world, they spread the message by talking rather than writing. And in any case, many of them thought that Jesus had indicated that the world was going to end quite soon, so what would be the point of writing books?

However, the world did not end, and Jesus' expected return did not take place, but the people of God lost none of their enthusiasm for Jesus' message. Then, of course, the first witnesses started to die off. The apostle James was martyred by Herod in AD 42, and Peter probably in the aftermath of the Great Fire of Rome in 64. After that, the question arose of how to pass on the message; and perhaps some people felt the need to have something in their hands to give to those who were instructing new converts. And so the author whom we know as 'Mark' put down on paper, or rather dictated onto papyrus, an account of Jesus' life. It was not quite as you or I would do it, but the shape of what he did was good enough to be used as a basis by Luke and Matthew for their Gospels. The author of John's Gospel may also have known Mark and the other two, but he produced something rather different. But they all tell the same basic story, of Jesus from his baptism to his death and the emptiness of his tomb on that momentous Sunday morning. It is recognisably the same story and, more importantly, it is recognisably the same person whom we encounter as we listen to all four of these Gospels.

Now these Gospels were very likely written to particular communities in particular circumstances (although it must be said that this statement, like almost anything else you might wish to say as a firm conclusion of biblical scholarship, is firmly contested by at least some experts in the field). As you read them, and as you notice the differences between them, simply ask yourself, what kind of a group was *this* Gospel written for?

And that, of course, raises the important question of why there are four of them. Think back to your grandmother's funeral, unless that lady is still healthily among us. What happens at the funeral of someone we love is that, if the mood is right, people get together and tell stories about her. Many of those stories will be true; and all of them will fill out the picture of the grandmother or great-great aunt or former teacher, or whoever it was we are remembering. And the rich vein of stories brings the dead person powerfully back to mind.

Now here is a striking thing: from almost as early as we can tell, there have been four Gospels. And the idea of reducing the four to one, doubtless in the interests of greater efficiency or 'getting back to the original', goes back at least to the second century. Irenaeus in that century said that we need four Gospels because there are four winds and four points of the compass. The Church has always insisted on keeping all four and has, in my view, shown immense wisdom in doing so, precisely because of all their differences and their unique angles on the mystery of Jesus.

But before these narratives appeared (and I hope that you are going to read them all as you follow this book), Christians had done some writing of a different sort. Or rather, primarily one Christian, called Paul. Just to clarify the question of what to call him, we learn from Acts that he had the Jewish name of 'Saul', and he only seems to have taken on the name by which we know him best after some time as a member of the Christian Church. This fiery character, who claimed to have met Jesus after Jesus' death and fell head over heels in love with him, spent the rest of his life walking and sailing round the world, telling people about Jesus. When anyone took any notice, he would stay a while in that place – normally a largish Greek city – and organise the group of believers so that its enthusiasm would not evaporate for lack of structure. And once he had moved on (and Paul was always moving on, desperate to tell other people about his beloved Jesus), he kept in touch by post (there was no other way of doing it) and dealt with problems as they arose. That is the source of the seven (or thirteen) Pauline letters that the tradition has handed down to us.

There is one all-important event that we need to bear in mind when we think about the origins of the New Testament, namely the terrible fact of the destruction of Jerusalem and of its beloved Temple. That was a traumatic moment; our Jewish brothers and sisters still mourn for what happened in AD 70, when the Romans took terrible revenge on the Jewish nationalists who had tried to reassert Israel's independence after far too many years (more than a century by that time) of Roman occupation.

And it was not just traumatic for the Jews; or rather, we should say that among the Jewish groups who found it traumatic was that group of Jesus people we now call 'Christians', meaning those Jews who were convinced that God's Messiah had come, and that after he had been crucified by the Romans, God had raised him from the dead, proving that Jesus was after all God's Messiah, or 'Christ' (both words mean 'Anointed One', in Hebrew and Greek respectively). So that group started to be called, possibly originally by their enemies, 'Christians', a title they still bear proudly today.

And so as one group of Jews coped with the Temple's terrible destruction by replacing it with what they called *Mishnah*, the 'repetition of the Law', this other group, the Jesus-group or 'Christians', replaced the Temple with the resurrected person of Christ. That made enormous sense to them. For AD 70 was a terrible moment: the Temple that had been so horrifically destroyed was thought to have been God's gift, which could therefore never be brought low. It had been rebuilt after a previous destruction, back in the sixth century BC, and then extravagantly refurbished and enormously expanded by Herod the Great towards the end of the first century, with beautiful marble fronts that were said to reflect the rays of the setting sun as far away as the distant Mediterranean Sea. It was a place of unimaginable holiness; the religious and political centre of the nation. So the Jesus-group, increasingly known as 'Christians', reflected on the power of the great God who had done the unimaginable and raised Jesus from the dead, and they came to realise that Jesus himself was the new Temple, 'not made by hands' the phrase that they often used. That tragedy, and the meaning that God brought out of it, is there between the lines of our New Testament.

What I propose to do in this book is to look at nearly all of the 27 documents that make up our New Testament library, with one exception, which I will talk about in a moment. In addition, I am going to talk about other and wider issues, such as the question of 'inspiration' and whether we can trust the New Testament, and whether we still need the Old Testament if we have the New Testament. There will also be a chapter on the absolutely central issue of the Resurrection of Jesus, without which we should not have a New Testament at all.

The one exception to which I have just referred is the letter of Jude, which you will find towards the end of your New Testament (and I hope you have one, and that it is open – you will need it to accompany this book), between 3 John and the Apocalypse (or Revelation). Look it up, read it, and then ask yourself two questions. First, why was this letter included in the New Testament? Second, why is it not very often read? It is only fair to warn you that we shall not attempt to answer these questions in the course of the book. Your challenge is to find an answer for yourself!

One last question may occur to you, and you will often hear it raised in our secular age. The question is this: surely the New Testament is a prejudiced witness, so how can we really believe what it is telling us? Are there any outside sources that we can consult?

Well, yes, there are, as a matter of fact, but I don't advise you to put too much weight on them. Certainly we have witnesses to the Jesus story who are not Christians. For example, what we call the 'rabbinic authors' – those great people who made it possible for our great mother religion of Judaism to survive, after the Temple's destruction, down into the present day – know about Jesus. They know he was executed, though they tend to say it was for 'witchcraft', which is, when you think about it, a kind of confirmation of the gospel claim that Jesus worked miracles.

Then there is another Jewish writer, Titus Flavius Josephus, who, in his book *The Antiquities of the Jews*, written in the last decade of the first century AD, mentions Jesus. He is a fascinating character, profoundly Jewish, though he increasingly sided with Rome, and he knew Judaism well. He fought against the Romans in the first Jewish War (66-70), at least until he saw which way things were going; then he went over to the Roman side, and wrote his version of how that War had gone. This makes him, of course, a very good witness, though not always an unprejudiced one. In *The Antiquities*, which he wrote some 20 or 30 years later to persuade Romans of the civilised nature of their erstwhile Jewish opponents, he twice mentions Jesus. In the first place, he wrote something, later corrupted by Christian interpolation, that originally seems to have gone something like this: 'Jesus the Messiah was a wise teacher who was crucified by Pilate.' Later, there is a reference to the execution of James, 'the brother of Jesus, who was called Christ'. So he clearly knew about Jesus, and along with the rabbinic writings is another Jewish source for the existence of Jesus, and for his death under Pontius Pilate.

But there were others, from the imperial power of Rome and its literate and competent historians. The distinguished (if not unprejudiced) Roman historian Suetonius certainly knew about Christians, and he also knew that the unbalanced emperor Gaius (or Caligula – 'Little Boot') had expelled the Jews from Rome for causing trouble, with someone called 'Chrestus', presumably 'Christ', as an *agent provocateur*. Suetonius thought Christianity was what he called a *superstitio*, which is a slightly damaging word for 'religion'; and although he did not have much regard for the Emperor Nero, on the whole he thought that when Nero executed Christians after the Great Fire of Rome in AD 64, they had it coming to them.

Then there is Tacitus. Tacitus is another upper class Roman, roughly contemporary with Suetonius, and a friend of Pliny, who also knew about Christians and did not have much good to say about them. In his *Annals*, a splendidly written account of the history of Rome from Tiberius to Nero, Tacitus mentions the execution of Jesus by Pontius Pilate under Tiberius. Naturally, not all scholars agree (you will find they never do in this field), but the consensus is that Tacitus got it right, and confirms what we find in the Gospels about Jesus' death.

So there you have it, some fairly solid non-Christian evidence of the existence of Jesus and of his death by crucifixion during the reign of Tiberius. End of story, you might think. Well, no, actually. You see, not every scholar agrees that these references are authentic, and some argue that Christian scribes have interpolated the texts.

That means we are driven back to the Gospels. Is that a bad thing? Not really, for with the four Gospels we actually have more information about Jesus than we have about his contemporary the Emperor Tiberius. Now obviously you could argue that the evidence is prejudiced, in the sense that each of the Gospel writers is, in their different way, devoted to Jesus. Even so, there is enough there, and enough difference of angle, for us to be able to get close to the facts about Jesus, and to form a recognisable picture of him.

That is not the whole story, however, for I want this book to offer you a challenge. Read the whole of the New Testament, and ask yourself this question (I can't give you the answer; only you can do this): does my reading of this library of 27 texts bring me any closer to recognising this strange character, the Galilean rabbi called 'Jesus of Nazareth'? And, if so, do I feel in any way drawn to give my life over to that man?

That, or something like that, is what I hope this book might do for you. But in all events I hope you will enjoy it. I shall not try in this book to say everything that could be said about our New Testament, only to encourage you to open its pages.

One final note: Bible quotations are my own translation (although they may not necessarily coincide with what you will find in my published translation[1]). Allow the different variations to give you a feel of the richness of the text.

Questions

1. What do you think the New Testament is for?

2. Do you think the New Testament is 'true'?

3. If we have a New Testament, does that mean we don't really need an Old Testament?

4. Does the New Testament provide us with 'pictures of the early Church'?

---

1. Published by Kevin Mayhew, 2013.

CHAPTER 1

Starting with Paul (because he came first): the letter to the Galatians

There are two reasons why we always tend to think of the Gospels coming first:

- They come first in the New Testament.
- The life of Jesus logically comes prior to later reflections on the implications of that life.

However, the first person we know of as having put down on paper the implications of Jesus' message was the prickly, passionate and powerful personality, head over heels in love with Jesus, whom we know as Saul or Paul, from Tarsus, in what is today South Central Turkey, a little more than ten miles from the sea.

We need, however, to offer a word of warning about that phrase, 'the implications of Jesus' life'. You are not to think of Paul as sitting in an office or a library, thinking his way in a leisurely manner through difficult theological questions. For Paul was always responding, often in a hurry, to a crisis here or there in one or other of his churches. His letters therefore are not to be seen as carefully worked out treatises, balanced against what he says elsewhere; rather he is always talking about *this particular situation*, in Thessalonica or Corinth, for example, and dictating a response in haste.

And that word 'dictating' is another warning. Paul could certainly read, and he also had the related skill of being able to make intelligible marks on a page, but he had to use a professional scribe. On one occasion, in the very important letter to the Romans, we know the name of this scribe. In Romans 16:22 Tertius, with some courage, puts his head above the parapet. Occasionally Paul grabs the pen, as at Galatians 6:11 where he laughs at his own inability to write small letters; and compare 1 Corinthians 16:21; Colossians 4:18; 2 Thessalonians 3:17; Philemon 19. Imagine him striding up and down and pouring the stuff out, possibly in the limited space allowed by a tent-maker's shop (see Acts 18:3).

So that is Paul. Now – what about Galatians? It seems to come early in the list of Paul's letters; some scholars think it may have been first, though most put 1 Thessalonians as the first of his surviving letters. I shall be looking at that one in the next chapter. Why Galatians at this point in our investigation? Simply because it is so explosive!

It may be good to explain the structure of letters in the ancient world, which is largely borne out in those literary letters that survive (by Cicero, for example) and in the enormous number of papyrus letters which have survived in the Egyptian sands, in the rubbish dumps to which they were despatched, thanks to the dry climate in those parts. Not all the papyri have yet been transcribed, but they show the following general pattern.

They begin, unlike our letters, with the name of the author (so you are not allowed to accuse Paul of arrogance when the first word of his letters is 'Paul'!). This is followed by greetings to the audience, then thanksgiving for their good qualities or whatever. Next comes what you might call the 'main body' of the letter, and it ends with the final salutations.

Paul makes use of this basic structure and develops it in a way that admirably fits his purpose. In particular he builds up what I have called the 'main body'; good examples of this, and much longer than a standard letter in the ancient world, would be the section of argumentation in Romans 1–15 or the relevant portions of 1 Corinthians.

The only exceptions to this pattern are Galatians and 2 Corinthians, where Paul is so cross with his audience that he does not offer any thanks for their good qualities.

To make this point, look at Galatians 1:6, where we hear him roar, 'I'm **astonished** that you are so quickly transferring from the one who called you in the grace of Christ, and have gone to another gospel'. Then read 3:1-5, which is a series of angry questions: 'You stupid Galatians – who has bewitched you?' 'Are you so stupid? Starting with the Spirit – are you ending up with the flesh?' 'The one who gave you a generous supply of the Spirit and who performed miracles among you – was it because of doing what the Law says, or was it because you listened obediently?'

So that is the real and undisguised Paul. We should be grateful to those who annoyed him, because it is only when he is cross that he indulges in autobiography, which otherwise he rather avoids. For another example of Paul's telling his own story, look at 2 Corinthians 11:9–12:13, about his sufferings on the mission, *and* his mystical experiences in the 'third heaven' (especially 2 Corinthians 12:2-4). Now why is he so cross? In both cases, Paul gives us the reason: his correspondents have been playing with what he calls 'another gospel' (2 Corinthians 11:4; Galatians 1:6), and Paul simply will not have that.

In this chapter we are looking at Galatians, so let me just concentrate on the passage from this letter: Galatians 1:10–2:14. I suggest you have it open in front of you, and check what I am saying. We need to know that Paul is trying to prove to them that his gospel came from God and Jesus Christ, not from human beings (1:1, 10-12). This is what he tells us:

First, Paul starts with the proud claim that he is 'a slave of Christ' (1:10; compare Romans 1:1 and Philippians 1:1 for the same proud claim). Secondly, he insists that this is a gospel message from God and from Jesus Christ. Thirdly, Paul remains a convinced Jew, who persecuted God's Church (1:13; remember that Paul was always a Jew, to the end of his life). Fourthly, he is convinced that in him God chose to reveal his Son (1:15-16), and also that God gave him the job of preaching to non-Jews (1:16). Next he tells us that he spent some time in Arabia (1:17); it is hard to be sure where this might be, but a possibility is that it might be the Nabatean kingdom that was centred on the lovely city of Petra. The main reason for thinking this, to be honest, is that Paul, like Luke, was a city boy rather than a Galilean peasant, and in the vast and largely desert area that was known as 'Arabia' at that time, Petra best meets the criteria for a likely place for him to surface.

After that, we gather, he went back to Damascus (1:17) where, according to Acts 9:3-22, he had originally been converted and started preaching that Jesus was indeed the Son of God. Then, after three years, he says, he went up to Jerusalem (1:18; we may reflect that he took his time about it). At that point, he talked to Kephas, which is the Aramaic for 'Peter' or 'Rock', for a fortnight (and would not one have loved to be a fly on the wall?) and then to 'James the brother of the Lord'.

After that, he says, he 'went into the regions of Syria', perhaps Antioch, where he would later spend a good deal of time, and Cilicia, possibly his native Tarsus (1:21). At that point, we gather (1:22), the Judean churches didn't know him by sight, so presumably he had kept his head down.

Then, after 14 years (2:1, although it is hard to be sure when that period started) he went back to Jerusalem with his valued co-workers, Barnabas and Titus (both of whom are mentioned in Acts). The purpose of this meeting (which may or may not have been the one referred to in Acts 15) was to check out Paul's gospel (2:2). This was in some way connected with a crisis about circumcision, for Paul makes the point (2:3) that Titus was not compelled to be circumcised. One of the issues in the letter to the Galatians is that some people had been insisting that you could not be a follower of Jesus unless you had been circumcised (5:3, 6; 6:12, 13, 15, 16). But we have to admit that they will have known the situation far better than we do.

After that (2:6, 9) we learn that he does not have much time for the 'so-called pillars [of the Church]'; but he is well aware that he needs their recognition: you can hear the note of pride, or possibly relief, when he tells the Galatians that James and Kephas and John 'gave me and Barnabas the right hand of solidarity:

we were to go to the Gentiles and they to the Jews' (2:9). And there is another matter, that they 'wanted us to look after the poor' (2:10); and Paul sharply points out his enthusiasm for that project (2:10; compare 1 Corinthians 16:1).

At some later point, there was a crisis with Kephas at Antioch; it seems (2:11) that Paul confronted him face to face for hypocrisy: for at the beginning he had been eating with Gentiles, but when people came from James he retreated and set himself apart (2:12). Even Barnabas, with whom Paul would later have a disagreement (Acts 15:36-39) fell into the trap. 'How come you're forcing Gentiles to play the Jew?' Now it must be said that this reference to 'play the Jew' (in Greek the word is *Judaise*) sounds offensive to our ears – but we must remember that *Paul was always a Jew.*

Do you see how Paul's annoyance has him spilling the beans? So why is he so annoyed? As he said to both the Galatians and the Corinthians, it was a question of getting the gospel wrong. There is another way to put it. For Paul, Galatians is about *freedom*: see 5:1; 2:4: 'spy out our freedom . . . in order to enslave us'. Paul, as we have seen, is a slave only to Jesus Christ.

That is why Paul is so cross; at times the emotion runs so high that his argument is not altogether clear. At other times he uses language that he might later have regretted; for example at 5:12 he hopes that those who are disturbing the Galatians about the need for circumcision 'might castrate themselves'.

There is also some quite dense argumentation, which you may perhaps find difficult to follow: for example, what he says in chapter 3 about the Law and the curse, or in chapter 4 about Abraham's wives and what they stand for. Read them slowly and carefully.

If you really want to get into the heart of this letter and to be captivated by Paul's genius, have a look at the following passages and understand why he still exercises such a hold on us today:

- 2:20: 'It is no longer I that live; it is Christ that lives in me.'

- 3:27, 28: 'all of you who have been baptised into Christ have put on Christ. There is no such thing as "Jew or Greek", no such thing as "slave or free", no such thing as "male or female".' So all human categories of race, religion, gender and class are artificial and not to be taken seriously.

- 4:19, where Paul compares himself as a mother to the Galatians.

- Or 5:16-26, when he explains to the Galatians what the gospel offers. He contrasts the 'works' of the flesh against the 'fruits of the Spirit'. I'll leave you to read for yourselves the works of the flesh; but listen to the beautiful list of the fruits of the Spirit (5:22-23): 'Love, joy, peace, patience, kindliness [that word would have sounded like 'Christlikeness' in the original Greek], goodness, faith, gentleness, and self-control'.

To be honest, it is very difficult for us to be sure that we can construct precisely what was going on in Galatia that had got Paul so cross. Scholars often talk of 'listening to one side of the telephone conversation': we can hear what Paul is saying, but not what his opponents were arguing. As you read Galatians, don't worry too much about what the issue was; instead, savour those lovely lines, be captivated by Paul's passion for Jesus, and try to understand why people are still drawn to this great lover today.

Questions

1. Does Paul come across to you as a real human being in this letter? If so, why?

2. Why do you think Paul was so cross with the Galatians?

3. What was the basic issue in the letter to the Galatians?

CHAPTER 2

Paul's earliest letter and his shortest: 1 Thessalonians and Philemon

It seems quite important to open these two letters with both awe and care. In the case of Philemon, we have here perhaps Paul's most charming letter; it is hardly more than a postcard, but it packs a punch. 1 Thessalonians demands our respect because many if not most scholars believe it was the first of Paul's letters to be written (or dictated). So when you hear it or read it, you are dealing with the first surviving attempt of a Christian reflecting on and writing down the implications of the gospel message.

When was this letter written? We don't really know, I'm afraid, as Paul and his secretary unaccountably omitted a date stamp, but AD 51 is often suggested, based on the picture given us in Acts 17:1-15, where Paul preaches in Thessalonica and then has to flee, first to Beroea and then to Athens. Some people think our existing 1 Thessalonians may in fact be two separate letters combined. However, though I admire the attention to detail shown by these scholars, I am not convinced that their evidence is all that compelling. In any case, your reading of this letter (which is all that matters as far as this book is concerned) may not be very greatly affected by it. The fact is that for two millennia people have been able to read this as a single letter, and I suggest that we continue to do so.

One thing that you might like to do is have a look at the map of Northern Greece, and see how Paul's journey from Troas in modern Turkey will have taken him across to Neapolis, then to Philippi, where Paul tells us (in 1 Thessalonians 2:2) he came under stress in his attempt to preach the gospel. Then he moved (presumably walked) 100 miles along the great Roman road, the Via Egnatia, and arrived in Thessalonica where, evidently, he met with some success. It is possible that the hassle he had to endure meant an untimely departure from Thessalonica, and that is why the letter is so affectionate.

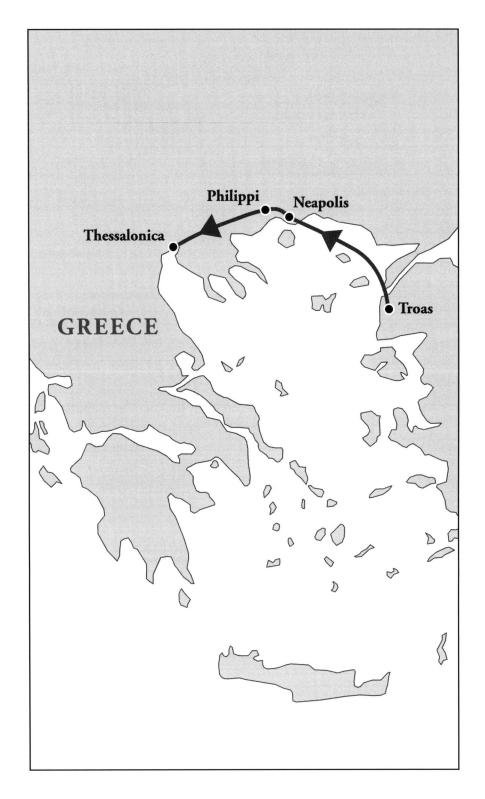

We do not have space here to say everything that is to be said about the letter, but what I should like to do is just pick out a few points that shed light on Paul and on his relationship with fellow Christians. The reason for that is that people are often beset with misgivings about Paul, and feel that he is somehow 'out to get them'. As we shall see, it is unlikely that the Thessalonians would have said that of him.

The letter starts with apparently three authors (Paul, Silvanus and Timothy, 1:1), but it is Paul alone who counts, since Silvanus is not mentioned again, and Timothy resurfaces only at 3:6, as a messenger boy. The letter is addressed to the 'assembly' or 'church' in Thessalonica, rather than to particular individuals. The word *ekklesia* in Greek, from which we derive English words like 'ecclesiastical', is of great importance to Paul: it refers to a group of Christians in a particular place, and it was always his desire to make sure that they were united, otherwise Christ would not be present. It is also the word used in the Septuagint, the Greek translation of the Old Testament, for the assembly of God's people in the desert. This may serve as a reminder of how very much Paul saw himself and the Christian people in the context of the Old Testament people of God.

You might notice the bracketing, in a single breath in verse 1, of 'God the Father and the Lord Jesus Christ'. One of the questions that the early Christians, including Paul of course, always had to ask was about the relationship of Jesus to God, and whether they had abandoned their old Jewish monotheism. Here Paul may be feeling his way to an answer.

One thing that everyone knows about Paul, because it is in 1 Corinthians 13, which is read at every wedding that you have ever attended, is the threesome of the great theological virtues of faith, hope, and love. You will be interested to notice that they are already here in 1 Thessalonians, for at 1:3 he speaks (with gratitude) of 'the work of faith, the labour of love, and perseverance in hope'.

It is moreover an unusual letter in that it seems to have two thanksgivings, if you look at 1:2 and 2:13. Perhaps no one had told Paul that he was only allowed one (actually that seems to be the main reason why some people think we have parts of two letters here). The great thing for us here is to see and relish the gratitude that is very much a part of who Paul is, and of his journey with God.

The Thessalonians would certainly not have been able to accuse Paul of ingratitude; he tells them, for example, that he is 'orphaned' because of being separated from them (2:17), 'in person, but not in my heart', and how he 'longed enormously to see your faces, with immense desire'. He is well aware of the great merits of the Thessalonians: he describes himself as being an 'infant' (or, just possibly, 'gentle', depending on what manuscript reading you opt for at 2:7). And he is immensely grateful (see 1:9) for the way they received the gospel, which, we learn, has gone out not only to Macedonia (meaning for Paul the northern part of Greece, where Thessalonica is), but also to Achaea, which is the southern part, where Corinth is.

We also learn that they were not a Jewish group, but Gentiles, since Paul speaks of them as 'turning away from idols' (1:9). He tells us, too, that they are expecting Jesus to come again soon: 'waiting for his Son from heaven, whom God raised from the dead' (1:10). So Paul is very fond of this group, because they have got it right; and you might look at 3:1-7 for his unfeigned affection for them.

Most of the letter is a matter of reminding them what he had taught them when he was with them, including the example he gave them by 'working night and day, so as not to put a burden on you when we preached the gospel of God' (2:9). There is, however, one slice of evidently new teaching. The reason for this may be that they had written to him with a difficulty, or that he had heard of the problem on the grapevine or from Timothy. For at 4:13 he speaks of 'those who have fallen asleep'. Now perhaps some had died since he left them, and they were worrying about the fate of these people, or were concerned that they had failed in some way. So Paul carefully reminds them of the central importance of Jesus' death, and argues that 'God will bring those who have fallen asleep through Jesus with him' (4:14). And, building on various hints in Jewish apocalyptic literature, he gives a picture of what the second coming might be like (4:16):

- at a command

- at the voice of an archangel

- and at God's trumpet-call,

he will come down from heaven and the dead in Christ shall rise first. Then he goes on, 'we who are left will be snatched up in the clouds to meet the Lord in the air' (4:17). So it will come, he tells them. On the other hand, he insists that they are not to expect to know when it will be (5:1). The main thing is the solidarity of the group, as he concludes (5:11), 'therefore comfort each other, and build each other up into one'.

Like many Christian groups down the centuries, it seems that the Thessalonians have had disciplinary problems: at 5:12 they are told to 'recognise those who labour among you and who admonish you'. And they are all instructed to 'admonish the disorderly' (5:14). So you may be reassured to know that there is nothing new about divisions in the Church!

The letter ends 'the grace of Our Lord Jesus Christ be with you'. And they need it, this unconditional love of God (and of Jesus) that is so close to the heart of his theology. It is a wonderful letter, and I suggest you spend some time with it.

Now we can conclude this chapter with a letter that is even more charming than 1 Thessalonians, namely the letter to Philemon. We do not know when or where it was written, except that Paul was in prison – which happened to him a good deal, it seems – and he calls himself 'an old man' (verse 9), which may be a bid for sympathy from his audience.

Who was this audience? Well, Philemon, for sure, who is the addressee, and who is described as 'beloved and a co-worker', which may make him feel good. However, there is also a lady called Apphia, possibly Mrs Philemon, and one Archippus, so it is not completely private for Philemon himself, especially since the letter is also addressed to the 'congregation/church [*ekklesia* once more] in your house'. We have to imagine this letter being read out in public, with everyone watching Philemon to see how he is reacting. For he is being asked to accept Onesimus as a brother. And you may, if you wish, imagine Philemon, in the middle of the assembly, leaping from his seat and saying, 'As a *what*?!' For, if we are reading the letter correctly, Onesimus is a runaway slave, and therefore a thing, not a person, one who deserved the most dire punishments.

The point Paul makes is that the gospel transforms our relationships and shows up the irrelevance of terms such as 'slave' and 'master'. Paul pursues his aim with all kinds of clever little wordplays. For example, he commends Philemon for having (it is hard to get the translation right here) 'given rest to the innards of the saints'. So we imagine Philemon purring with pleasure; but at verse 12, Onesimus is described as 'my innards'; we notice that his name is only revealed at the end of a long description of him as 'my child, whom I have begotten here in prison'. Then, as the letter comes to a conclusion, when the nature of Paul's request is now alarmingly clear, he uses the phrase again, as he asks Philemon to 'give rest to my innards' (verse 20). And of course this unfortunate church worthy is absolutely trapped. Paul says, 'I could give you an order, but I won't.' Imagine yourself in his boots: what would you have done? What *could* you do?

There is another set of wordplays that we may also admire, for the name Onesimus means 'useful' or 'profitable', and after his name is mentioned for the first time there are a couple of puns on that idea, for he is described as 'once unprofitable, but now well profitable to both you and me' (verse 11). Not only that, but those two words would have sounded in Greek like 'unchristian' and 'well Christian' or 'Christlike'. In verse 20 there is another play on the name Onesimus, when Paul asks 'that I may *profit* in the Lord'. He also says, at the outset (verse 8), 'I have every right to command you what is right, but out of love, I am rather imploring you.' And towards the end, 'receive him like me' (verse 17). So if Philemon has anything in mind like branding Onesimus, or chopping his hands off, or executing him – which was possible for runaway slaves – then he had better think again, because he would be doing it to Paul!

Finally, if Philemon is listening, and one imagines that by now he is being very attentive indeed, there is a bit of menace: 'make a guest room ready for me – for I am hoping that through your prayers I'll be given you as a free gift' (verse 22). Put yourself in Philemon's place: if you had had this letter read out in your presence, what would you do? I suppose that the fact that we still have it, and it was not torn up, means that he took notice.

There is one further question that will have struck you. What about slavery? Should not Paul have spent a bit more energy on attacking the institution rather than liberating just this one slave? Possibly, but there are two points you might like to consider. The first is that if Jesus is coming back very soon indeed, by next Wednesday at the latest, then there are more urgent things to attend to than undermining that essential economic institution of the Roman Empire. The second is that if we have properly understood the gospel – indeed, if we have understood Paul in this letter – we should realise that it is quite impossible to have slaves. Now it is true that Christians have not always quite grasped this, but then we are desperately slow to think outside our own selfish interests. But I suggest you read carefully through this lovely letter and see what you think. And remember: Paul is on his way!

Questions

1. How would you describe the relationship between Paul and the Christians in Thessalonica?

2. Does it make a difference that 1 Thessalonians may be Paul's first surviving letter?

3. How would you guess Philemon responded to the letter addressed to him?

4. Should Paul, in your opinion, have done more to bring an end to the institution of slavery?

CHAPTER 3

Romans:
an attempt to be diplomatic

Now we come to what is perhaps Paul's most influential letter, one that exercised immense influence on St Augustine, and through him on the religious controversies of the sixteenth century. You need to be warned, however, that this letter is far from easy. So my advice is that you should not be content with just reading it once, but should keep coming back to it, especially the parts you find difficult.

It may be good to start by asking what the letter is about. Down the ages there have been various suggestions:

- It is all part of the aftermath of the letter to the Galatians. The issue of circumcision is treated in Galatians (at 5:2, for example) and in Romans (3:1, 2). Paul's somewhat robust approach may well have caused upset, especially perhaps in Jerusalem, whose Jewish Christian community was close to Rome in some ways. And the Jerusalem community was important to Paul because of the question of the collection for the poor Christians there.

- Another suggestion is that Romans is a summary of all Paul's thought. The great Reformer Melanchthon described it as a *compendium rei Christianae*, a summary of Christianity. That view is not widely held today, because too many key elements of Paul's thought are missing, but it still surfaces from time to time.

- A third suggestion is that Romans offers an account of what God has done in Christ. This probably comes close to the truth, although it is a bit vague as it stands. It may be best to explain here that the Church in Rome was originally a Jewish one, but in AD 49 the Emperor Claudius expelled Jews, or perhaps Jewish Christians, from Rome, because of squabbling among them. So it is possible that the Gentile Christians had come into their own and taken over the leadership of the Church. So when Jewish Christians were allowed back, under Nero's leadership, there will probably have been tension, and that may well be the background of the letter.

It may be good to begin by observing Paul in his diplomat's hat; this is a rare phenomenon for this rumbustious apostle, so it is worth observing. Look at the following remarks, and marvel at Paul's attempt to win the Romans over. Consider the flattering tone of these verses:

- 1:8: 'Your faith is announced in all the world.'

- 1:9, 10: 'God is my witness . . . asking in my prayers that somehow one day I may succeed by God's will in coming to you.'

- 1:11: 'For I *long* to see you.' Here the alert observer will see that the diplomatic mask slips, as Paul asserts that it is 'in order to give you a spiritual gift, for you to be strengthened'. In the following verse he remembers that he is trying to be diplomatic.

- 1:12: 'I mean to be comforted among you, through the faith that is in each of us, yours and mine.'

- 1:15: 'I am longing to preach the gospel to you people in Rome.' Here the mask has slipped slightly, and once more he is insisting on his mastery of the gospel and that therefore they have something to learn from him. We should notice his difficulty: Paul did not found the church in Rome, and in any event it may be that he thinks they have heard about the intemperate language of the letter to the Galatians.

It is clear that Paul is enormously, and quite genuinely, keen to come to Rome, and that is the impression we also receive throughout Acts of the Apostles. To pave the way for that he explains his travel plans at the end of the letter. Look at 15:14: 'I am persuaded about all of you that you are jam-packed with goodness, and filled with all knowledge.' That is Paul being super-diplomatic. But the next two verses tell us that he is worried, because of his mission to the Gentiles:

I have written to you a bit more audaciously, so as to remind you because of the grace that was given me by God – for me to be a minister of Christ Jesus to the Gentiles, doing the sacred work of the gospel of God, in order that the offering of the Gentiles might become acceptable, consecrated by the Holy Spirit.

Several of the words in that passage are cultic words, referring to the Temple services. They are taken from the Greek Bible that the Jewish Christians of Rome would have had at their fingertips, and we may see this as Paul sending a signal to them.

Then he expresses the urgency of his travel plans (15:23): 'having had a desire to come to you, these many years' (diplomacy again, you see). Then, however, to prevent them thinking that he's going to be imposing on them for ever and a day, he mentions a planned visit to Spain (15:24), and expresses a hope that they will send him on his way.

There is another issue, however, and that is the tricky business of Jerusalem. Paul introduces it in this way: 'Now I am on my way to Jerusalem, in the service of the saints' (15:25). That sounds all right, and indeed it is, for Paul is determined to bring his collection to the Jerusalem church. He often expresses his enthusiasm for this project, as we can see at 1 Corinthians 16:1, 2; 2 Corinthians 8–9; Galatians 2:10; Philippians 4:10-19 (though here the collection is for Paul himself). But here, and we should rub our eyes when we read it, Paul is actually afraid that the Jerusalem church might *refuse* his offering. So he begs the Roman church (15:30, 31), 'through Our Lord Jesus Christ and through the love of the Spirit', in his very solemn phrase, 'to fight at my side with your prayers for me to God, that I may be delivered from the unbelievers in Judaea'. It turns out that what he is hoping for is that 'my service of offering for Jerusalem may become acceptable to the saints, and so I may come to you through God's will, to relax in your company' (15:32).

Then it sounds as though the letter is coming to an end, as Paul writes, 'May the God of peace be with all of you. Amen' (15:33). And if he is worried about hostility in both Jerusalem and Rome, then that is an excellent prayer on which to conclude.

However, we have not quite finished; and once again the reason is diplomatic. For Paul now produces a long list of names. Quite often he ends his letter with salutations of this sort; see, for example, 1 Corinthians 16:19; Philippians 4:21, 22; Colossians 4:15-17; 1 Thessalonians 5:26; Philemon 23, 24. But this list in Romans is quite different, and much longer, and crosses a number of boundaries.

The first name mentioned is that of Phoebe, who is described as 'a fellow Christian and deacon of the church which is in Cenchreae'. Cenchreae is the easternmost harbour that serves the city of Corinth, from which this letter is written; and it looks as though its deacon may be the one who carried this important letter to the important city of Rome, for the Romans are asked to 'give her a welcome in the Lord, worthy of the saints, and offer her anything at all that she has need of' (16:1, 2). We discover that this lady has been 'a benefactress of many people, including myself'.

She is clearly important; and she is also, we should notice, a woman, and may serve to check the too-ready assumption that Christianity has been against women from the outset. Other women mentioned in this important chapter are Prisca, Maria, Tryphaena and Tryphosa, who may be sisters, Junia, 'conspicuous among the apostles' (16:7), Persis, and the sister of Nereus. Nor is this the only sense in which the list is inclusive, for we also have those who are probably Jews: the husband and wife team of Prisca and Aquila; Herodion, Apelles, and the house of Aristoboulos (the last two names are often given to Jewish people). The name Maria might also be Jewish, translating the Hebrew Miriam. Most of the group have Greek names, and some of them are the kinds of names that could be given to slaves: Epainetus (which means 'praiseworthy'), Stachys, Apelles, Narcissus, the name of a freedman who was famous under Nero, Asynkritos, Phlegon, Hermes, Patrobus, Hermas, Philologus, Nereus, and Olympus. There are Latin names too: Junia, already mentioned, and her husband Andronicus, Maria, which might be the feminine of Marius, Ampliatus, Urbanus, Rufus, who might just be the son of Simon of Cyrene, and Julia. Most of these come from the lower end of society; but a few might be among the wheelers and dealers: Narcissus, Herodion, Aristoboulos and Julia, a name often given to women members of the ruling Julio-Claudian dynasty.

Those are the names of the people whom Paul is greeting, and they constitute a wide range, socially and in other ways. His strategy, we presume, is to make the Romans aware that there are people there who can vouch for him. And the people who send their greetings from Corinth to Rome are likewise multiracial: Timothy, Lucius, Jason and Sosipater are all Greek, and possibly Jewish; then there is Tertius, the secretary who took the letter down at Paul's dictation, who has the nerve to stick his head above the parapet and send his greetings to Rome. His name means 'Third'. There is another name, Quartus, which means 'Fourth'; that could, I suppose, conceivably be a brother of Tertius, if their parents were a little short of imagination when it came to naming their offspring. And there are two other names: Gaius (16:23) is Latin, and this passage may suggest that he owns a house big enough to hold the entire Corinthian church; he may be the same as the one who is mentioned at 1 Corinthians 1:14 as having been baptised by Paul. The other is Erastus, here described as the 'city treasurer'. He is presumably fairly high on the social scale, especially if he is to be identified with someone of the same name referred to in a first-century inscription uncovered in Corinth, who describes himself as an 'aedile', which might be the same person. For us, the important point is that Paul is pulling out all the stops in his diplomatic onslaught, persuading the Romans that he is someone to reckon with.

So that is the context in which this remarkable letter seems to have been written. What I suggest you do now is to read slowly through it, probably several times. The best thing may be if, without telling you what I think Paul is saying, I give you the rough shape of the letter, to divide your reading into manageable pieces.

The first chapter is, clearly, of immense importance. For in it Paul sets out where we are going; proudly he describes himself, in the very first line, as a 'slave of Jesus Christ, called as an apostle, set apart for the gospel of God'; he stresses the continuity of this gospel with the old story of Israel and its God. This story finds its fulfilment, according to Paul (1:4) in the person of his beloved, 'who was set apart as Son of God in power, in accordance with the Spirit of Holiness, because of the Resurrection from the dead, Jesus Christ our Lord, through whom we received grace and a mission for the obedience of faith among all the Gentiles on behalf of his name'. In 1:16, 17 Paul then offers what many people think is a summary of his message: 'For I am not ashamed of the gospel; for it is God's power, for all those who believe, Jews first and then Greeks; for God's righteousness is being revealed, from faith to faith, as it is written, "The one who is just will live out of faith."' (When you have read the letter, come back to this, and see whether you agree that this does indeed summarise it.)

After that, Paul talks about the need that the Gentiles have for what God offers in Jesus. Now remember that a good many Jewish Christians will have been there when Phoebe (or whoever) read the letter out, they will have applauded as they heard 'Jews first, and then Greeks', and they will have felt even better as Paul laid into the Gentiles about their need to avoid God's anger. However, the boot is on the other foot in chapter 2, 'So you are without any defence, anyone who condemns', and they will suddenly have realised that Paul was now attacking his fellow Jews! The point is that all of us, whether Jew or non-Jew, need what God is offering to us in Jesus. And so we come to the difficult argument of chapters 3 and 4. Read carefully through it, several times over, until you think you have understood it; and then read it some more, because it is not as difficult as you suppose.

Then you should move on to chapter 5; and for the next four chapters, Paul is telling the Roman church, both Gentiles and Jews, what are the grounds for their confidence. This is likewise not terribly easy, but keep going, and when you get to the end of chapter 8, reward yourself by reading several times the lovely verses (8:31-39) with which it concludes.

After that, the more thoughtful listeners will have seen a problem: if it is indeed 'first for Jews and then for non-Jews', what about the plain fact, in Paul's day and in ours, that for the most part Jews have not been seized by the gospel message? In the next three chapters Paul gives expression to his longing for his fellow Jews to come into Christ, concluding with a lovely hymn, again to be read several times, about the wonderful purposes of God (11:33-36).

We are almost there now. The rest of the letter explores, in various different ways, the implications of all this for the Roman Christian community, with all their tensions and difficulties. You might go slowly through it, down to 15:13, and make a list of the number of issues that Paul raises, and see if you can get a feel for the kind of community he was dealing with. You will not regret it.

Questions

1. What kind of document do you think Romans is?

2. Why do you suppose it has been so influential in the history of Christianity?

3. Which bit of Romans do you find most striking?

CHAPTER 4

1 Corinthians:
dealing with a divided church

It is to be hoped that by now you are coming to see that Paul was dealing with real issues besetting real people. Now we are going to look at an embarrassingly real church with uncomfortably real problems: that of Corinth, the great harbour city on the isthmus that separates the northern half of Greece from the Peloponnese, its southern half. The biggest of these problems, though by no means the only one, was the fact that they were squabbling. We tend to assume that everything was all tickety-boo in the early Church, and then look with sadness and embarrassment at our present plight, muttering, 'If only we were back in the good old days.' But look again: those good old days never existed, and Christians have always found reasons to be divided.

This was particularly true in the case of Corinth. The place was enormously wealthy, and a lively port city, with all the vices that might imply. You might like to have a look at a map, and see how, if you were travelling from the Black Sea to somewhere like Rome, with timber or spices or wheat, you could unload your cargo at Cenchreae in the East (where Phoebe came from in Romans 16:2), then send it on wagons through the city to Lechaeum in the West, paying taxes as you go, simply to avoid the much trickier navigation round the Peloponnese, the bottom end of Greece.

Like many such cities, Corinth was notorious, at several periods of its history, for a lively sex life and considerable social divisions. The population is thought to have been one-third slaves, one-third free and one-third 'freedmen' or former slaves, and we assume that the Christian community had roughly the same demographics. So it is not surprising, with this very divided society, that they fought; and, as I say, the fighting was their biggest problem. Paul tries to solve the divisions in all (both, I suppose we should say) his surviving letters to that community. We'll have a look at Paul's tactics for dealing with fighting, but there were other problems as well.

Sadly, it looks as though Paul did not manage to put an end to the squabbles. His last surviving written words to the community you know by heart: 'the grace of Our Lord Jesus Christ, the love of God, and the solidarity of the Holy Spirit be with you all', he says at 2 Corinthians 13:13, presumably because they were deaf to grace, immune to love, and had made a right mess of their Christian solidarity. And half a century later, Clement wrote from Rome to Corinth because they were still fighting.

Let us go through Paul's first letter now, and see how he deals with their disunity. As you do so, you might like to remember that they had written to Paul a perhaps rather complacent letter and were waiting for his reply. As you read, you might imagine yourself summoned by a Corinthian fellow Christian to Gaius' house, because 'Paul's reply has come', and you are curious to see how he is going to reply. In fact, you are going to get rather a shock.

It starts all right: 'Paul, called as an apostle of Jesus Christ, and Sosthenes the brother' (and here we may pause to notice that poor Sosthenes never appears again in the entire letter) 'to the assembly of God which is in Corinth'. Soon after that, however, if they were paying attention, they may have noted something rather odd: a series of passive verbs, making the point that anything they have done right is not their doing but God's. So he refers to the Corinthian Christians as 'those who *have been made* holy', '*called* to be saints', and speaks of 'the grace which *has been given* you'. He tells them that 'you *have been enriched* in every way', and that 'the witness of Christ *has been made strong* in you so you *lack no free gift* (this is not a passive, but the implication is the same), and 'Christ will strengthen you to the end so *you'll be acquitted*', and 'through whom *you have been called* into the fellowship of his son'. If you listen carefully, you can probably hear them wondering, 'What about all our spiritual achievements – isn't Paul going to congratulate us?'

Just as that thought comes into their minds, he really lets them have it: 'I beg you all . . . to say the same thing and that there be no division among you' (1:10). Paul tells them that he knows about their quarrels: 'Chloe's people have told me' (and for sure at that point there is an angry muttering of 'that sneak Chloe!'), and that they have divided into parties: 'I'm for Paul', 'I'm for Apollos', 'I'm for Kephas'; and Paul makes his grim little joke – 'Well, *I'm* for Christ.'

So that is the problem. How does Paul respond to it? In a number of ways, as it turns out. First, he tells them (and this will not have gone down well in Corinth) that 'the rhetoric of the cross is stupidity' (1:18); and that when he arrived in Corinth from a tricky experience in Athens, 'I decided to know nothing but Jesus Christ – and him crucified' (2:2).

Secondly, they must be prepared to be foolish (everywhere in the letter – but see 3:18, for example).

Thirdly, Paul and Apollos are only servants, working in God's garden, or God's building (3:7-17; 4:1).

Fourth, they are reminded, several times (8:1; 10:23; 14:4), that the only thing that matters is to build up the body.

Fifth, they are told that because of their divisions, when they come together it is not the Lord's Supper that they are eating (11:20).

Sixth, Paul draws for them, with considerable humour and originality, the picture of the body (12:12-31).

And his last attempt to stop the fighting is that beautiful hymn to love, which is likely read at every wedding you have ever attended, and which precisely fits the Corinthian situation, but to which they never bothered to listen.

There were, however, other issues on which Paul had to challenge them. Early on he speaks of the immaturity that is revealed by their squabbles (3:1). Then there is, as there always must be, the question of sex. We don't know from where he received his information – possibly Chloe again – but he had heard that one of the Christians was committing incest with his stepmother (5:1), and others were using prostitutes (6:16-20). He was, moreover, simply horrified to learn that they had been taking each other to court (6:1). Only when we get to the beginning of chapter 7 does he condescend to answer their letter, in a slightly offhand way: 'Now – with regard to things that you wrote about'. Here they have been asking, perhaps a shade naively, whether all sex is bad. Chapter 7 is mainly given over to that tricky question (and the answer is 'no', since you ask).

There is another difficult issue that you might not think really topical in our world, about whether it is permitted to eat food that has been offered in the temples. There are two aspects to this: the first is that such meat was often sold on by the priests to whom it was given, so it could be a cheap way for citizens to come by some protein. Second, if you are a Christian in Corinth, and a friend invites you to a meal in the temple of Asclepius, for example, is it permissible to accept? The difficulty is that someone walking past might look in and see you (8:10), for the temple dining rooms were open to the outside, and think that you have betrayed Christ. Paul's answer is interesting: he is well aware that false 'gods' don't really exist (8:4), but even so, in case he might damage a sensitive fellow Christian, he says that he is ready to abstain from meat (8:13). We are not to share a table with demons (10:14-22).

Another tricky issue is whether Paul was right to refuse money from the Corinthians (9:1-18). On the whole this is a rather rare complaint from Christians, that their church leaders are not accepting enough of their money – but there you are.

Corinthian women could be a problem for him, too, for it seems that some of them were not wearing a veil. This is not, today, a major problem for us, but if you look at 11:2-16 you will see that Paul is getting very hot under the collar, and perhaps feeling that his arguments are not all that strong. It may be, as some scholars suggest, that there was homosexual cross-dressing going on at Corinth. If that was the case, then Paul would not have thought that at all a good idea.

Yet another issue (and by now the Corinthians may have regretted asking the reader to give them the contents of the letter) was that they had social divisions at the Eucharist, so that (11:21) some were going hungry while others were drunk! Probably the slaves would arrive late from their work, while the more well-to-do could get their feet under Gaius' table a bit earlier.

Another problem was how to discern the spirits. This is a very important question for all religious people, and Paul gives some eminently sensible guidelines concerning their attitude to Jesus and leading in the direction of unity.

Yet another problem was chaos in the liturgy, with people showing off their skills at speaking in tongues. Read slowly through chapter 14 to get the picture here.

And, with a bit of a shock, there is an instruction, which some people feel did not come from Paul, that the women are to remain silent in church (14:34). We must be honest here and say that we do not know what Paul might have meant by this, though presumably the Corinthians knew what he was talking about. Certainly back in chapter 11:4, 5 Paul was happy for both men and women to prophesy and pray in the assembly, so the text remains mysterious. Many scholars simply want to excise it, but that is an option that should only be taken when there is no other choice.

Then in chapter 15, when we are almost at the very end, Paul has to deal with some crazy people in Corinth who doubt the resurrection of those who have died. Now for Paul, as he carefully explains, Resurrection is absolutely central to the gospel: no Resurrection, no Christianity is the way he sees it.

Another painful issue is that of getting the collection to Jerusalem. We have seen elsewhere in this book that this is a matter of great personal importance to Paul, but look at what he says in chapter 16:1-4. He says, 'Every Sunday, each of you should put aside, piling up whatever you can afford.' In other words, they don't trust each other sufficiently to take the money to their weekly assembly. And, it seems, they do not trust Paul, either! For he says, 'When I turn up, the accounts can be done; and I'll commission anyone you approve to bring your act of kindness to Jerusalem', and then, 'If it is appropriate for me to go as well, they will travel with me.' This is great self-sacrifice on his part, for the collection, as we have seen, really mattered to him.

Lastly, they have to be told to respect Timothy (16:10), Apollos (16:12) and 'the house of Stephanas' (16:15-18).

Paul deals with his much-loved Christians skilfully and on the whole compassionately, but it was not easy for him, and we may find common ground with him in our churches today. Read this letter as a treatise of our times.

Questions

1. Does 1 Corinthians speak to us today?

2. What do you think were the main problems at Corinth?

3. What is Paul's attitude to women here?

CHAPTER 5

2 Corinthians and Philippians: rather different challenges

Each of Paul's letters is different, and that is because the community he is writing to in each case is different. If we watch him carefully, we can see how he does it, thinking on his feet in response to various crises. So Paul does not always say the same thing in his letters; they are 'occasional', by which we mean that they are written to particular communities with particular problems.

In 2 Corinthians, the main problem seems to be something of a breakdown in relations between Paul and this slightly dysfunctional community, of which he was really very fond, despite everything. And there was quite a correspondence between them, it seems. If you look at 1 Corinthians 5:9-11, you will see that there was a letter previous to 1 Corinthians. And it seems that things had not gone well since then. For one thing, 2 Corinthians starts with the other side complaining that Paul had not turned up as soon as he had promised (which suggests that they were also quite fond of him, of course). At the end of 1 Corinthians (16:5-9), he had indicated that he was going to come quite soon, and would spend a good period of time with them. But in the meantime other Christian apostles (he calls them, derisively, 'super-apostles' at 2 Corinthians 12:11) had come to Corinth and attacked Paul and, to his fury, the Corinthians had believed them! When that happened, Paul wrote a letter in his defence; some scholars think that we can find bits of that letter at 2 Corinthians 2:14; 6:13; 7:2-4, and some material about the collection for Jerusalem in chapters 8 and 9.

(That reminds me: you do not need to worry too much when scholars break up the letters of Paul in this way. You are quite entitled to insist on doing what Christians have done for 2000 years and read the letter as a single unit. It works perfectly well that way, but I just thought it might be interesting to you to look at it from another angle.)

Anyway, back to 2 Corinthians. After that angry letter, it seems that Paul visited Corinth and was publicly insulted (2 Corinthians 2:5-8 will give you the details). So he went back to Ephesus and wrote another letter, 'with many tears', as he says at 2:4, and that letter is referred to in 7:8-13. That seems to have done the trick, for eventually Paul met up with Titus, who had been acting as something of a 'go-between', in Macedonia, though he had hoped to meet him sooner. From him Paul discovered that the crisis was over, and that the Corinthians were back on track and repentant. You'll see the details if you read 7:5-16, and you will breathe a sigh of relief with Paul as you take it in.

Because of that, we think that Paul then wrote a joyful letter, and those scholars who like to excavate bits and stitch them together think that it may have been 1:1, 2, 13; 7:5-16. Anyway, it seems that after that he finally got back to Corinth.

So whether you break up the letter or not, you can see easily enough that there are many different moods. If you look at the opening verses (1:3-8), you will see an alternation of words that mean 'tribulation' and words that mean something like 'comfort' or 'consolation', and that may help you to catch the mood of this epistle.

You will also notice that in places Paul is actually quite cross. As in Galatians, there is no 'thanksgiving' in this letter; the nearest he gets is a blessing to God at 1:3. For other evidence, just look at 1:17, 18, about the accusation that he did not keep his promise; or 2:1; or 10:8-18, dealing with the attacks made upon him; and then see what he says about those 'super-apostles' at 11:5-15 and 12:11.

As I have said before, however, when Paul gets cross, he 'does' autobiography, and for that we must be grateful to those who annoyed him. Read slowly through 11:16–12:10, and you will see what I mean, especially when he is talking about the things that have been done to him because of his mission (11:23-33). Or read what he goes on to say (12:1-10), very reluctantly, about his own mystical experiences. When you hear this, especially his admission about the 'thorn in the flesh', you just know that he is telling the unvarnished truth.

Finally, if you ever find yourself wondering how to raise money for a good cause, just read through chapters 8 and 9. The Corinthians were not short of a shilling or two, but they had very deep pockets, and perhaps didn't really trust Paul. What he is doing in these two chapters is shaming them into generosity. When you have read those two chapters, see if you think they would have come up with the money for the poor of Jerusalem.

One last thing: if you want to understand Paul, just see what he says about his task, at 4:5. There you will see it: 'Christ Jesus as Lord, and ourselves as your slaves because of Jesus'. That is all you need to know.

Bear that in mind when you come to read Philippians. Philippi was a big Roman town on the way to Thessalonica, and from Acts 16 we gather that Paul, along with Timothy and Silas, endured a great deal of suffering there, including flogging and imprisonment. The Philippians, however, were very fond of him, and had proved extraordinarily generous to him (see 2:25 and 4:10-15 for the evidence). One thing we should recall is that Paul was writing from prison (see 1:7, 13, 14, 17), and, as was generally the case in prisons in the ancient world, faced death. Despite that uncertain future and confined existence, this is easily Paul's most joyful letter; just look at the number of times he uses the word 'rejoice': 2:18; 3:1; 4:4 (x 2!), as well as 1:25 and 2:2 for the noun 'joy'. Then read through the rest of the letter and judge the mood for yourself. We have no way of telling where Paul was in prison, at Ephesus or Rome or somewhere else, and nor does it matter all that much. What counts is the love, for Christ and for his Philippians, which radiates from this remarkable letter. Read 1:20, 21 to grasp the importance of Christ for him, even to the point of embracing death.

Now one of the best-known passages in Philippians is the great 'hymn to Christ', which you will find at 2:5-11. You probably know it by heart. But look a bit closer at the context: in the opening verses of that chapter, Paul is speaking of 'comfort' and 'consolation' and 'solidarity' and 'pity' and 'joy' (2:1, 2), and asking the Philippians to 'think the same thing' (which he had already asked, unsuccessfully, of the Corinthians), presumably because some of them had been quarrelling. So what Paul does is to remind them of Jesus and ask them to 'think what Jesus thought'. He does this by quoting (scholars think) a hymn that was already known to them, which emphasises Jesus' very high status ('Lord – to the glory of God the Father'), and at the same time his readiness to let go of his status of equality with God. This is meant to persuade the Philippians to 'have the same love, not quarrelling . . . but in humility thinking others as better than you are' (2:2, 3; that may have been a shock to some of them).

Does Paul tell us anything more about the quarrelling that was going on? It seems that he does, because at 4:2, two ladies, Evodia and Syntyche, whom he describes in glowing terms as great 'fighters with me in the gospel, along with Clement and the rest of my fellow workers' (4:3), are exhorted to 'think the same thing in the Lord'. So presumably they had not been thinking the same as each other.

There is one more thing about this passage. Women seem to have been important in the church at Philippi, right from its very beginning in the house of the wealthy purple-dye merchant, Lydia, who more or less forced Paul and Barnabas to found the church there. Then there are Evodia and Syntyche, of course, of whom Paul evidently approves as pastoral workers, even if they are fighting.

There is a further interesting possibility, that Mrs Paul may be there in Philippi. For just as he is asking the two of them to 'think the same in the Lord', he turns to someone whom he addresses, possibly as 'noble Syzygus' or, possibly, as 'noble yoke-fellow' (4:3). For Syzygus is not attested as a name in Greek, but it is used to refer to cattle or horses who are together 'under the yoke', and is often used to mean a spouse. Could that be Paul's wife, who perhaps feels unable to go rushing round the Mediterranean with him, but keeps home for him and looks after the children, so that on his occasional visits he has somewhere for a bit of rest?

Now I know that as I write this you are thumbing through 1 Corinthians 7 and looking at verse 8, where Paul talks to the 'unmarried and widows' and tells them that it is 'good for them to remain as I am'. That is often read as referring to Paul's celibacy, but it might just, Corinth being Corinth and its inhabitants rather over-inclined to indulge themselves sexually, be that he is saying that unlike some of *them* he doesn't need to go off to the prostitutes when he is separated from his wife. And indeed, when Paul is talking about the rights of apostles at 9:5, he asks, 'Don't I have the right to eat and drink, and the right to take a Christian wife around with me, just like the other apostles, and the brothers of the Lord, and Kephas?' The Corinthians might have pointed out to him that that would not be much of an argument if in fact he had no wife at all! I can't prove it, but it is something for you to think about when you try to form your view of Paul. Certainly Philippi, well set up for Paul's travelling, and clearly a community of which he was very fond, would have been just the sort of place where his wife might very well find a home.

Finally, as you read through Philippians, never forget that Paul is writing from a Roman prison, and look out for evidence of his attitude to the Roman Empire. It looks as though Paul felt drawn to Rome, and felt that his apostolic work was incomplete until he had preached the gospel there. But at the same time he was well aware that his values were not those of the Empire, which at that stage was starting to allow even emperors to be worshipped as gods, something that Paul, as a good Jew, could not possibly tolerate. So there is a clash of cultures here, and if you look carefully, you can see it. For he speaks at 1:13 of his 'chains becoming obvious in Christ to the whole Praetorium'; and that Latin word stands symbolically for Roman imperial power.

But Paul is well aware that his values are not those of Rome (except that according to Acts 22:28 Paul was very proud of being a citizen), for one very good reason, namely that for him Jesus was *Kyrios*, or Lord, and not any tuppenny-halfpenny 'emperor'. So, almost deliberately, one feels, Paul insists that Jesus is Lord, not just at the climax of his great hymn to Christ in chapter 2, but also at 1:2, 14; 2:19, 24, 29; 3:1, 8, 20; 4:1, 2, 4, 5, 10 and 23.

Once (1:26) Paul talks about his *parousia*, which means 'presence', but was a regular term for the visit of an emperor to a far off town or city state. And twice he uses the word for 'citizenship', which was obviously a very important idea in the Roman world. The first time is at 1:27, when he uses the verb, and tells the Philippians, in connection with his *parousia*, to 'live out your citizenship in a manner worthy of the gospel', and that is just before he goes into the great hymn to Christ as 'Lord'. Then at 3:20, he makes it clear just how different Christians are from the Roman vision of the world, for he says 'our city state/citizenship is in heaven', and goes on, 'from where we are also waiting for a Saviour, Our Lord Jesus Christ'. Both 'Saviour' and 'Lord', of course, were used of the emperor at this time, and I don't think the Philippians will have missed the point.

So Philippians is a thoroughly subversive document, and I hope you will notice that as you read it. Much more important, however, is the joy that wells up from it, even though Paul is in prison, and I hope that it is the joy above all that will seize you as you read this lovely letter.

Questions

1. What differences do you notice between the first and second letters to the Corinthians?

2. Do you think that the Corinthians will have contributed generously to the collection?

3. What is the prevailing mood of Philippians, in your view?

4. What does Philippians tell us about Paul's attitude to the Roman Empire?

CHAPTER 6

The disputed Pauline letters

As you will already have gathered, of the 13 letters attributed to Paul in our New Testament, only seven are undisputed as coming from him. You may find yourself stirring uneasily at this and wondering if the New Testament is not committing some kind of a fraud on us, pretending to be something that it is not. So in this chapter I should like to look with you at this question of 'pseudonymity', or ascribing a letter to someone who did not write it, and then look at 2 Thessalonians, Colossians and Ephesians to see some of the reasons why scholars think that they may not be from Paul himself. Finally, I want to briefly tell you why I think you should read each letter.

So first let's look at 'pseudonymity', or writing a letter in someone else's name. If you are anything like me, you would probably prefer all the letters ascribed to Paul to have actually been written by him, but we have to live in the real world. We should remember that in the Jewish culture that produced our New Testament, producing a text in someone else's name was not uncommon: for example, the various books of Enoch, the Apocalypse of Abraham, and various 'Testaments' attributed to various characters of Israel's past, such as Moses or the 12 sons of Jacob. And in any case, since the three letters we are looking at are part of our New Testament, that means that the Church thinks that they are good for us to read and ponder. So let us do just that.

What about 2 Thessalonians? One scholar said that 'the problem with 2 Thessalonians is 1 Thessalonians'. Given the existence of both of them, it is hard to see how to fit them into what we know of Paul's career. 2 Thessalonians is much less warm and personal than 1 Thessalonians; it is clearly intended as a successor to 1 Thessalonians (2:15), and it seems to imitate it a bit, with two thanksgivings and some very similar vocabulary. However, if it was not written by Paul, Marcion and Polycarp in the second century AD knew of this letter, and assumed that it was by him.

So why should you read it? One thing that the author stresses is the importance of work, even if the world is coming to an end quite soon. He is concerned to tone down the expectations of Jesus coming back soon, and makes a slogan of 'no work, no food' (3:10). You might like to read reflectively through 3:1-5 and listen to the confidence that is there.

Colossians is also thought by some scholars to come from a pen other than Paul's. Why is this? Sometimes, I have to say, you get the feeling that scholars find it a little too 'Catholic' for comfort, with its sense of the Church universal rather than the local churches which scholars detect in the genuinely Pauline letters. The style, too, is a bit different, with long sentences and strings of words that mean more or less the same thing, words that we do not find in the seven letters that are universally agreed to be by Paul. But we have to say that Paul seems to have had a long career as an apostle of Jesus Christ, and we know for certain that he wrote more letters than survive in our New Testament, so we should be cautious of making too many over-confident statements about style or indeed about theology on the basis of so small a sample. It is a lovely letter, and we should certainly be the poorer without it. So whether you decide for or against its origin in the apostle to the Gentiles, make sure you read it carefully and get to know it well.

What can we say about it? Colossae was a smallish town, not far from Laodicea and Hierapolis, and about 100 miles inland from Ephesus in modern Turkey. As in most of his letters, Paul starts with a 'thanksgiving': 'having heard of your faith in Christ Jesus and the love which you have for all the saints'. If you want an example of a long sentence, have a look at 1:3-8, which has no break in Greek, but in English translations often ends up as several sentences.

One of the loveliest passages in the letter is the 'hymn' (if that is indeed what it is, and it is another long sentence) from 1:15-20, to Christ, 'image of the unseen God, the firstborn of all creation'. Many scholars regard this as a meditation on the first words of the Bible, 'in the beginning', applied to Jesus, who was present at creation and is therefore superior to all that threatens us, including, perhaps, the sinister angelic powers that were part of the teaching of the opponents in Colossae, 'thrones and lordships, rules and authorities . . . in order that he might be in every respect Number One'. Notice in particular the development of the idea of the 'body' from 1 Corinthians: 'he is the head of the Body, the Church', which is a step further than the idea of the body in that letter. Notice also Jesus' lofty relationship to God: 'in him the fullness was pleased to dwell, and through him to reconcile everything to him, after making peace through the blood of the cross'. Rather than worry about whether Paul could have written that passage, just sit with it and let it speak to you today.

As you read through it, allow yourself to be startled by Paul's idea that 'I am filling up what is lacking in Christ's afflictions, in my flesh, on behalf of his body, which is the Church' (1:24). We don't normally think of there being anything missing from Jesus' sufferings, but that is not to say that Paul could not have expressed himself in this rather striking way.

When you read through chapter 2, try to see what you think might be going on in Colossae that the author wants to defeat. Now scholars have several views on the matter, but they generally suppose that there was a shaky amalgam of offbeat

Jewish and pagan ideas, reflecting the mixture of cultures in that part of the province of Asia.

You will find a lovely passage to pray through at the opening of chapter 3: 'Given that you have been raised with Christ, seek the things above, where Christ is seated on the right side of God.' Then he encourages them to behave in various appropriate ways and to avoid certain vices. There is a passage you might wish to reflect on, about how to operate within families, telling husbands and wives, children and parents, and slaves and their masters how they are to coexist. That you will find at 3:18–4:1, and if you look very carefully at it you will see that it fundamentally asserts the equality of all the baptised, and not the superiority of men over women, adults over children, and slave owners over their slaves, as is often supposed. That then leads into a lovely exhortation (4:2-5): 'Persist in prayer, remaining awake in thanksgiving, and praying for us, that God may open a door of the word for us, to speak the mystery of Christ . . . Deal wisely with outsiders.'

Whoever wrote this, it is a lovely letter, and we should be grateful to those who preserved it for us.

Lovelier yet is the letter to the Ephesians, which can be described as 'a magnificent expression of the Pauline vision'. If Paul did not write it (and we have to admit that a majority of scholars believe it was from someone else's pen), then at least whoever wrote it thoroughly understood what Paul was about. The difficulty about ascribing it to Paul is that it seems to be based on Colossians, which is hard to understand if Paul wrote it. Like Colossians it has quite long sentences, and seems a bit too impersonal. Scholars also point to 'non-Pauline' vocabulary, but that is an argument that requires handling with care. You are, however, permitted to think that Paul wrote Ephesians, and it is not a silly thing to suppose.

Why should we read it at all? Well, for one thing, it is a good deal easier to read than the letter to the Romans! And although it can come across as a little impersonal, it offers a lovely vision of what God has done in Christ. You will find, if you are interested in statistics of this sort, the longest sentence in the entire New Testament at Ephesians 1:3-14. Read through it and admire the author's ability to keep the sentence under control; but, much more important, relish the beauty of his thought about what God has done in Christ. As you read it, get a feel for the author's strong sense of the universal Church, and for his lofty Christology, and how Christ and the Church are not to be separated.

One very interesting passage that you will not, I am sure, regret reading is 2:11-22. As you go through it, remember the Temple in Jerusalem and its concentric walls keeping Gentiles, women and laymen out of the holy of holies, and see how our author meditates on that in terms of what Jesus has done for us:

You, gentiles in the flesh, the ones known as 'uncircumcision' by those known as 'circumcision', were alienated from belonging to Israel, and strangers to the covenant of promise, with no hope, and no God in the world.

He then contrasts that with their present state: 'As it is, in Christ Jesus, you who were once a long way off are now near in the blood of Christ.' And see how he plays with the image of the walls round the Temple; instead of being any longer divided, both sides are

reconciled to God in one body through the cross . . . so you are no longer immigrants or strangers; instead you are fellow-citizens of the saints, and members of God's household, built on the foundation of the apostles and prophets, with Christ himself as the cornerstone.

This is a simply magnificent vision, and the great thing is that we should read it rather than worry about who wrote it. Read carefully through 3:14-19 and see the magnificent climax it reaches: 'to know the love of Christ that surpasses all knowledge, that you may be filled with all the fullness of God'.

Then in chapter 4, the author goes in for some lovely moral exhortation as to how his readers are to behave:

anxious to preserve the unity of the Spirit, in the bond of peace: one body, and one Spirit, just as you have been called in one hope of your calling: one Lord, one faith, one baptism, one God and father of all, who is over all and through all and in all.
(4:3-6)

That is the context in which we must read all the moral exhortation that now follows, and the famous 'household code', which you will find at 5:21–6:9. There are two important things to remember as you read it. The first is how it begins: 'You are all to be subordinated to each other in the fear of Christ.' So when he goes through the three pairs, wife–husband, child–parent, slave–master, we need to have the intelligence to see that he is not commanding the subordination of the weak to the strong, but rather a community where each loves the other and helps them. Look carefully at 6:5-9 and listen to it with the ears of a slave. You will, if you do that, realise that Paul is making a very clever point, using the Greek word *kyrios*, which means both 'Lord' and 'slave owner', to remind both slaves and their masters in the Church that, although they may have 'lords' whom they have to obey, they are not just to please human beings 'but as *Christ's* slaves doing *God's* will'. The slave owners do not come into the reckoning here; indeed, they, 'the lords', are reminded that they are to behave properly, 'knowing that they and you have a Lord in heaven – and he is not a snob'. There is no comfort here for the upper classes that want to keep their superior place.

One last passage for you to read is 6:13-20, where the writer draws a picture of a soldier putting on his armour for battle: 'Take God's panoply', it begins, and then goes through every item of the combatant's apparel, to show how prepared they have to be as they go into war. It is a lovely passage, and is an excellent way to end your reading of this remarkable letter.

Questions

1. Do you think it matters if Paul did not write 2 Thessalonians, Colossians or Ephesians?

2. What do these letters have to say to us today?

3. Is it possible to hear Paul's voice in these three letters?

The pastoral letters

Now we come to the three letters that have been known since at least the time of Thomas Aquinas as 'the pastorals', to Timothy and Titus. They are so called because they give advice to 'pastors' on how to do their shepherding job.

I have to tell you that you will find very few scholars nowadays who will argue that as these letters stand they are written by Paul. The basic arguments are that the vocabulary and style are at a rather more exalted level than we normally find in Paul, and that in them is a high proportion of words that are not to be found in the letters that everyone agrees in ascribing to Paul. They say that in the pastorals there is no sense of preparing for Jesus' imminent return, and that there is correspondingly much more interest in Church structures (because if you don't think that everything is coming to an end quite soon, then you have to look at how to structure the Church).

So there is, you will find, a good deal of talk about 'bishops' and 'deacons'. Or, rather, that is the way we transcribe those Greek words; in fact, the two words mean something like 'overseers' and 'servants'. In addition, there is a role for women, under the heading of 'widows', and what it says sounds very much as though they have a formal role in church (1 Timothy 5:3-15). However, you will also notice that the author has misgivings about allowing women much say in church: look at what he says about the teaching role of women (1 Timothy 2:11, 12): 'Let a woman remain in peace, in all submission. I do not permit a woman to teach, nor to have authority over males, but to be at peace.' Then he gives his reasons, which we may not find immediately convincing:

> For it was Adam that was created first, then Eve. And it was not Adam who was deceived, but the woman who was deceived at the transgression. But she will be saved through childbirth, if they remain in faith and love and holiness, with sobriety.

Texts of this sort should remind us that we do not know the whole context, and that the author and his audience did. They might find themselves rather surprised if they heard that we interpreted it as meaning that women are not allowed to teach or preach in the twenty-first century.

As always, we have to start by asking what kind of documents they are. I should tell you that scholars think that they are not at all the same sort of thing, and that 2 Timothy in particular, which shows no sign of knowing 1 Timothy, is different from the other two, and both of them are hard to fit into what else we know of Paul's biography. You must, of course, make up your mind about that when you read them. One thing that is clear is that the author and those whom he addresses (apparently the heads of the Christian community in Ephesus and Crete respectively) are facing the urgent need to get the structure of the church right, and that as part of an effort to keep hold of the basic insight into who Jesus was. The clear implication is that in order to get Jesus right you have to make sure that the right sort of officials are in place.

Why should we read these letters? They have some splendid phrases, it must be said, and contain lines that have come into many of our most familiar hymns, so ordinary Christians obviously feel at ease with them, whatever scholars may say. 'Fight the good fight' (1 Timothy 6:12), for example, rings several bells. And many widowed Christians will be able to echo what the author says at 1 Timothy 5:5: 'The real widow, the one who has been left alone, is the one who has put her hope in God and remains at her intercession and prayers night and day.' One exhortation that retains its relevance today is the stress on praying for those in authority 'in order that we may live a quiet and peaceful life, in all piety and respectfulness' (1 Timothy 2:2). It is certainly the case that those who govern today need our prayers.

In addition, the author of 1 Timothy outlines the qualities required in church officials, the *episkopoi* (3:1-7) and the *diakonoi* (3:8-13). For some reason, in a seminary where I used to teach, the students would always giggle nervously when they heard these instructions being read out, especially the injunction that these officials were not to be too much given to drink. That is not, however, the main point: the key thing is that it is not enough simply to find yourself thinking, 'It would be a good idea if they made me a bishop.' You have to recognise that not just anyone can do it. Institutions have their problems, as we all know, and when this letter was written the early Church was starting to come to grips with those problems. The important thing, for us as for them, is that we must always come back to Jesus, 'who appeared in the flesh, and was justified in the spirit, who appeared to angels, who was proclaimed among the Gentiles, who found faith in the world, and was taken up in glory' (3:16).

In addition to this, widows, as I say, seem to have had a definite role in the church. This letter insists above all that they have to keep their eyes on God (5:3-16), and elders must be treated properly (5:17-19). For some reason, elders are to receive double pay, and Timothy is not to hear any accusations against them, except on the basis of two or three witnesses (5:17, 19). This last instruction had uncomfortable implications when it was read in a way that evaded accusations concerning the sexual abuse of children. But, once again, we have to read these lines in their original context. The same is true, of course, of the well-known advice to Timothy against drinking neat water, but to take a little wine with it, possibly to kill the germs.

2 Timothy, as I say, is a different letter, much warmer and with a stronger pastoral instinct. Read, for example, the author's sense of his vocation as 'herald and apostle and teacher' (1:11) and try to apply it to your own life. And read the reference to Timothy's mother and grandmother, Lois and Eunice (1:5), and be warmed by those family relations that helped the growth of the early Church. The author reports something of what happened to Paul in his apostolate:

> You have followed my teaching, my leadership, my purpose, my endurance, my love, my stamina, my persecutions and sufferings that happened to me in Antioch, at Iconium, and at Lystra. I endured them all, and from them all the Lord delivered me.
> (3:10, 11)

Autobiographical fragments such as these make some scholars think that we have here a letter based on genuine fragments from Paul himself. And look at the request at 4:11, 13 that Timothy should bring with him, when he comes, not only Mark but also the 'cloak that I left behind at Troas, at Carpus' house, and the scrolls, and especially the parchments'. It is hard to imagine this being used in a letter that was a straight forgery.

Notice also the insistence, one that we should do well to heed today, on the importance of the true gospel (1:9-18), and the need for authentic teaching (2:1-7), especially when the false teachers are claiming that for them the Resurrection has already happened (2:18). There is a lovely meditation on the author's imminent death, which we should do well to read again and again:

> For I am already poured out like a libation, and the time for my dissolution has drawn near. I have fought the good fight, I have completed the Marathon; I have kept the faith. For the rest there is stored up for me the Gold Medal of righteousness, which the Lord, the just judge will give me on that day; and not just to me, but to all those who have loved his appearing.
> (4:6-8).

Then there is the letter to Titus, of whom we know from the other Pauline letters. He was pastor of the Christians in Crete, and was the one to carry Paul's 'tearful letter' to Corinth, where he managed to produce a diplomatic reconciliation. If you want to know why (as I understand the matter) there are no churches on the island of Crete built in honour of St Paul, have a look at 1:12, where you will read that, 'Cretans were always liars, evil beasts, and idle gluttons.'

Now it may be that this is a quotation from a Cretan prophet, but the inhabitants of the island were far from impressed, and have never forgiven St Paul.

As with the two other pastoral letters, there is emphasis on the existence of false teachers, described as 'many disorderly people, utterers of vain words, and mind-beguilers', which is splendid (if not particularly Pauline) language, so you can tell that he is not pleased. In particular he singles out 'those of the circumcision, whom it is necessary to silence, for they turn over whole houses, teaching what they should not, for the sake of base profit' (1:10, 11). Titus is to make sure that they do 'not pay attention to Jewish stories and commandments, belonging to people who pervert the truth' (1:14).

And for the author, as in the other two letters, the reason for getting the right sort of teachers is connected with the need to get the doctrine right. Whether this comes from Paul's pen or not, you can see that this is not the kind of issue that would be to the forefront in the earliest part of this ministry. This is how the author expresses it: 'you are to utter what is appropriate for healthy teaching' (2:1). Then, because he clearly makes a link with the right sort of teaching, he gets back to the right sort of teacher. So male elders are to be temperate, serious, sober and healthy in faith, love, and endurance; while female elders are to be

> fitting for priesthood in their array, not slanderers, or enslaved by much wine, good teachers, to give the young women instruction to love their husbands and their children: sober, chaste, working at the house, good, and with a proper relationship to their husbands, to prevent God's word from being insulted.
> (2:1-5)

Even the young men are to be 'sober', and 'slaves subordinated to their own masters, giving satisfaction in every respect, and not answering back'. Likewise Titus is to remind people to be 'subordinated to rulers and authorities, to be obedient, and ready for every good work, and show gentleness to all human beings.'

Now you may at this point be getting a bit restive, and feeling that all this stuff about getting orthodox teaching correct is a bit 'old-fashioned', and that getting the right sort of person into office is perhaps a bit overdone. You may also wonder what is the point of being subordinated to the secular authorities. Should not the Church be a bit more prophetic? Should we not challenge those who are in power? Well, perhaps, but we have to beware of transferring the needs of our time to those of another era; we should be prepared to make a distinction between the kind of teaching that was necessary in Jesus' day, which was all rather exciting and radical, and the kind of teaching that was required in another era, when the Church was trying to settle into something a bit more stable and long-lasting. Being Catholic means, as James Joyce said, 'Here comes everybody', so we need not suppose that there is just one correct approach to doctrine or to the holding of church office or to the powers that be.

If you want one passage in the letter to Titus that makes it worth your while coming back to it again and again, you might try the following, which you will find at 3:4-7:

> When the kindness [or you could read this as 'Christlikeness'] and loving-kindness of our Saviour God appeared, it was not because of any deeds that we ourselves have done in righteousness, but in accordance with his own mercy he saved us, through a washing that gave us rebirth, and of the renewal of the Holy Spirit, which he poured out abundantly upon us, through Jesus Christ our Saviour, so that we might be made righteous by his grace, and might become heirs in the hope of eternal life.

It is not elegantly expressed, but you could do a great deal worse than to sit with it and get inside it.

Questions

1. Does it matter to you whether or not Paul wrote these three letters?

2. Do the 'pastoral letters' have anything to say to us today?

3. Is 'institutionalisation' in the Church necessarily a bad thing?

CHAPTER 8

Mark:
the inventor of the Gospel form

So now we come ('and about time too', you may say) at last to the Gospels. We start, appropriately enough, with Mark, who was the first to write a Gospel, and whom we may therefore reasonably call its inventor.

In this chapter, I am going to invite you to think about Mark's Gospel's strange beginning, and its even stranger ending. For Mark is (there is no getting away from it) 'the strangest Gospel'. Look at how it begins, with the word 'Beginning', which must inevitably have reminded his first hearers of the opening words of the Bible.

> The beginning of the good news of Jesus Messiah, Son of God.
> As it is written in Isaiah the prophet:
> 'Look – I am sending my messenger before your face,
> who will prepare your way,
> the voice of one crying in the desert:
> "Prepare the way of the Lord –
> make straight his paths"'.
> John came, baptising in the desert, and proclaiming a baptism of
> repentance for forgiveness of sins.

So we discover that it is the beginning of the 'good news' or 'gospel'. Now this word echoes a Hebrew term from the Old Testament, about what God has done; but it also challenges a word used in the Roman Empire about the great things that the Emperor has done. So it is a subversive Gospel that we are starting to look at, one that is built on the Old Testament and its story of God; but it is also one that challenges the dominance of the Roman Empire.

And then, we learn, it is the good news of Jesus Messiah; which is to say that the only people to whom the document is of any interest are those who have actually heard of Jesus. Finally, in many but not all manuscripts, Jesus is described as 'Son of God'; whether or not this is what Mark wrote in this first verse, it is certainly what he believed.

Then it becomes a little odder, because Mark tells us that it is 'as it was written in the prophet Isaiah', but quotes the line, 'Look! I am sending my messenger before your face, who will prepare your way'; but as Mark's first hearers will have known, that was not from Isaiah but from Malachi or Exodus. And then, finally, we get to Isaiah with the next line, about 'a voice of one crying in the desert, prepare the way of the Lord'.

That seems fine, but the oddity continues when, instead of meeting Jesus, we are introduced rather to John the Baptist (so we are supposed to know who he is, evidently). He is also in the desert, so presumably the voice in the previous verse was his. And he has a message: 'repentance for the forgiveness of sins' (1:4), which is addressed to 'all the Judean region and all the Jerusalemites, confessing their sins'. And these, of course, are the people who will pay the least attention to Jesus in the rest of the Gospel.

Then we discover what John is wearing: 'camel hair and a leather girdle around his loins'. The alert reader will remember that this is what the prophet Elijah was wearing in 2 Kings 1:8 when Ahaziah received a grim oracle about his health prospects. So John the Baptist fits into the story of those people whom God has sent in the past.

And now, at last, we hear about Jesus: 'There is coming the One Stronger than Me after me, of whom I am not fit to stoop down and untie the thong of his sandals. I baptised you with water, but he is going to baptise you with the Holy Spirit.' (1:7, 8)

Finally, then, Jesus (from Nazareth of Galilee) erupts onto the stage, but instead of his doing something exciting, we are simply told that 'he was baptised in the Jordan by John', which is a bit of an anti-climax for the reader. Then God takes a hand in the story, for 'immediately coming up out of the water he saw the heavens opening [so we know that God is at work] and the Spirit like a dove coming down upon him'. Next we are allowed to eavesdrop on what God says to Jesus: 'You are my Son, the Beloved; in you I am well pleased.' According to the rules of storytelling, we now know, therefore, that Jesus is a good thing, and that he fits the old story of God and the people of God. We probably also have a hint that the story is going to be an uncomfortable one, as we can see in the text:

> And immediately coming up out of the water,
> he saw the heavens being divided,
> and the Spirit like a dove coming down to him.
> And a voice came from the heavens [so it's God talking]:
> 'you are my Son, the Beloved: I am well pleased in you'.

That last line is a clear reference to the first of the Songs of the Suffering Servant (Isaiah 42:1); so the discomfort hits Jesus immediately, even if God is talking to him.

Now see what follows:

And immediately the Spirit hurls him out into the desert.

We notice the word 'immediately' [which, by the way, is Mark's favourite adverb] and that very strong verb 'hurls' as a description of how Jesus goes out into the desert. Then we read, 'And he was being tested by Satan; and he was with the wild beasts; and the angels were serving him.' So Jesus is not in charge of his own mission. He shares the human experience of temptation. He has endured the loneliness of being with the wild beasts, but the helpful presence of the angels means that he is on God's business. However, you may also find yourself saying, 'Wait a minute – what about that business of the invitation to "turn these stones into bread"?' If that is the case, you have forgotten that Mark tells the story rather differently from Matthew and Luke, who have Jesus tempted in three rather specific ways. So you might like to read what those two evangelists have to say about it all.

But here we are at verse 13 of chapter 1, and Jesus has not done anything at all yet, so you may be feeling that this is all a bit strange, since this Gospel is supposed to be about him. Only now does Mark at last permit us to see Jesus actually doing something, but we should notice the circumstances: 'after John had been handed over' (in chapter 6 we shall discover that he was beheaded on Herod's orders, so this too is rather strange). And what does Jesus do? He goes back to his home region of Galilee, and Mark tells us that he is 'preaching the gospel of God, and saying, "The time has been fulfilled, and the Reign of God has drawn near. Repent and believe in the gospel."' We don't at the moment know what the gospel is that we are to believe in, but we are ready for anything, and we know that God is at work here, in this strange tale.

Then it gets stranger, for Jesus now gains followers, in the most remarkable way:

And as he was passing by the Sea of Galilee,
he saw Simon and Andrew, the brother of Simon,
casting their nets into the sea (for they were fishermen).
And Jesus said to them, 'Come here, after me;
and I am going to make you become fishers for human beings.'
And *immediately* they abandoned their nets – and they followed him!!
Then he went a little bit further onwards,
and he saw Jacob the son of Zebedee – and his brother John;
and them in the boat, repairing their nets.
And immediately he called them.
And they abandoned their father Zebedee in the boat,
with the hired servants.
And they went off after him!
(1:16-20)

We should pay some attention to the way Mark sets the scene. Jesus is walking by the Sea of Galilee (every time you encounter this lake in Mark's Gospel, be aware that something strange is going to happen) and sees two sets of brothers: first Simon and Andrew, exercising their profession as fishermen, and then 'Jacob the son of Zebedee and John his brother'. It is an extraordinary episode; there is even a little joke on Jesus' part, telling these professional fishers that they are now going to fish for human beings instead of their normal quarry.

In addition, of course, you have all been well brought up, and you know that when a strange man asks you to follow him, the correct response is to call either the police or the men in white coats. But that does not happen; instead, both sets of brothers obey the summons, to our astonishment; indeed, the sons of Zebedee abandon not just their nets, but also the boats, their father and the hired servants. So now this strange new project has one leader and four followers.

Nor does the strangeness end there. For Jesus now enters the synagogue on the Sabbath. Later in the Gospels we shall learn that virtually every time this happens, there is going to be trouble. And there are signs of it here: 'He started to teach.' That sounds simple enough, but why is he teaching, if all is well? Then we discover that Jesus' teaching makes a very considerable impact: 'they were amazed at his teaching'. That sounds all right, until we discover the reason for their astonishment, which is simply that 'he was teaching like one who has authority'. That word, 'authority', runs all the way through Mark's Gospel, and is precisely the dividing line between Jesus and his opponents. You may remember, for example, that at 11:27, 28 Jesus is interrogated by the religious establishment ('the chief priests and the scribes and the elders'), after he has made his gesture of expelling the commercial interests from the Temple. And they ask him, 'By what authority are you doing these things? Or who gave you the authority to do these things?' The reader, of course, knows the answer: Jesus' authority comes from God, and that trumps all human authority, but that will not pacify his opponents, and Jesus is shortly going to die because of this.

So he is 'teaching like one who has authority', and then Mark slips in a comment: 'not like the scribes'. This is the first time we have met these characters, but quite soon we shall work out that they represent the opposition, and that their presence means trouble. For the moment, though, it is our task to remember what we heard at Jesus' baptism, that he is God's beloved Son, 'in whom I am well pleased'. But, to our astonishment, this brings him into conflict with the religious authorities.

Nor does the conflict end here, for we are still in the synagogue, and Jesus has his first battle with demons, which once again culminates in the verdict: 'a new teaching, with authority: he even commands the unclean spirits – and they obey him!' This is a very strange Gospel, and we shall do well to live with the strangeness, a battle between God and the opponents of God.

There is much more to talk about in this extraordinary Gospel, but for the moment I should like to leap ahead 15 chapters and look at how it ends; for Jesus is going to die, and the last verses take us to the tomb in which he was subsequently placed on the last Friday of his life. If you look at your copy of the Bible, you will find that there are perhaps three endings given to the Gospel. There is the 'short ending', which has the women reporting 'concisely' back to Peter about what they have seen, and Jesus himself giving them their mission. Then there is the 'long ending', which is generally printed as 16:9-20. If you look closely at that, you will see that it is taken from other Gospels, especially Luke, but also Acts, Matthew and John.[2]

But neither of these endings sounds like Mark, and it looks as though they were added because Mark's original ending seemed a bit puzzling to his early readers. I want to suggest to you that this very odd ending is precisely what Mark originally intended. This was almost certainly 16:1-8, a very strange passage that we shall now read together.

It starts, 'when the Sabbath was finally over' (and I think we can hear the impatience of the women in this phrase), Mary Magdalene and the other two 'went and bought spices', in order to come and anoint him. So they did not believe in the Resurrection (because otherwise they would not have tried to anoint the corpse). Then we watch them as 'very early on the first day of the week, they come to the tomb', and we admire their courage (the male followers of Jesus are nowhere to be seen just now, having disappeared on the last train to Galilee on the Thursday night). When they get there, Mark comments that 'the sun has risen'. Now this may be Mark's little joke: 'You're a bit late, ladies'; but if that is indeed the case, we should avoid laughing too loudly and reflect on where the men are at this point.

The next thing that Mark does is to allow us to overhear, as he did at Jesus' baptism, when we eavesdropped on what the Father said to him. There are many other places where Mark gives us this privilege, in order to understand what is going on in the story. At this point, what we overhear is the women wondering how to get rid of the stone that Joseph of Arimathea had rolled in front of the door. Now it is no good the male readers of the Gospel chiming in, 'You should have thought of that, ladies,' because the men, who might have been stone-pushers, are completely off the scene.

All is well, however (this is, after all, the story of God), because 'looking up' (and we need to know that this verb can also mean 'recovering their sight'; see Mark 10:51, 52), 'they see that the stone has been rolled away'. That phrase,

---

2. It is only fair to warn the reader that since writing these words I have come across the interesting work of Nicholas P. Lunn, *The Original Ending of Mark: A New Case for the Authenticity of Mark 16:9-20*, James Clarke & Co, Cambridge, 2015, which offers an arresting challenge to my claim that the 'long ending' is not written by Mark.

'has been rolled away', is what they call a 'divine passive'; so we are meant to understand that God has intervened. Then the evangelist comments, 'For it was very big.' Now you will not believe this, but there are scholars, sober and apparently in their right minds, who claim that that comment, 'For it was very big', really belongs in the previous verse, when they were worrying about getting the stone rolled away. That is to miss the point: Mark is drawing our attention to how easily and effortlessly God acts – and that may be in a context of his writing for an audience who are wondering seriously whether God can cope.

So, the stone thus deftly removed, they now go into the tomb; and we must bless these courageous ladies, for in their culture they might have expected to find demons, or vultures, or perhaps just a decomposing body. There are none of these things, however; instead, when they went into the tomb, 'they saw a young man'. Now the last time we heard this particular word, it was applied to one of Jesus' followers, at the arrest in Gethsemane, who in terror ran away naked, leaving behind a 'shroud'. This seems, however, to be a different young man; for we learn that the person in the tomb greeting the ladies is 'sitting on the right', which, incidentally, is what Jesus had predicted, in his trial before the High Priest, would happen to the Son of Man. Not only that, but the 'young man' is wearing a white garment, possibly reminding us what had happened at the Transfiguration (9:2-9), at that moment when God told Peter, James and John that Jesus was indeed his beloved Son, and that they must listen to him.

We are not finished with the young man, however, for the women 'were amazed', which in this Gospel is a regular term for what happens when human beings encounter the divine. And the young man, like so many angels in the Old Testament, tells them, 'Don't be amazed', a command which he backs up by revealing that he knows what is going on here, for he says, 'It's Jesus you are looking for, the crucified one.' We do not need to be told that he has it right, for we saw them set off with their spices. But if someone is sitting in the tomb armed with this knowledge, then that makes an immense difference, and we learn (once more) that God is after all in this strange story. At this point we are almost not surprised when we hear the Easter proclamation, 'He has been raised – he is not here.' Dimly we remember that on each of the three occasions when Jesus predicted his Passion (which we shall be looking at in a later chapter), he also predicted his Resurrection, but we did not notice it. And as evidence of Jesus' absence, the 'young man' points to 'the place where they put him', and there is nothing there: no decomposing corpse, nor a body torn by dogs or vultures, just an empty tomb.

Then the women are given a job to do: 'Off you go and tell his disciples.' We remember that the disciples have all disappeared and wonder how this is to be done; and the young man continues, 'and Peter'. Now of course, the last time we saw Peter, he had been, despite his energetic posturing beforehand, cursing and swearing the most terrible oaths that he had no idea who this Jesus person might be. So Peter and the disciples are here very gently brought back onside, and once more belong to Jesus' group to which they had been called at the beginning. And we learn that 'he is going before you into Galilee'. Now 'Galilee' is where the whole adventure had started, and now they are to go back, armed with a deeper understanding of the Jesus story: 'You will see him there.'

But it is not just for them; it is also for the reader, for you and me. We are now invited to go back to the beginning of the Gospel, and to read it with new eyes.

And what happens? The ending of the Gospel is perhaps the strangest of all; for as the narrator continues we hear him say, to our astonishment, 'They went out and ran away from the tomb. For trembling and amazement had seized them. And they said nothing to nobody. For they were afraid . . .'

And where does that leave you and me? This is a very strange Gospel.

Questions

1. What does Mark's beginning tell us about what we are about to read?

2. What do you think of Mark's ending? Where did he intend his Gospel to end?

3. Do you agree that Mark is a very strange Gospel?

CHAPTER 9

The Marcan sandwich

In this chapter, I should like to look with you at a device that Mark often uses as a way of encouraging his listeners to pay attention. It is called the 'sandwich', or, if you like impressive-sounding phrases, 'interpretative intercalation'. This is a device whereby Mark wraps one story round another, and the clue for the hearer is to interpret one story by the other. I am going to talk about just five of these 'sandwiches', and then at the end I will mention a couple of other possibilities. Scholars often find other 'sandwiches', and as you read the text of Mark, you might look out for other possibilities.

Let me start with perhaps the most obvious of these 'sandwiches'. It comes in chapter 5, just after the cure of the Gerasene demoniac, as Jesus returns by boat across the sea. Mark here gives us two stories. The first, what you might call the 'bread', is that of a sick daughter; the second, the filling of the sandwich, is that of the woman with the haemorrhage. They are both striking stories, but they gain enormously in impact if we read them together.

When Jesus gets off the boat, he is once more beset by crowds, 'by the sea', and is approached by 'one of the synagogue-rulers'. 'Aha!' you think. 'Now there is going to be trouble.' But hold on, and watch. For one thing, the ruler is given a name, and we were not expecting that. For another thing, the name is Jairus, which means something like 'the Lord gives light'. Then we see that instead of attacking Jesus, 'he falls at his feet and begs him many times, saying, "My little daughter is at the end: come and put your hands on her, that she may be saved, and live."' So we are not surprised when Jesus 'went off with him'.

At this point, the crowds reappear, 'and they were pressing upon him'; but here they function as cover for the woman whose story is the 'filling' of the sandwich. She is, we learn, one who 'is with a flow of blood for 12 years', which means that she is ritually impure. Mark takes us deeper into her situation, and immediately wins our sympathy: 'She had suffered at the hands of many doctors, and spent all that she had, and was not helped, but had got worse.' Then we watch with horror as she creeps up in the crowd (where she should not be, of course, because of her ritual impurity), and 'touched his cloak'. This means that Jesus is now ritually impure.

Then Mark, as he often does, allows us to overhear the woman's thoughts, and once more gains our sympathy for her: 'If I just touch his clothes, I'm going to be saved' (and we notice that she uses the same word that Jairus used when asking Jesus on behalf of his daughter). The result is electrifying: 'And immediately the fountain of her blood was dried up, and she knew in her body that she was healed of her scourge.'

The story does not end there, however (and the alert reader notices that she has not yet been 'saved', which is what both she and Jairus were looking for). Jesus feels the power going out of him, and enquires 'whodunit?' His disciples jeer at him, pointing to the crowd, but Jesus takes no notice of them at all. The Greek now makes it clear that he knows it is a woman who has touched him. So at last she comes forward and admits what she has done. We wait to see what will happen, and breathe a sigh of relief when Jesus calls her 'daughter', and says, 'Your faith has *saved* you,' which was, you remember, what she was looking for in the first place. Jesus continues, 'Go in peace – and be healed of your scourge,' showing a very precise sympathy for what she has endured.

The lady now disappears off stage, and we return to our first story. We think we know what will happen, but instead, 'they come from the synagogue-ruler's house and tell him', in words that are not exactly from the Manual of Bereavement Counselling, 'Your daughter's dead – stop bothering the Teacher.' Jesus, once again, ignores the obvious comment and simply says to Jairus, 'Don't be afraid, only have faith.' Then he narrows the audience, getting rid of everyone bar Peter, James and John, his 'inner cabinet'.

There is another crowd in the house, 'wailing and weeping', and when Jesus tells them 'she is not dead but sleeping', they mock, as his disciples had just done. So he gets rid of them all, except for the girl's parents, and goes into where the child is. Ignoring rules of social propriety, he takes her by the hand and tells her in Aramaic, 'Little girl, I'm telling you, rise.' The inevitable happens: 'And immediately she arose and walked!'

There are four results: first, we are told her age, which is 12, that is to say that she has been alive as long as the other woman has had her affliction. Second, this is greeted with 'great amazement'. Third, perhaps least likely of all, Jesus commands them to an impossible silence. Finally, in a lovely touch, 'He said that she was to be given food.'

So there we have the sandwich, and we can already see how the two stories together take us deeper into the strange tale of Jesus, who brings salvation as well as healing, who does not mind about ritual impurity, who is open to everyone, even synagogue-rulers, who is jeered at for his pains, and who issues impossible instructions about not telling anybody. This is the hero of this very strange Gospel.

You get the point, and there is no need for us to cover the remaining stories in quite so much detail. The next one to look at is at 3:20-35, and it is a very strange sandwich. It starts (look at 3:20, 21) with 'his people' trying to arrest

Jesus, thinking he is crazy because he doesn't have time to eat. We should remember that in that culture, if a member of the family does not eat, that reflects on their honour. Then comes the 'filling' of the sandwich, where 'scribes from Jerusalem' (a phrase that already tells us they are up to no good) accuse him of 'having Beelzeboul, and casting out demons by the prince of demons'. Effortlessly he rebuts their accusation, proving that it is impossible for Satan to cast out Satan, and warning them that this is the worst kind of blasphemy. After that, the 'bread' of the sandwich is completed by the arrival of his mother and brothers, and Jesus is heard to redefine family in terms of those who 'perform God's will'. This is a strange combination of stories, but together they take us deeper into the mystery.

The same thing happens with our next sandwich, 6:7-33. The 'bread' consists of sending the Twelve out in twos on their first mission, with authority over unclean spirits and instructions to travel light. They go off, and to fill the space until they return, Mark inserts the lively story of the execution of John the Baptist, which, if you look carefully, is really about who Jesus is and what is his likely fate. Read this story attentively and notice that it takes John off stage for the last time, but also tells us what is likely to happen when disciples do what God wants them to do, culminating in the disgusting picture of the Baptist's head being presented on a dish to Mrs Herod and her unengaging daughter. Once John's disciples have safely buried their unfortunate leader, Jesus' disciples come back in triumph and are invited to a bit of peace, which, as a matter of fact, is never given to them.

From reading these two stories together, we learn something about the nature of our mission as disciples and something about the hostility we may expect to arouse, and perhaps also a glimpse of what will happen to Jesus in the end.

The next sandwich story I'd like you to look at is a good way down the line, at 11:11-25. Jesus has entered Jerusalem, which we have foreseen for a while, and we have already been told that this means death at the hands of the 'chief priests and scribes' (10:33) – that is to say, the Temple authorities. Now the Messiah actually comes to the Temple and, to our astonishment (this is a very strange story), 'he looked round at everything, and because the hour was late he went out to Bethany with the Twelve'. Then he comes back the next day and we have the extraordinary story of the cursing of the unfortunate fig tree, which is, sandwich-like, wrapped round Jesus' expulsion of the sellers and buyers from the Temple and the overturning of the tables of the commercial interests. This moment of prophetic challenge is then hammered home with a quotation from Isaiah about 'a house of prayer' and Jesus' departure from the city. The rest of the story is picked up the following day (11:20), with the discovery that the fig tree is now 'dried up from the roots', and Peter manages to notice it.

This is a strange story, until we realise that the fig tree, the ancient symbol of Israel, stands for the Temple's failure to be 'a house of prayer', so we are not to imagine that Jesus is petulantly punishing the tree for not producing its fruit when the time is not right. All Jesus will say is, 'Have faith in God . . . and may your Father, the one in the heavens, forgive your trespasses.' That, incidentally, is the nearest that Mark's Gospel gets to quoting the Lord's Prayer.

Our final sandwich opens the story of Jesus' Passion. If we look at 14:1, 2, we see the background: 'Passover and Unleavened Bread', and the plan on the part of the high priests and scribes to kill Jesus by guile, with the proviso that they do not want it to be during the festival because of the danger of popular unrest. Then we go to verse 10, and we see that the story runs on quite naturally, with Judas Iscariot volunteering to help them in their plan.

In between, at verses 3-9, it looks as though Mark has placed the captivating story of the anointing at Bethany, 'at the house of Simon the leper'. Once again Jesus is in an impure setting, made more risky by the sudden appearance of a woman where no woman should be, with an extravagant quantity of the best oil. Her generosity is underlined by the fact that she 'broke the alabaster jar', meaning that the entire quantity has to be used. Then she anoints him (as Messiah, we presume), and that leads to an element that we have seen in each of these sandwiches, namely a certain hostility from the establishment. Here it is a complaint about the very high value of the anointing oil, which could, they say, 'have been given to the poor'. Jesus then rereads the woman's gesture; he does not deny that it was a Messianic anointing, but reveals what kind of a Messiah he is, namely one who has to die: 'she took the myrrh ahead of time to anoint my body for its burial'. Then he decrees that this woman is to be immortalised for her generosity: 'what she has done will be spoken of in memory of her'. The contrast between the establishment plot to kill Jesus and the woman's loving attentiveness to the dying Messiah gives us the lens through which we are to read the subsequent story of how the religious and political authorities apparently succeeded in their objective. This is a sandwich of immense importance in assisting us to understand how Mark's Gospel works, at this climax of the narrative.

As I say, these are not the only possible examples of Marcan sandwiches, but they will give you an idea of how our evangelist works. Here are some more examples, though they are a little different because they stretch out over a longer portion of the text. The first you will find at 1:10,11, at the baptism of Jesus, where Jesus sees 'the heavens tearing open and the Spirit coming down like a dove, and the voice from heaven tells him, "You are my Son, the Beloved"'. Then turn to the end, to 15:38, 39, when the same word for 'tearing open' is used, this time with regard to the 'veil of the sanctuary'. Clearly we are to understand this as God's comment on the Passion of Jesus. But see what happens next: a voice, not from heaven, but from a professional soldier, a centurion who is accustomed to the death of foolish criminals, who declares, unbelievably, 'Truly, this man was Son of God'. These two texts, taken together, bracket the entire Gospel with the affirmation of Jesus' identity as a dying Messiah. It is a very remarkable sandwich.

Another sandwich I should like you to look at for yourselves begins and ends with a cure of a blind person. The first takes place at 8:22-26, at Bethsaida. The cure is not mentioned in Matthew or Luke, possibly because it involves the use of spittle and because the cure is not at first complete, because initially the healed man sees people 'walking like trees' before Jesus touches him a second time, and the cure is complete. The second healing is that of Bartimaeus (10:46-52); this takes place immediately after James and John have shown their catastrophic failure to understand Jesus by demanding top places in his hierarchy. On the way out of Jericho we encounter the blind beggar sitting '*beside* the road'. Like others in the sandwiches we have looked at, he encounters some hostility: the crowds tell him to 'shut up'. He persists, however ('Son of David, have mercy on me'). Then, at Jesus' call, he takes off his clothes, blunders naked through the crowd, and has his sight restored. Then he follows Jesus *on* the road; so he is now a disciple. And where is the road leading? Why, to Jerusalem, where we arrive in the very next verse (11:1). And we have long known that in Jerusalem Jesus is going to die.

That is the 'bread' of this sandwich. And what is the filling in the middle? It is the threefold prediction, each time followed by catastrophic misunderstanding on the part of the disciples, that Jesus is a dying Messiah. The blindness of the two men who make up the outside of the sandwich is matched by the blindness of the disciples, who have no real understanding that Jesus must die, and that his Messiahship has nothing to do with gaining status and everything to do with what God wants.

See how the sandwich helps us to hear Mark's story better. Do you think there are any other texts like this in this strange Gospel?

Questions

1. Does Mark's use of the 'sandwich' device help us to understand the Gospel better?

2. Do you think Mark is doing this deliberately?

3. Can you see any other 'sandwiches' in the text of Mark?

CHAPTER 10

Mark's Passion story

From what we have already seen in the preceding chapters, we know that the Passion is of huge importance in this strange Gospel. Just count the number of verses in chapters 14 and 15 given over to the story and you will see what scholars mean by calling this Gospel a 'Passion Narrative with an extended introduction'. So in this chapter I will say a bit about how the Passion Narrative works in Mark's Gospel. But it goes wider and deeper than that, for in chapters 8–10 it is bracketed, you may remember from the previous chapter, by two healings of blind men, who perhaps stand for the blindness of those readers who are reluctant to face the truth about Jesus. And before that, the theme of the Passion is played out in what I like to call various 'straws in the wind', which indicate that Jesus has enemies.

First, then, the 'straws in the wind':

At 1:22 Jesus is described as teaching 'not as the scribes'. (We have not heard of these characters before, but we know it means trouble.) And see 1:24 – the battle lines are drawn (compare 3:11, where the unclean spirits recognise him: 'You are the Son of God'). So scribes and demons are put on very much the same level, as fundamentally hostile to Jesus.

The next time we hear of the scribes is at 2:6, 7 when 'some of the scribes' make the allegation of 'blasphemy' against Jesus. This is followed in 2:16 by Mark's mention of the 'scribes of the Pharisees', and in verse 18, where it is just the Pharisees who complain.

Another 'straw in the wind' is found at 3:2, in the synagogue. Notice that '*they* [unidentified] were watching him', and see Jesus' anger in verse 5. So we are not surprised, although it is a bit sudden, when at the end of that story (3:6) we hear that 'The Pharisees went out immediately, and made a plot with the Herodians against him how they might destroy him.' We can already see the way the wind is blowing. This is, of course, very much of a piece with 3:22, where we hear the verdict of the 'scribes from Jerusalem' (and we know enough by this time to be aware that this means death), that 'he has Beelzeboul'. See once again the connection between Jesus' opponents and unclean spirits.

Jesus, you see, is not a very comfortable person to have around, so at 5:17 the Gerasenes beg Jesus to leave (not religious authorities, this time). One response to him is mockery (see 5:31 and 5:40, where it is not the religious authorities who are opposed to him, but his disciples in the first place, and the mourners at Jairus' house in the second).

Then at 6:3 Jesus encounters rejection in Nazareth (family and friends rather than authorities). And we have already looked at 6:14-29, the story of the death of John the Baptist, foreshadowing Jesus' death. Then there are the constant arguments: at 7:1-15, for example, with Pharisees and some scribes, and some more Pharisees arguing with Jesus, at 8:11, where it is presented as a question of authority. This dispute is picked up at 8:15, where the disciples are sharply told, 'Beware of the yeast of the Pharisees and the yeast of Herod', which they misinterpret as a rebuke for their failure to bring a picnic. All of these are straws in the wind, which make it no surprise when things turn darker in the second half of the Gospel.

For almost exactly halfway through the Gospel, at 8:29, the question is put to all of the disciples, 'Who do you say I am?' On their behalf, Peter gets it right: 'the Messiah', but when Jesus goes on to predict his sufferings, Peter will not have it. And from this point on, the tone of the Gospel changes abruptly; the crowds that were everywhere in the first half virtually disappear, there are now hardly any miracles, and the three predictions of Jesus' Passion overshadow everything else as Jesus attempts, without much success, to teach his reluctant disciples.

After each of the Passion predictions the disciples get it badly wrong, and have to be rebuked. At 8:32, 33 Peter responds by grabbing hold of Jesus 'and began to rebuke him'. Jesus rebukes him back (Mark uses the same word here), and tells him, 'Get behind me, Satan', which sounds pretty damning, except that it may simply be a repeat of the invitation to discipleship, for 'you are not thinking God-thoughts but human thoughts'.

The second prediction (9:30-32) takes place after the Transfiguration, which might have given at least the 'inner cabinet' the right idea, at 9:2-13. The response of the disciples is fairly catastrophic, as Jesus is compelled gently to show them by asking a gentle question: 'What were you arguing about on the way?' This silences them, because they know they have got it wrong – they were arguing '*on the way*' about which of them was Mr Big, and they have to be gently educated by Jesus using a child as a visual aid.

The third Passion prediction takes place in chapter 10:32-34. It is followed by two blunders on the part of the disciples, the first by James and John, bidding for the best places on either side of Jesus when he comes in his glory. That is the first blunder, because it is not to be like that in the kingdom, so Jesus explains about drinking the cup and being baptised, which *we* know is all about death. And when Jesus' death comes, the two brothers will be nowhere to be seen, and on Jesus' right and left there will be two convicted thieves. Then comes the second blunder, as the other ten disciples get annoyed at this bid for power, and they all have to have it explained to them (once more) that in the Jesus movement, leadership is all a matter of service and slavery.

And now, with the happy example of Bartimaeus, we are in Jerusalem and into the Passion Narrative, where the Gospel has been aiming all this time.

This moment was, as we saw, foreshadowed at 3:6, when the Pharisees and Herodians decided that Jesus had to die. Perhaps there was a hint of it also at his baptism: if 'my son, the Beloved' (1:11) is meant to echo the 'Suffering Servant' of Second Isaiah (42:1). We cannot grasp the Jesus of Mark unless we also grasp the Cross. Moreover, it is because of the Cross that Mark's Gospel is worth reading in a broken world where there is too much suffering: all human life is in this marvellous story. The evangelist is asking a double question: why should Jesus suffer? And why should we?

Mark almost certainly had existing material before him, but you can feel his hand at work. We saw in the previous chapter how he uses his 'sandwiching' technique to insert a passage right at the beginning (14:3-9), to help us read the Passion Narrative.

There are also some marvellous stories here. Again, this is typical of Mark. Notice how these stories both advance the narrative and create a sombre mood; the evangelist does not just tell stories for stories' sake. See the following stories, and consider the atmosphere that they create:

Jesus in charge	14:12-16 (organising the Passover meal)
A moment of sadness	14:17-21 (prediction of betrayal)
The shadow of death	14:22-26 ('This is my body, my blood of the covenant, poured out for many')
Abandonment	14:50 ('and they all abandoned him and fled').

Two of the best stories in Mark's Passion Narrative are those of Gethsemane (14:32-42) and Peter's denial (14:66-72). Both these stories have a threefold structure. With the second story, notice how skilfully Mark builds up the atmosphere: 14:29-31 ('even if all of them trip up – Not Me!'). And Mark makes a clear contrast between the Peter story and the parallel narrative about Jesus (14:53-65), as the following table should make clear:

Jesus	Reference	Peter	Reference
Is led	53	Follows from afar	54
Confronts high priests, elders, scribes	53	Sits with servants; is confronted by a slave girl	54; 66
-	-	Warms himself	54
Is falsely accused	56, 57	Is correctly identified	67, 69, 70
Is silent	61	Says too much	68, 70, 71
Eventually proclaims that *Ego Eimi*, and cites Scripture	62	Curses and swears and lies	68, 70, 71
Is deliberately condemned to death	1, 55, 64	Weeps	72
Is mocked, hit, and eventually killed	65 &c.	Gets off scot free	-

Then there is the phrase 'King of the Jews', which Mark uses with some skill; it does not appear until almost the end, and then it figures quite prominently: on the lips of the soldiers, mockingly, and the civil administrator, questioningly, before, finally, being placed above the cross, as 'the inscription of his criminal case':

15:2 'Are you the King of the Jews?' (Pilate)

15:9 'Shall I release the King of the Jews for you?' (Pilate)

15:12 'What am I to do with the King of the Jews?' (Pilate)

15:18 'Hail, the King of the Jews!' (soldiers)

15:26 'The King of the Jews' (the Roman verdict).

Then things go from bad to worse, as Jesus is mocked by soldiers (15:16-20), passers-by (29, 30), high priests (31, 32) and even his fellow convicts (32b). Finally, at 15:34, comes the terrible moment of abandonment: *Elohi, Elohi, lema sabachtani?* It is often supposed that Jesus is here quoting Psalm 22, which ends, like almost all the psalms of lament, in a great act of confidence; but although the psalm has clearly affected the way Mark tells the Passion story, we should notice that Jesus cites the psalm here in his native Aramaic rather than in the

Hebrew in which he would have learnt the psalm. So I assume Mark means us to take this prayer quite literally, as an expression of Jesus' sense that he has been abandoned even by God.

However, it turns out that all is not quite at an end. For then we notice (what we may have been too stunned to observe earlier) the reference to 'Alexander and Rufus' at 15:21. The fact that they are mentioned at all means that they are known to Mark's community and that in turn presumably means that something happened to their father, the African Simon, on that Friday afternoon. After that, all kinds of things start to happen that renew our awareness that this is not the end of the story:

- 15:39: The Christological climax, when the centurion asserts that 'truly this fellow was Son of God'.

- 15:40, 41, 47: We realise that Jesus was not, after all, quite alone: the faithful women were there.

- Lastly, at 15:43: the mysterious figure of Joseph of Arimathea emerges from the woodwork.

In these moments we are given a glimpse (no more than that – unless we recall that each of the Passion predictions included a reference to Resurrection) of ultimate victory . . .

This is a bleak and powerful story that hints at God's future.

Questions

1. What do you notice most about the way Mark tells the story of Jesus' Passion?

2. Why did Jesus have to die, in Mark's view?

3. What are the signs of hope in Mark's Passion Narrative?

CHAPTER 11

Questions and counter-questions in Mark

We have seen, then, that Mark is a very strange Gospel, which makes its way by asking questions of the reader. What I should like to do in this final chapter on Mark is to make a list of some of these questions and show how they invite us to 'fill in the blanks', as a way of going deeper into the mystery of Jesus. I shall not be listing all of the questions in the Gospel, and you can look through the text for the ones I have missed. Very often, you will notice, the questions are answered with counter-questions, which offer a different angle.

The point is this: if you chase up the questions in the Gospel, the gaps where Mark allows you, the reader, to fill in, then you will draw very close to what he is doing. I want to suggest to you that Mark is dealing with just two basic questions: 'Who is Jesus?' and 'What must Jesus' disciples be like?' I think that by the end you may find yourself agreeing that the text of Mark's Gospel leads us towards an answer to both of those basic questions, about Jesus and about his disciples.

The first question you will find is at 1:24, where the demons ask, 'What have you to do with us, Jesus of Nazareth?' (And you will find the same question on the lips of the Gerasene demoniac at 5:7). Then listen to the exclamation of the crowds (1:27): 'What is this? A new teaching with authority?' Both of these questions force the reader or hearer to ask who Jesus is, and in particular what is his relationship to the demons.

At 2:7 there is a really important question. When the paralysed man has been let down through the roof, Jesus is heard to say, 'Child, your sins are forgiven you.' Suddenly there are scribes present, who ask this important question: 'Why is he talking like this? He is blaspheming! Who can forgive sins, except One, namely God?' If you listen carefully, you can hear Mark saying, 'Exactly.' Jesus responds with a counter-question: 'Which is easier . . . ?' and then effortlessly demonstrates his power by freeing the man to walk again. Once again, the question takes us into the heart of the mystery of Jesus.

There are other questions, too: in 2:16, 'Why does he eat with tax-collectors and sinners?' or 2:18, 'Why do your disciples not fast?' This produces another counter-question: 'Can the wedding guests fast?' And compare another aggressive question from the religious authorities: 'Why are they doing what is unlawful on the Sabbath?' and Jesus' counter-question: 'Have you never read what David did?' which locates the question squarely in its Old Testament background

(2:24-26, and compare 7:5 for an example of the same sort of question). These questions help us to explore the deeper question of who Jesus is, and, clearly, what his disciples must be like.

Sometimes there is a question that is implicit rather than explicit. A good example is, 'They watched him' (3:2, in the synagogue). The 'watching' is evidently an implicit question about who Jesus is and what is his authority, and in its turn it provokes a devastating counter-question from Jesus (3:4): 'Is it permitted on the Sabbath to do good or to do evil?' This once again takes us deeper into the mystery.

At 3:22 we find another implicit question from Jesus' enemies: 'He has Beelzeboul, and by the ruler of demons he casts out demons.' This provokes the counter-question from Jesus, 'How can Satan cast out Satan?' The reader is forced here to pause and reflect.

Occasionally there is a really big question. Look at 4:35-41. After Jesus has given his parable discourse, they have all got into the boat from which he has been preaching, and Jesus is fast asleep when the storm hits. They wake him in a panic; with absolute authority he calms the storm as though it were an over-exuberant dog, telling the sea, 'Be silent! Be muzzled!' The disciples' response is formulated as a question, and the reader is invited to attempt an answer: 'Who is this, then, that the wind and the sea obey him?'

There are smaller questions too, of course, but each of them helps us to develop the picture. At 5:9 Jesus asks the demons, 'What is your name?' and effortlessly gains power over them. At 5:30 Jesus asks, 'Who touched my clothes?' as the woman with the haemorrhage is cured. And at Jairus' house Jesus asks the mourners, 'Why are you mourning and weeping?' At 6:3 Jesus' compatriots in Nazareth ask, 'Where did he get all this?' The answer to that question is not given, but the reader is once more invited to 'fill in the gap' and work out the source of Jesus' power. At 6:37 when the disciples are told to feed the 5000, they ask, incredulously, 'Are we to go off and buy 200 denarii's worth of bread and give them to eat?' Jesus, once more, offers a counter-question: 'How many loaves do you have?' (and compare 8:4, 5). Or listen to the volley of sharp questions uttered by Jesus in the boat at 8:17-21 ('Why are you arguing?' 'Do you not yet understand or get it?' 'Do you have your heart hardened?' 'Do you not remember?' 'How many baskets?' and 'Do you not yet understand?'), which serve to reveal the ignorance of his dim-witted disciples.

Another really big question emerges at 8:27, 29: first, 'Who do people say I am?' and then, 'What about you? Who do you say I am?' Once again these two questions hold together the two basic questions of the Gospel, about who Jesus is and about who his disciples must be. As we saw in a previous chapter, Peter does his best, with 'You are the Messiah', but cannot cope with the kind of Messiah that Jesus is, namely one who is to suffer and die.

Questions are important. Notice the reaction of the disciples to the second Passion prediction at 9:30-32: 'They did not know the thing. And they were afraid to ask.' Clearly this carries the implication that we are supposed to ask questions when they occur to us. Immediately afterwards, Jesus' question is greeted with silence: 'What were you talking about on the way?' For they were dealing with the question about which of them was Mr Big. And that is the wrong question.

Jesus' religious opponents reappear at 10:2, when Pharisees raise with him the question, 'Is it permissible for a husband to divorce his wife?' The evangelist comments, though we might have guessed it, that they were 'testing him', and so we are not really surprised when Jesus answers with a counter-question: 'What did Moses command you?'

Likewise there is the rich man, who asks (10:17), 'Good Teacher, what am I to do in order to inherit eternal life?' That is clearly the wrong question, and not at all what Mark's Jesus is about, and so he too receives a counter-question: 'Why do you call me good?' This should give the reader pause for thought. Then Jesus is moved to reflect on the impossibility of rich people entering the kingdom of God, which provokes another question from the disciples: 'And so who can be saved?' (10:26).

James and John make an implicit question, for they want 'whatever we ask you' (10:35-45). It produces a counter-question: 'What do you want me to do for you?' So they are enabled to reveal the extent of their hunger for power. Jesus puts the same question later in the chapter to blind Bartimaeus (10:51), who simply wants 'that I may see again'.

Once we get to Jerusalem and Jesus performs his prophetic gesture in the Temple, the question that surfaced right at the beginning, about Jesus' authority, reappears (10:27-33). We who hear or read the story know the answer to the question, because we have heard the voice of God say, 'You are my beloved Son.' So when we hear the high priests and scribes and elders asking, 'By what authority? Who gave you this authority?' we rejoice at Jesus' counter-question about John the Baptist, and notice how this absolutely stumps them. 'We don't know,' they say, and the reader goes deeper into the mystery.

This, then, as the tension rises, and Jesus' death at the hand of the establishment comes evidently closer, provokes a further series of questions and counter-questions. The Pharisees and Herodians get together at 12:14, and ask, 'Is there authority to pay census-tax to Caesar or not?' This is a lethal question, aimed at either his life or his prestige (if he says 'no', then he can be sent straight to Pilate; if 'yes', then he has lost all street credibility with his compatriots). So we are not surprised that they receive a counter-question: 'Why are you testing me? Whose likeness is it?' The same thing happens in response to the next trick question, from Sadducees on 'resurrection', and the counter-question, 'Is not this why you are wrong? That you do not know the Scripture?' The Sadducees, of course, only accept the Torah, the first five books of the Bible. Brilliantly, Jesus takes a text from Exodus, the second of those five books, and offers a most original interpretation of it to demonstrate that 'He is God not of the dead but of the living.'

The next question also bids fair to be a trap, for a scribe asks it, and so far scribes have always meant trouble. The question takes the tricky form of 'What is the Number One commandment of all?' Jesus does not hesitate and produces in answer the Shema: 'Hear O Israel: the Lord your God is One God, and you are to love the Lord your God with all your heart . . .' He even gives a second commandment into the bargain: 'You are to love your neighbour as yourself.' To our astonishment, there is a rare meeting of minds here, and the scribe applauds him. In turn he is told, 'You are not far from the kingdom of God.' This has the remarkable effect that 'No one any longer dared to ask him a question' (12:34).

Things become more and more threatening, and the next question comes from the disciples, who gaze admiringly at Herod's Temple. Their implicit question about the size of its stones and buildings produces a counter-question from Jesus: 'Do you see these great buildings?' and he plunges into his account of the end time. And when they are stunned by that, they have another question, which he does not really answer: 'When will this happen? What signs will there be?' (13:1-8).

Immediately after this we are into the story of Jesus' Passion. When it starts with his anointing at Bethany there are more questions: 'Why this waste of oil?' (14:4), and the counter-question from Jesus: 'Why do you give her hassle?' (14:6). There is a slightly dim-witted question at 14:12 from the disciples: 'Where do you want us to prepare for you to eat the Passover?' (They should have thought of that, given that Jerusalem was always absolutely full at the festival.)

Then, as we go deeper into the darkness, there are other questions that continue the journey into who Jesus is and into what his disciples must be like. So when they are told that one of them is to betray him, the disciples ask, 'It isn't me, is it?' When Jesus prays he has to ask Peter (14:37), 'Simon, are you sleeping? Did you not have the strength to stay awake for a single hour?' At 14:48 the arresting party is asked, 'Have you come out as against a robber?'

Then we come to the trial before the Sanhedrin, and before Pilate. The High Priest asks several questions in order to trap him: 'Have you no answer? What are they testifying? Are you the Messiah, the Son of the Blessed One?' (14:60, 61). And when Jesus is finally persuaded to tell the truth, a final, damning question: 'What need do we still have of witnesses?' (14:63).

Then there are the questions asked by Pilate: 'Are you the King of the Jews?' 'Do you want me to release the King of the Jews to you?' 'What am I to do with the one you call King of the Jews?' and 'What evil has he done?' (15:2-14). Each of these questions from Jesus' executioner takes us deeper into the mystery of Jesus' identity.

In that connection the next question is very big indeed, for we hear Jesus bellow '*Elohi, Elohi, lema sabachtani*' (15:34), which Mark kindly translates for us: 'My God, my God – why have you abandoned me?' This is the opening line of Psalm 22, which ends with a great song of hope, but I do not think that the hope is what Mark is emphasising here, since he has Jesus speaking his native Aramaic, rather than the Hebrew in which he would have learnt the psalms. It seems to me that this question is meant to underline the utter loneliness and sense of abandonment that Jesus feels at this point. But, we should notice, he is at least still talking to God, whom at Gethsemane he addressed as 'Abba, Father'.

And so, finally, to the biggest question mark of all. It is a passage that we looked at previously, where the brave women go to Jesus' tomb, at 16:1-8. They are, you will remember, given a job to do: to tell Jesus' disciples – and Peter – what has happened. Yet Mark ends his Gospel with the statement, 'And they said nothing to nobody – for they were afraid.' And what do you, Reader or Hearer, make of that? For the implicit question is addressed to you: are you going to be afraid, with trembling and amazement? Or are you going to tell the disciples what has happened?

There is the question.

Questions

1. What are the questions that Mark's Gospel is seeking to answer?

2. Is it true to say that Mark uses his questions and counter-questions to enable the reader to understand what the Gospel is about?

3. Why are there so many questions in this Gospel, do you think?

CHAPTER 12

Matthew: something of a schoolmaster?

Now we come to Matthew's Gospel. We do not know much about this author, except what we can guess from his work; even his name may only be an intelligent second-century surmise based on the fact that at 9:9 he gives the name of Matthew to the tax-collector whom Mark and Luke know as Levi. However, since it is virtually certain that he was working on a version of Mark's Gospel, and may indeed be said to be Mark's first revising editor, we can guess a bit about him on the basis of what he does to Mark's text.

Sometimes he corrects Mark's Greek, and I always imagine a rather pained expression on his face as he does so. For example, you can see him up to his schoolmasterly ways at 13:31, 32 on the mustard-seed when he corrects Mark 4:32, where we have a slightly ungrammatical hanging participle ('who, when it is sown upon the earth, being smaller'), which Matthew changes to 'he sowed it in his field. [This seed] is smaller than all other seeds . . .'. It is a tiny example, but you get the picture.

Sometimes Matthew corrects Mark's theology. At Matthew 13:58 he changes what he found in Mark's account of the PR disaster in Nazareth (Mark 6:1-6) – 'and he was unable to do *any* miracle there' – to 'he did not do *many* miracles there, because of their unbelief'.

But there is something else that Matthew does. To illustrate it, I'd like to look at the following five verses, because they reveal something really important about Matthew:

7:28:   'and it happened when Jesus had finished these words . . .'

11:1:   'and it happened when Jesus had finished giving instructions to his twelve disciples . . .'

13:53: 'and it happened when Jesus had finished these parables . . .'

19:1:   'and it happened when Jesus had finished these words . . .'

26:1:   'and it happened when Jesus had finished *all* these words . . .'

These are not quite identical, and the last one acts as a kind of summary, with the addition of the word 'all'. Do you see what has happened? If you look through

Mark's Gospel, you will see that he often refers to Jesus as a 'teacher' and describes him as 'teaching'. Now Matthew clearly approves of Mark, because he has taken over his basic outline, from the baptism by John to the empty tomb, but if you listen carefully you can hear him complaining, 'Yes, Mark, but you don't say what Jesus taught!' So he adds the five great discourses that give a new shape to Matthew's Gospel, and he ends each of them with the verses that we have quoted, as a kind of signal to the reader of what he has done. The first discourse is the loveliest and best, what we call the 'Sermon on the Mount', which you will find at chapters 5–7. The second, which Matthew ends by talking about 'giving instructions to the Twelve' is the 'Missionary Discourse', when the 12 apostles are sent out 'to the lost sheep of the house of Israel' (10:5-42). The third is the great 'Parable Discourse' (13:3-53). At the end of that (and he has added some parables to the rather small number that he found in Mark 4), he does two things. First, like every trainee teacher Jesus asks his hearers, 'Have you understood all this? (13:51). Like schoolboys down the generations they give the expected answer, and fortunately he does not test them on it. Then he adds a second comment, for he says, 'Therefore every scribe discipled in the kingdom of the heavens is like a person, a householder, who brings out of his treasury new things and old.' I would like to suggest to you that Matthew sees himself as doing just this, bringing out the old story of God and the people of God and telling it in a new way to bring in the absolutely new thing that is the story of Jesus. So we might hear a little touch of Matthean autobiography in this verse.

Then the fourth line that we quoted comes after the end of chapter 18, what they sometimes call the 'Church Discourse'. To be honest it is a little untidier than the rest, since it is interrupted a couple of times by dumb questions from the disciples, but it does cover the question of how you deal with other people in the Church, including, in response to a question from Peter, how often you have to forgive them. That is the famous parable of the Unforgiving Servant, which I should like you to read now; I hope you agree that it may have a slightly comic edge to it:

> Because of this, the kingdom of the heavens has been likened to a man, a king who wanted to draw up accounts with his slaves. And when he had begun to draw them up, there was brought to him one man who was in debt to the tune of ten thousands of talents [this is a fantastic sum, and not the kind of debt that the king should have permitted to be run up]. And because he had no way of repaying, the Lord ordered him to be sold, and his wife, and his children, and everything that he possessed, and the money restored. So the slave fell down and worshipped him, saying 'Have patience with me – and I shall pay you back the whole lot' [repaying a sum of this magnitude would of course be quite out of the question].

And the Lord of that slave had compassion on him and let him off and remitted the debt for him.

Then that slave went out and found one of his fellow slaves who owed him a hundred denarii [a much more probable sum]. And he grabbed hold of him and throttled him, saying, 'Repay anything you owe.' So his fellow slave fell down and begged him, saying, 'Have patience with me and I'll pay you back' [where have we heard these words before?]. But he did not want to, but went out and threw him into prison, until he should repay what was owed. So his fellow slaves, when they saw what had happened, were very pained, and they came and revealed all that had happened to their Lord.

Then his Lord summoned him and says to him, 'Wicked slave! I let you off all that debt, since you begged me. Ought you not to have had mercy on your fellow slave, in just the same way as I had mercy on you?' And in a rage, his Lord handed him over to the torturers [who are known, of course, to have a profound effect on the bank balance] until he should pay back all that was owed. And this is how my Heavenly Father will deal with you, unless each of you lets off your brother [or sister] from your hearts.

(Matthew 18:23-35, in response to Peter's question: 'How many times is my brother [or sister] to sin against me and I am to forgive them? As many as seven times?')

Finally there is the last discourse, which may include chapter 23, the seven terrible woes against the scribes and Pharisees, and clearly includes chapters 24 and 25, about the end time and staying alert. Here we find two parables that appear only in Matthew's Gospel, namely the Ten Virgins and the Sheep and the Goats.

I should like you now to read that last parable. It depicts a familiar sight that you will see even today in the Judean desert:

And when the Son of Man comes in his glory, and all his angels with him, then he will sit on his throne of glory. And all the nations [or Gentiles] are going to be gathered in his presence; and he is going to separate them from each other, just as the shepherd separates the sheep from the goats.

And he is going to stand the sheep on his right, and the goats on the left. Then the king will say to those on his right, 'Come here, you who are blessed of my Father; inherit the kingdom that was prepared for you from the creation of the world. For I was hungry, and you gave me something to eat; I was thirsty and you gave me a drink. I was an immigrant, and you gathered me in; I was naked and you gave me clothes; I was sick and you visited me; I was in prison, and you came to me.'

Then the righteous will answer him, saying, 'Lord, when did we see you hungry and nourished you, or thirsty and gave you a drink? When did we see you an immigrant and gather you in, or naked and gave you clothes? When did we see you sick or in prison and we came to you?'

And the king is going to answer and tell them, 'Amen I am telling you; insofar as you acted to one of these my brothers or sisters, even the least of them, you did it to me.'

Then he is going to say to the ones on the left, 'Get away from me, you accursed ones, into the eternal fire prepared for the devil and his messengers. For I was hungry, and you did not give me anything to eat; I was thirsty and you did not give me a drink; I was an immigrant and you did not gather me in, naked and you did not put clothes on me, sick and in prison and you did not visit me.'

Then they in their turn will answer him, saying, 'Lord, when did we see you hungry or thirsty or an immigrant or naked or sick or in prison and we did not serve you?' Then he is going to reply to them saying, 'Amen I am telling you, insofar as you failed to do it to one of these littlest ones, you failed to do it to me.'

And they will go off into eternal punishment – but the righteous to eternal life.
(Matthew 25:31-46)

As I say, it is possible that the discourse might also include the slightly chilling chapter 23, the seven 'woes' against the scribes and Pharisees, and the final lament over Jerusalem (23:37-39).

So look at those five discourses, and the difference they make to the overall shape of the Gospel. We do not have time here to go through all of them, but it might be worth pausing for a while to look a little more closely at the first of them, the Sermon on the Mount. People often find it rather difficult to get hold of the structure, and I want to make a suggestion to you about how to grasp it.

People often find the Sermon on the Mount very difficult to grasp; it has a very puzzling shape (partly because Matthew is collecting material from various places), and the shape goes like this.

- All is clear up to 6:18, including an electrifying new vision (5:2-12) , which goes something like this:

  Congratulations to the poor in spirit – for theirs is the kingdom of the heaven.
  Congratulations to those who mourn – for they are going to be comforted.

Congratulations to the gentle – for they are going to inherit the land.

Congratulations to those who are hungry and thirsty for righteousness – for they are going to be sated.

Congratulations to the merciful – for they are going to be mercied.

Congratulations to the pure in heart – for they are going to see God.

Congratulations to the peacemakers – for they are going to be called children of God.

Congratulations to those who are persecuted in the cause of righteousness – for theirs is the kingdom of the heavens.

Congratulations to you when they revile you and persecute you and say all kinds of bad things against you in my cause. Rejoice and exult – for your reward is great in the heavens. For this is how they persecuted the prophets who came before you.

'You are the salt of the earth and the light of the world . . .'

and then Matthew emphasises that he is still telling the old story of God and the people of God, as we hear Jesus say, 'Don't think I have come to abolish the Law or the Prophets.' Here we are very likely eavesdropping on Matthew's controversy with what is sometimes called the 'synagogue across the road', fellow Jews who accuse him of having 'sold the pass'. This is how it goes:

> Don't think I have come to abolish the Law or the Prophets; I didn't come to destroy, but to fulfil. For Amen I'm telling you: until the heaven and the earth pass away, not one iota, or one punctuation mark is going to pass away from the Law, until it is all done. So anyone who undoes one of the least of these commandments and teaches people [to do] the same, is going to be called 'least' in the Kingdom of the Heavens. But whoever performs it and teaches it, that person is going to be called Mr Big in the Kingdom of the Heavens. For I am telling you that unless your righteousness overflows far more than that of the scribes and Pharisees, no way will you enter into the Kingdom of the Heavens.

After that the shape falls away a bit, as we have:

- Six Antitheses (5:21-48): 'You have heard it said . . .' Radical reinterpretation of Israel's Scripture. What matters is what goes on inside a person.

- Three pillars of Judaism, then as now, namely almsgiving, prayer and fasting (6:1-18), with a neat pattern of 'do it in secret and your heavenly father will see you', awkwardly broken up by Matthew's version of the Lord's Prayer.

This is followed by:

- A bunch of seemingly rather unrelated sayings (6:19–7:27). So it seems rather to fall apart.

However, we need to notice the oddity of 6:9-15, for I think Matthew is giving us a clue here. The Lord's Prayer completely interrupts what the evangelist has been building up, the pattern of observing those great pillars of Judaism, which are almsgiving, fasting and prayer, where there is some very sound teaching about doing these important things in secret, for God, and not to show off for other people.

But the broken structure itself gives us the clue: the very centre of the Sermon on the Mount is the Lord's Prayer. Once you see that, the whole thing starts to make sense: God's fatherhood, so important to Jesus, is the central insight, and everything else is related to it (in other words, Matthew is telling the old and new story of God and the people of God).

If you see it in this way, the unrelated sayings at the end of the Sermon start to make sense in the context of God as Father.

- 6:19-21: Treasure up treasures in heaven (what the Father offers – 'give us this day . . .')

- 6:22, 23: The light of the body is the eye, which opens you to God's creation.

- 6:24: God and Mammon: there is only one God (the old problem of idolatry in Israel), and so no one can serve two 'lords' . . . you cannot be the slave of God and Mammon. *Mammon* is an Aramaic word for money, with its root in the word that gives us 'Amen', and it refers to any alternative 'god' in which we think we can put our trust.

- 6:25-34: Not worrying about what to eat or drink or wear because God is Father.

- 7:1-6: Not judging, because we are all *brothers and sisters.*

- 7:7-11: Ask and you will receive, seek and you will find, knock and it will be opened to you: the moral here is that we are not to doubt, because God is our Father.

- 7:12-14: The Golden Rule – 'Everything that you want people to do for you, you yourselves should do for them.' It is typical of Matthew that he ends, 'for this is the Law and the Prophets'. Once again, this is the old story of God and the people of God. This saying and the one about entering by the Narrow Gate carry the same idea; that we should implicitly trust the Father.

- This idea also helps us to understand the next saying, in 7:15-20, about trees and their fruit (if you belong to the Father): 'from their fruits you shall know them'.

- 7:21-23: Jesus is not to be taken for granted ('Lord, Lord'). (We must beware of relying on Mammon, rather than on the one whom Jesus calls 'Father'.)

- 7:24-27: Two possible foundations: reality (Father) or unreality (Mammon).

Then we come to the final parable of two ways of building: on rock or on sand. This image will have spoken clearly to a Palestinian audience, applied to 'the one who hears these words of mine and does them'.

So the whole of the Sermon on the Mount turns out to be a meditation constructed on the Lord's Prayer, which has been put, slightly artificially, right at its very middle. I hope that makes it a little easier for you to read.

One last thing: you should notice the comment from the crowds at the end of this great Sermon: 'they were amazed at his teaching; for he was teaching them like one who had authority, and not like their scribes' (7:28). Now if you look at Mark 1:22, Matthew has taken these words more or less precisely from the text of Mark, but Mark does not indicate what Jesus taught; indeed, when that remark is repeated at Mark 1:27, it refers not to teaching but to Jesus' authority over unclean spirits.

And there are other 'schoolmasterly' aspects to this Gospel. Matthew is, as we have seen, a skilled organiser of his material. He leans heavily on the Old Testament, and often, especially in his opening two chapters, emphasises that 'this was to fulfil ...' He has, as all good teachers should have, a sense of humour, such as in the idea of 'lilies of the field' toiling and spinning (6:28), or the contrast between the 'tiny speck' in your brother's eye and the huge plank of timber in your own (7:3, 4). Or what about the idea of Pharisees straining out a gnat while effortlessly swallowing a camel (23:24)? This should provoke at least a wry smile from us.

In that culture, a teacher teaches while seated: (Matthew 5:1; 13:1, 2; 15:29; and contrast with the parallel passages in Mark 3:13; 4:1, 2; 7:31, 32). Matthew has made a serious point of this, and Matthew the teacher can be detected emphasising that Jesus, too, is a teacher.

Questions

1. Is Matthew something of a schoolmaster, do you think?

2. What has Matthew done by adding his five great discourses to what he found in Mark?

3. What do you think is the 'shape' of the Sermon on the Mount?

CHAPTER 13

Matthew's beginning and ending

We have seen that Matthew took Mark's basic structure, so he presumably approved of it. We have also seen, however, that he thought there was material missing, and so he took it upon himself to add his five great discourses, to give the feeling of Jesus the teacher. But there are other additions that he makes, and in some ways the most striking are the two chapters he puts at the beginning of his Gospel, and the way he ends it, taking up from Mark's remarkable ending ('they said nothing to nobody – for they were afraid' – Mark 16:8).

So it is probably worth our while to have a look at what this evangelist has added. The first thing we meet is what some people dismiss, rather hastily, as 'the most boring bit of the New Testament'. Because Matthew comes as the first of those 27 documents, some people probably open it, turn to page 1, find Matthew's genealogy and close it for good. If that is you, may I invite you to have another look at it?

Matthew gives a heading to his Gospel, which can be translated as something like 'The book of the origin of Jesus Messiah, Son of David, Son of Abraham'. Now that already tells us a good deal about what we are going to hear: firstly, that there is writing, and it must be read to us. Secondly, we have to know who Jesus Christ is; and, thirdly, Matthew is telling us something very important to him when he describes Jesus as 'Son of David, son of Abraham'. The important thing is that Jesus sums up all Jewish history (Matthew, remember, is telling the old story of God and the people of God in a new way).

We also need to notice that Jesus' ancestry is traced through David, who was the founder of the royal dynasty and from whom, it was assumed, the Messiah would be descended. Then there is Abraham, who received his first calling in Genesis 12, and who was promised that he would be the ancestor of descendants as many as the stars (Genesis 15:5). Matthew traces the descent of these two senior figures, 14 generations from each of them (and 14, you will be aware, is not just an astounding mathematical coincidence, but 2 x 7, or double the perfect number). Then look at the third group, which is headed not by the name of an ancestor, but by 'after the deportation to Babylon'. Count carefully the number of generations in this section and you will find that there are only 13, not 14: Jesus is the fourteenth; what Matthew seems to be saying here is that Jesus is the real fulfilment of the promise that was made to Abraham and seemingly fulfilled in the brilliant reign of David and his son Solomon, then apparently utterly lost in that terrible moment of the deportation to Babylon, when everything that Israel thought it could rely on – city, Temple and a royal line of succession – was snatched from them. After that disaster, Matthew is telling us (and his first hearers would have had no difficulty in reading the code), the whole of Israel's history as people of God is summed up in the coming of Jesus the Messiah.

To put this in context, it may be necessary to remind ourselves that what is sometimes referred to as 'the synagogue across the road' (Matthew's fellow Jews in Antioch, or wherever he was writing) may well have been telling him that he has sold the pass of their Jewish identity. Matthew is determined not to let that view go unchallenged. And what better way to make his point than to place Jesus so very solidly at the heart of Jewish history, in all its ups and downs?

There is one other point to notice. Quite unusually, there are four women named in this genealogy. There is Tamar, a Canaanite lady who (for perfectly good reasons) pretended to be a prostitute. There is Rahab, the lady in Jericho who actually was a member of that ancient profession. There is Ruth, from Moab, who got up to some obscure activity late at night with Boaz, and became the great-grandmother of King David. Finally there is Mrs Uriah, the wife of David's Hittite general. David seduced her and then had Uriah murdered because he would not play ball and help David get away with what he had done.

What is Matthew saying here? Some suggest that all these women had some kind of sexual irregularity, and so the fact that Mary is pregnant when she is only engaged to Joseph, not married, fits in with the general truth that God writes straight with crooked lines, as the saying goes. Others point to the fact that in various ways the women are on the edge of Israelite society, and that fits with the idea that Matthew's Church is opening out to the Gentile world. More recently, other scholars have argued that Matthew uses the women, including Mary, as a feminist counter-narrative, to challenge the domination of men in the story. It does not matter which of these solutions you adopt (or you may think of another of your own); the important thing is that you should see that this section is perhaps not quite as boring as one might have supposed.

Having provided this impressive overture, Matthew then offers us no fewer than five scenes before we get to John the Baptist, where Mark's Gospel starts. Look at these five scenes and ask yourself, 'What is Matthew doing here?'

They are as follows:

- 1:18-24: Jesus' birth

- 2:1-12: The Magi come from the East

- 2:13-15: The flight into Egypt

- 2:16-18: The slaying of the children

- 2:19-23: The return from Egypt to Nazareth

Read carefully through all of these and notice how Matthew operates. Feel the shock at the announcement of Mary's pregnancy, and feel the relief at the end of verse 18 when we are told that the child is of the Holy Spirit. Feel Joseph's pain, and how it is suddenly relieved by the presence of the Lord's angel in a dream. Joseph silently does what he is told to do (and is therefore a model for all who read this Gospel). We cannot look at everything, but you might just notice the citation from Isaiah 7:14: 'a young woman/virgin shall conceive and bear a son; and they shall call his name "Emmanuel"'. Then Matthew helpfully adds a translation: 'God with us'. Remember that, for we shall come back to it at the end of this chapter.

The second scene is an extraordinary one: the Magi cause a terrible shock in Jerusalem by asking to be allowed to 'worship' (you might need to remember that word too) the new King of the Jews. This was not the most diplomatic question they could have asked, because there is a King of the Jews happily reigning, and his name is Herod, and he does not normally tolerate any threat to his reign. So he pretends that he too wants to worship the dear little child, consults his religious experts, discovers that the Messiah is to be born in Bethlehem (so he believes that the Magi are on to something), and sends them on their way. Happily, God is in charge, and so the Magi, having given their three gifts (which is why you thought there were three of them), go home by another route.

Then we have the third scene, the flight into Egypt, and this is not at all as it should be. You are supposed to flee *from* Egypt, if you are part of Jewish history, not *to* it; and if you go by night, that is a reminder for us of the first Exodus, except that this one is going in the wrong direction. Once again, Matthew draws our attention to the fulfilment of Scripture.

The fourth scene is the horrible story of the murder of the innocent children. This story is not known from other sources, but what we know of Herod (mainly from the Jewish historian Josephus) tells us that he was perfectly capable of such an action.

Finally, the fifth scene brings Jesus to Nazareth, from where he will emerge at 3:13. This happens on the perfectly sensible grounds that Archelaus was currently king in Judea. He was even worse than his father, so much so that even the Romans noticed and sacked him. So Jesus ends up in Nazareth. As always, Matthew has a Scripture quotation to offer (2:23); but if you track it down, the nearest equivalent is probably Judges 13:5. Why does Matthew use this quotation? I am not sure, but try this: the text refers to the birth of Samson; and Samson, you may remember, dies with his arms outstretched, a great victory for God against his enemies (Judges 16:30). And Jesus, of course, dies with arms outstretched . . .

So I suggest that you sit with these five scenes and ask yourself what Matthew is doing when he places them so carefully at the beginning of Jesus' life, immediately after that extraordinary genealogy with its stress on what God is doing in the story of Jesus.

And now, what of the ending? Once again, we should look at it carefully, trying to work out what Matthew is up to.

What follows is a deliberately crude and literal translation of the final five verses of the Gospel:

> But they, the eleven disciples, journeyed to Galilee

- Eleven: the number should, of course, be 12; but Judas has gone missing. This is a reminder that the Church always limps.

- Galilee: the place where Jesus' mission started, what Matthew, citing Isaiah, calls 'Galilee of the Gentiles' (4:15).

> to the mountain which he had appointed for them, Jesus

- Mountain: this is a very important idea in Matthew's Gospel. We meet it at 4:8, where it is the site of Jesus' third temptation; 5:1, at the beginning of the Sermon on the Mount; 14:23, where Jesus goes up to pray after the feeding of the 5000; 15:29, where Jesus encounters large numbers of sick people and heals them, before the feeding of the 4000; 17:1 where the Transfiguration takes place; 21:1, the Mount of Olives, where Jesus orders his colt for the entry into Jerusalem; and 26:30, the Mount of Olives once more, where Jesus will predict the disciples' betrayal.

- Appointed: here the word simply gives the reassuring sense that Jesus is wholly in charge.

> And seeing him they **worshipped**

- This verb, 'worship', is an important one in Matthew's Gospel. It represents the correct attitude to Jesus. The first use of it is on the lips of the Magi (2:2), followed immediately (2:8) by a use of the word by Herod, who clearly means something quite different. The Magi perform this action for Jesus (2:11), and the devil (4:9) invites Jesus to do it to him. Mrs Zebedee (20:20) uses the gesture to ask a favour of Jesus on behalf of her sons. And the women (28:9) worship the risen Jesus.

> But they **doubted**

- Matthew here uses a rather rare word which also appears at 14:31, and nowhere else in the New Testament. In both cases, it refers to a failure on the part of the disciples.

   And coming forward Jesus said to them, 'It is given to me, all authority

- 'It is given' is what is technically known as a 'divine passive': in other words, this sentence makes the claim that Jesus' authority comes from God. This is a good way to end the Gospel.

   in heaven and on earth

- This phrase echoes, of course, the opening of the entire Bible (Genesis 1:1), and is another reminder that in Jesus the creator God, whose story is told throughout the Old Testament, is unmistakably operating for his people.

   Therefore journeying *disciple* all the Gentiles

- The word that I have translated 'disciple', as a slightly clumsy imperative, appears only in Matthew. The other two places where we find it are 13:52 where it refers to Matthew the 'discipled scribe', and in 27:57 concerning Joseph of Arimathea: 'a wealthy man . . . who was also himself discipled to Jesus'. The whole Gospel is thus held together. We should also notice the reference to 'Gentiles', who have not always received a favourable press in this Gospel (see 6:7; 10:5; 18:17). Now, at the end of the Gospel, Matthew, that most Jewish of evangelists, is reconciled to the fact that the message is to go out beyond the Judaism into which it was first preached.

   Baptising them into the name of the Father and of the Son and of the Holy Spirit

- Here we perhaps can detect a fragment of the liturgy of Matthew's Church.

   teaching them to keep everything whatsoever I have commanded you

- This presumably takes us back to the five great discourses that structure this Gospel, especially the Sermon on the Mount.

   And behold

- This word is an attention-attracting particle, frequently used in Matthew but all too often not translated in modern versions. This is a pity, since Matthew is quite serious about it.

   I am with you

- 'I am with you': the alert reader is taken back to the use of 'Emmanuel', helpfully translated by Matthew as 'God with us', in 1:23, quoting the prediction in Isaiah 7:14, and making a very high claim for Jesus' identity. This therefore links Matthew's beginning to his ending. (Compare also 18:20: 'Where two or three are gathered in my name, I am there in the middle of them.')

  all the days until the completion of the age.

- When is that? When you read Matthew's Gospel, and feel the presence of Jesus.

This is a remarkable ending to this extraordinary document. It is what enables us to continue reading it today.

Questions:

1. Why does Matthew start his Gospel in the way he does?

2. What is the importance for Matthew of the story of the Magi in chapter 2?

3. Does the way Matthew ends his Gospel, 'I am with you', make a difference to the way we read it?

CHAPTER 14

Matthew and the Church

Matthew is sometimes known as the 'Church gospel'. A sensible starting point here is the fact that the Greek word for 'church', *ekklesia*, appears three times in Matthew (16:18; 18:17) and in no other Gospel. The word is possibly better translated as 'congregation' or 'assembly', since that does greater justice to its background in the desert, but 'church' will do.

There are other senses in which Matthew is a 'church' gospel. For one thing, it comes first in the New Testament, and was the principal Gospel used for reading in church services until quite recently. This may have been connected with the fact that it was thought to come from the pen of one of the 12 apostles.

For another thing, it was a book very much at the service of the Church. Its probable setting (though one can never be sure of these things) is a time when a) the first witnesses were dying off, and b) there was a felt need to put something in the hands of teachers to help them instruct those apparently fairly large numbers of people who were attracted to this new movement.

Contrast the following two texts from this point of view:

1. Mark 8:27-30	2. Matthew 16:13-20
And Jesus went out, he and his disciples, into the villages of Caesarea Philippi. And on the way he asked his disciples, saying, 'Who do people say I am?' And they said to him, saying, 'John the Baptist, and others Elijah, and others that "It's one of the prophets."' And he asked them, 'But what about you? Who do you say I am?' Peter answered and said to him, 'You're the Messiah.'	And when Jesus had gone to the parts of Caesarea Philippi, he asked his disciples, 'Who do people say the Son of Man is?' And they said, 'Some [say] "John the Baptist" and others "Elijah", and others "Jeremiah or one of the prophets".' He says to them, 'What about you? Who do you say I am?' Simon Peter answered and said, 'You are the Messiah, the Son of the Living God.' And Jesus answered and said to him, 'Congratulations to you, Simon Bar-Jona, because it was not flesh and blood that revealed [this] to you. No – it was my Father, the one in Heaven.

	And I'm telling you, you are "Rock"; and on this "rock" I am going to build my ekklesia, and the gates of Hades are not going to be strong against it. I am going to give you the keys of the kingdom of the Heavens; and whatever you tie up on earth shall be tied up in the heavens. And whatever you untie on earth shall be untied in the heavens.'
And he rebuked them, that they were to say nothing about him.	Then he gave instructions to the disciples that they were to tell nobody that he was the Messiah.

For Mark, as we saw in a previous chapter, this episode in Caesarea Philippi comes right in the middle of the Gospel. Although Peter makes the correct response to Jesus' question, 'What about you – who do you say I am?' when he replies, 'You're the Messiah', Mark's interest is really in showing how Peter then gets it wrong.

Look now at how Matthew tells the story. Peter is here called 'Simon Peter', which adds a bit of formality, and he makes a much fuller declaration: 'You are the Messiah, the Son of the Living God.' Then Jesus comes in with a very fulsome response:

'You are to be congratulated, Simon Bar-Jona, because flesh and blood did not reveal it to you. No – it was my Father, the one in heaven. And I am telling you that you are "Rock", and on this Rock I am going to build my Church; and the gates of Hell shall not be strong against the Church. And I am going to give you the keys of the kingdom of the Heavens. And whatever you bind on earth will be bound in the heavens; and whatever you untie on earth will be untied in the heavens.'

Now a good deal of the language here sounds as though it comes from the Aramaic, so it may be that Matthew is using here an old tradition about Peter, rather than writing a new text to put Mark right.

Interestingly, Matthew's insertion balances what happens a few verses later, when Peter is unable to cope with Jesus' first prediction of his Passion: the one who was called 'Rock' is now a 'scandal'. Now, a 'scandal' is a tiny stone on which you stub your toe or trip over, rather than a rock. And the one of whom Jesus had said that the Church would be built on him as a base, and that the

Gates of Hades would not be strong against it, is now renamed, as 'Satan'. The one whom Jesus congratulated because he had a revelation from 'my Father' is now told that he is not, after all, thinking 'God thoughts' but 'human thoughts'. This is a very strong teaching about the Church, and we can see it a bit more clearly because we are able to detect how Matthew has used what he found in Mark.

The same is true if you look at the other passage where Matthew mentions 'Church': chapter 18. He has taken a good deal of material which appears in all kinds of different places in Mark and Luke and organised it into a treatise about the Church, even though he mentions the word only once. So a question from the disciples about who is biggest in the kingdom of heaven is turned into an exhortation to become like children (18:1-5). Then a Mark passage about not scandalising children, which is in a slightly different place in Mark (9:42-50), is organised into a much clearer teaching about scandals (18:6-9). Then Matthew takes the story of the lost sheep, which in Luke 15 is one of three parables about God celebrating the return of sinners, and makes it into a story about treating everyone in the Church with absolute respect (18:10-14). Then he deals with the question of what you do when a fellow Christian gets things wrong, and sets out a three-tier instruction, which is not in Mark or Luke: first, see the person alone; second, go with witnesses; third, tell the Church (18:15-18).

And there is more, for Jesus defines what it means to be 'Church': 'when two of you agree on earth about anything that they are asking for, it will happen to them from my Father, the One in the heavens'. And why? Because 'where there are two or three gathered in my name, there I am in the midst of them'. That is what Church means, and we remember Jesus' last words in the Gospel: 'I am with you until the end of the age.'

Finally in this chapter, Matthew puts on Peter's lips a question about how often to forgive a fellow Christian, and he caps it with the parable of the Unforgiving Servant (18:23-35), which does not appear in any other Gospel.

Do you see how Matthew's ability to organise material leaves us at the end of this chapter with a new grasp of his understanding of the idea of 'Church'?

Then there are other, smaller details. There are, for example, two parables about Church. Look at 25:1-13, the story of the Ten Virgins, and the need for the Church to stay awake and be ready for the coming of the bridegroom. This is only in Matthew, as is the next one, the story of the Sheep and the Goats (25:31-46), which is not really about the 'goats', but about those who unexpectedly discover that they have been giving Christ food and drink and hospitality and clothing and visiting him. That is the Church functioning as it should.

Occasionally, it seems, you can hear excerpts from the liturgy in Matthew's Church: *Kyrie Eleison* is echoed at 8:25 (Lord, save); 9:27 (Have mercy on us, Son of David); 14:30 (Lord, save me); 15:22 (Have mercy on me, Lord, Son of

David); 15:25 (Lord, help me); 17:15 (*Kyrie eleison* on my son); 20:30 (*Kyrie eleison*); and, of course, 'baptising them in the name of the Father, Son and Holy Ghost' (28:19).

And you can, I think, hear various warnings to the Church of Matthew's day. Look at 7:21-23: 'It's not everyone who says "Kyrie, Kyrie" to me who will enter the kingdom of heaven, but the one who does the will of my Father in Heaven.' Then there is that really difficult chapter 23, where six times Jesus bellows, 'Woe to you, scribes and Pharisees, hypocrites!' This is sometimes taken as Matthew's anti-Semitism, but Matthew is nothing if not a good Jewish boy. So when he says that the scribes and Pharisees sit on Moses' seat (23:2), we must take him seriously; and when he warns against 'imposing heavy burdens on people's shoulders' (23:4) and not lifting a finger to help; or when he forbids doing things to be seen by others (23:5), or wearing special clothes (23:5) and having the best seats at banquets (23:6), being called 'Rabbi' (23:8) or 'Father' (23:9), it is surely the Church of his own day that he is talking about. 'Everyone who exalts themselves is going to be humbled' (23:12), and warnings against closing the kingdom of heaven to others, or scouring the sea and the dry land in search of converts; or those who downgrade oaths, or make minute rules about tiny details of the Law, or who generally have a wrong sense of priorities (23:25), or who appear on the outside to be virtuous, when really they are rotten inside (23:28) could all be addressed to the Church in any age. All these charges could be laid against not just 'scribes and Pharisees', but religious people of any group, including Matthew's contemporary Church.

Finally, let us look at what Matthew has done in a story about Jesus walking on the water (14:22-33), in which he invites us to see the Church as a boat.

Mark 6:45-52 tells the story quite simply: after the feeding of the 5000, Jesus tells the disciples to go across to Bethsaida and he will get rid of the crowds. But it turns out that this is all about Jesus taking much-needed time to pray. They get into trouble with the waves, so Jesus walks across the sea to them. Mark mysteriously adds, 'He wanted to pass them by', although Matthew misses that out. In both narratives, the disciples panic because it is clearly a ghost, and Jesus calms them down by saying, 'Be brave – it is I.'

Matthew adds something that would certainly have spoken to the Church of his day. For he has Peter respond (14:28), 'Lord, if it is you, order me [*Kyrie keleuson* this time] to come to you on the waters.' Now the reader may reflect at this point that Peter might have thought things through a bit more before uttering this rather foolhardy challenge, but that is the way we are in the Church. And Jesus simply does what Peter asks, and says, 'Come.' And, as the Church does from time to time, Peter obeys the Lord 'and walked on the water, and came to Jesus' (as though it were the most natural thing in the world – 14:29).

Then good sense takes over, and Peter forgets about his confidence in Jesus: 'he saw the strong wind, and was afraid, and began to go under, and cried out saying, "Lord, save me!" [*Kyrie soson*]'. This is also what the Church does from time to time and, as always, Jesus 'stretched out his hand, took hold of him and says to him, "O you of little faith – why did you doubt?"', a question that can often be put to the Church. At that point Matthew rejoins Mark's version: Jesus (or in this case Jesus and a thoroughly bedraggled Peter) get on board the boat. Then Mark comments, 'they were excessively very much amazed in themselves'. Now look what Matthew does with that: 'Those in the boat worshipped him, saying, "Truly you are the Son of God."' We are surely not wrong in reading this as a picture of the way the Church operates in Matthew's view and in his lifetime.

Matthew is very much a Church gospel.

Questions

1. Is it helpful to think of Matthew as a 'Church gospel'?

2. Do you notice any differences between Matthew's approach and what he found in Mark?

3. In what other ways might Matthew be said to be a 'Church gospel'?

CHAPTER 15

Is Matthew's Gospel anti-Jewish?

Since the terrible events of the Holocaust, Christians have very properly been examining our consciences to see how we contributed to the disaster. And Matthew's Gospel has come in for its share of examination in this respect. Indeed, some people describe it as 'the most Jewish and the most anti-Jewish of the Gospels'.

Why would they call Matthew's Gospel anti-Jewish? Well, there is the famous scene, right at the centre of Matthew's infancy stories, where the Jewish King Herod is presented as believing the Magi; he is in no doubt that the Messiah, King of Israel, has indeed been born. Herod is shaken ('and all Jerusalem with him', 2:3), and is quite clear that any and every child who might conceivably be the newborn king must be exterminated. Of course, we have to be aware that many of Herod's fellow Jews would have had reservations about him; indeed, some of them would have doubted whether he was a Jew at all. Nevertheless, you could argue that from the beginning Matthew represents Jewish political authority as determined to destroy Jesus (in which objective they finally succeed by the end, of course).

Then Matthew picks up a usage of Mark, who talks about *their* synagogues, and greatly expands it (4:23; 9:35; 10:17; also 23:34, which is the famous passage addressed to the Pharisees, and talks about '*your* synagogues'). Matthew changes Mark's story (Mark 12:28-34) about the scribe who thought Jesus had got it right; in Matthew's version it is a 'lawyer' (never a good start), and the evangelist omits the meeting of minds between Jesus and the scribe (Matthew 22:34-40). Similarly, Jairus from Mark 5:22 is not given a name by Matthew, and is no longer a ruler of a synagogue, but a 'ruler' (9:18). Matthew 8:5-13, the story of the centurion's boy, becomes a platform for emphasising that Gentiles 'from east and west' will come into the kingdom 'and lie down with Abraham and Isaac and Jacob in the kingdom of the heavens, while the sons of the kingdom shall be expelled into the outer darkness'.

Then there is that terrible moment in Matthew's Passion Narrative where Pilate solemnly washes his hands of Jesus' innocent blood, while 'the whole people' say, 'His blood be on us and on our children' (27:25). Now it is true that down the centuries, many Christians have, alas, used this as an excuse to justify violence against the Jews, but both of them are resorting to well-tried Jewish texts: Pilate to Deuteronomy 21:6-8, and the people to 2 Samuel 14:9,

Jeremiah 26:15 and other such. In any event, by the time Matthew's Gospel was written, the destruction of Jerusalem had taken place, in AD 70, and will have been widely read as fulfilling their utterance.

Rather than as gross anti-Semitism, I should like you to read what you find in Matthew as yet another example of inner-Jewish debates such as you find in the first century on either side of the birth of Jesus. If you want examples, have a look at some of the things that the Qumran sectaries say about their fellow Jews, which makes what Matthew says about the Pharisees seem quite mild by contrast.

So I would like to suggest another way of looking at it, which is that Matthew is a deeply Jewish Gospel. The very fact of the way he begins his Gospel should give us the clue, for it seems difficult to claim that a text which starts with a rapid summary of Jewish history, in three groups of 14 and presenting Jesus as the climax of Jewish history, could possibly be anti-Jewish. Indeed, many scholars see Matthew as offering a Jesus who is a 'new Moses' and who, like his predecessor, goes up into the mountain, though admittedly whereas Moses went to *receive* the Law, Jesus is *giving* it. In addition, in Matthew's version of the Transfiguration Jesus appears just like Moses on Mount Sinai (17:2).

Matthew is quite clear in the Sermon on the Mount that Christians are to continue with the three great pillars of Jewish religion. So at 6:1-4 they are to give alms, as is expected of good Jews; but the thing they have to watch is 'not to perform your righteousness before human beings in order to put on a show for them. Otherwise, you'll get no reward from your Father, the One in the heavens.' Similarly, the second pillar, prayer, is warmly commended; but they are not to do it (6:5-15) 'like the actors . . . to make it obvious to others'. Then, as we have seen in an earlier chapter, Matthew places, rather awkwardly but firmly, right in the middle of the section on prayer, his version of the Lord's Prayer. It is a prayer that any Jew could say (except, of course, for the baggage that it carries today). And the third pillar of Jewish religious practice is also there: '*when* you fast', says Jesus – so there is to be no question of whether or not they will fast. The only thing is that they must not do it 'like actors, with long faces, and dirtying their countenances, to let human beings know' (6:16). So this is a very Jewish debate, and many of Jesus' fellow Jews will have applauded his sentiments.

At a very important moment, early in the Sermon on the Mount, we hear Jesus say, 'Do not think that I have come to destroy the Law or the Prophets' (5:17). Here one must imagine Matthew's fellow Jews from the 'synagogue across the road' charging him with selling the pass, and him energetically rebutting the accusation. His group of Christians are still Jews, still telling the old story of God and the people of God. Jesus uses very strong language about this:

I did not come to destroy but to fulfil. For Amen I'm telling you: until Heaven and earth pass away, not a single *yodh* [here I must explain that this is the Hebrew letter 'y', which is so small on ancient manuscripts that you cannot always be sure that it is not an ink blot] nor a single serif shall pass away from the Torah, until it all happens.

And indeed they are warned that anyone who undoes 'one of the least of these commandments [and Matthew uses the word for the prescriptions of the Old Testament] is going to be called least in the kingdom of the heavens' (5:19).

Incidentally, you will have noticed that Matthew frequently uses the term 'kingdom of the heavens' where Mark would say 'kingdom of God'. Remember that Jewish readers do not pronounce the sacred name of God, and it may be that Matthew deliberately makes the change from Mark in order to make the point. He does occasionally lapse and write 'kingdom of *God*' (12:28, for example); scholars are never short of an answer, and say that is because of 'redactional fatigue'. That is to say that Matthew gets fed up with pressing the 'replace' button on his computer, which I suppose might be the case.

So Matthew is a good Jew, but that is not to say that he does not have disagreements with his fellow Jews. They might, for example, have been startled to hear Jesus say, 'I am telling you that unless your righteousness [and that is a favourite word of Matthew's] is more abounding than that of the scribes and Pharisees [could they imagine a higher level of virtue than that?], no way will you enter into the kingdom of the heavens' (5:20).

Not only that, but Matthew expects his Christians to wear phylacteries (as long as they are not too ostentatiously wide – 23:5) and tassels on the end of their clothes (but not too long). Likewise he expects them to keep the Sabbath, for when Matthew's Jesus is talking about the end time, they are told to 'pray that your flight does not happen in winter or on the Sabbath' (24:20). The picture that emerges, then, is of a thoroughly observant Jewish group that will have been much like any other such group in the first century.

You can occasionally see this in the way Matthew rewrites Mark. Compare, for example, what you find in Mark 7:18, 19 where, after the remark about the food going into the latrine, we hear the evangelist's comment: '[thus] pronouncing all foods clean'. Matthew simply omits that (Matthew 15:17), which presumably means that his group kept kosher. And something similar happens when Matthew reports the Marcan story about the disciples plucking grain on the Sabbath: he omits Mark's very sharp comment that 'the Sabbath was for human beings, and not human beings for the Sabbath' (2:27), presumably on the grounds that it was rather too strong medicine.

Matthew is therefore thoroughly Jewish, and it makes no sense to describe him as anti-Jewish, except in an inner-Jewish context. In the story of the temptation in the desert, as scholars have remarked, Jesus and the devil are like rabbis swapping Scripture quotations ('I'll trump your "He will command his angels" with my "You shall not put the Lord your God to the test".'), and that makes for a very Jewish 'feel' to the episode. Or look through the Gospel and count the number of times that you meet the phrase, 'This was to fulfil what was spoken in the prophets.' Try to imagine Matthew selling the Jesus story to the 'synagogue across the road', and hammering home these citations. Or consider the fact that Matthew twice uses a citation of Hosea 6:6: 'I desire mercy and not sacrifice', which he quotes at 9:13 and 12:7 in a very Jewish way, both times in response to criticism from the Pharisees.

When Matthew tells the story of the temptation of Jesus, he and Luke both add three actual temptations to what they found in Mark. For Luke it is the Temple that forms the climax, but in Matthew there is a very important word, which we can translate as 'worship'. It is the word we first encountered when the Magi turned up in Jerusalem, wanting to 'worship' Jesus. In his response, Herod also uses that word 'worship', but we know what *he* means by that. The next time we meet the word, it is in chapter 4, the climax of the temptations. For Matthew, the final temptation is that Jesus should 'worship' the devil. Jesus' response is an interesting one: 'The Lord your God shall you worship, and him alone shall you adore.' But there is no indication anywhere in the Gospel that we are to disapprove when people 'worship' Jesus: a leper at 8:2, the ruler in 9:18, the disciples in the boat at 14:33, the Canaanite woman (of all people!) at 15:25; then there is the mother of the sons of Zebedee, asking a favour for her sons at 20:20, 21 (it was the two boys themselves in Mark's version), then the women at the tomb on Easter Sunday morning (28:9); and, finally, the 11 disciples, though Matthew adds that 'they doubted' (28:17). So 'worship' is an important word for Matthew, and a clue to the reader's proper attitude to Jesus. Read these texts and you can readily feel Matthew's Jewishness; but, as the idea of 'worshipping' Jesus indicates, being a member of the 'Jesus group' is in principle different from being any other kind of Jew.

We are dealing here with a Jewish group whom we have to call 'Christian', because they believe that the Messiah (or 'Christ' in Greek) has come. This group, possibly to its astonishment, finds that it is opening out to non-Jews: look at 4:15 ('Galilee of the Gentiles'), and how negative is the view of 'Gentiles' (6:32; 10:5; 10:18; 12:18, 21; 20:19, 25; 24:9). But at the same time there is a mission to the Gentiles: 24:14; 25:32; and, of course, in the very last words of the Gospel, 28:19, 20, when the Eleven are told to go out and preach the gospel to all the Gentiles.

Matthew's Jesus represents something very new in Judaism. Remember 13:52, about bringing forth new things and old? That is what Matthew is doing, for Jesus represents something very new in the old story of God and the people of God. What happened to Jesus, and by that I mean the Resurrection, entailed that suddenly the Jews who thought Jesus was the Messiah were living in a new world. They discovered that their monotheism, which they still cherished, had to be understood in a completely new way if they were to do justice to their own experience. And many of their fellow Jews thought that they had betrayed the ancient tradition.

Matthew did not agree, obviously, but if he thought for a moment that his views on Jesus and Judaism would give for a second any support to the view that Christianity meant getting rid of Jews by any means at all, he would have said that was simply missing the point. Matthew is a deeply faithful Jew.

Questions

1. Do you agree that Matthew's Gospel is 'anti-Jewish'?

2. Why is this an important question today?

3. What are the important texts in Matthew's Gospel for dealing with this question?

CHAPTER 16

Luke:
the supreme artist

It is a fair bet that if I were to ask you to list your favourite Gospel story, you would pick something from Luke's remarkable pen. For example, you would almost certainly mention the Prodigal Son from Luke 15:11-32, or the Good Samaritan (10:25-37). Or what about Paul's encounter with Jesus on the Damascus road, told for the first of three times at Acts 9:1-16? Then there is the lovely story of the Annunciation to Mary (Luke 1:26-38), which a thousand artists have attempted to portray. At the other end of the Gospel is the extraordinary narrative of the two disciples on the Emmaus road (24:13-32). Other enchanting pictures from this remarkable artist would include the Visitation of Mary to Elisabeth (1:39-56), which includes the subversive poem that we call the Magnificat, which the Church has used for its evening prayer for a millennium and a half. And the tale of Jesus' birth and placing in a feeding trough, as well as that of the shepherds who came to join in the fun, is engraved on the imagination of readers (2:1-20). Or there are the unforgettable stories of Lazarus and the Rich Man (16:19-31), the dishonest judge and the women who threatened him with a black eye (18:1-8), the Pharisee and the publican (18:9-14), Zacchaeus and his sycamore tree (19:1-10).

However, we are not to think of Luke as just someone who hangs our favourite paintings in his house, for he has a theological point to make to us. So have a look at each of these stories and see what you think Luke is using them to tell us. Can you discern any kind of common feature?

To help in this, I would like to go through with you some of the lovely stories that the evangelist gives us in his first two chapters, what we call the Infancy Narrative. The first of these is the beautifully drawn narrative of the annunciation to Zachary of the birth of John the Baptist (1:5-25), which starts us on the journey through the Gospel. Look at it carefully and make a list of the things that puzzle you. Then read that other annunciation, to Mary, and see the similarities and differences. After that, see how Luke brings the two stories together with the consummate artistry of the story of Mary going to visit Elisabeth in the hill country of Judah. You might like to notice, and perhaps be surprised by, the fact that it is Elisabeth, and not Zachary, who grips Luke's attention in this encounter between the two remarkable women. You may also be struck by the encounter between their two unborn sons.

The robust narrative continues with the feisty Elisabeth absolutely insisting that her son is not to be called Zachary (can you *imagine* a title like Zachary the Baptist?) but John. When the child's father assents to this and scribbles on a tablet to that effect, he immediately recovers his speech, which intrigues all the neighbours: 'they put it in their hearts, saying, "So what is this child going to be?" – for the hand of the Lord was with him' (1:66). Not only that, but Zachary's newly freed tongue pours forth that other great poem, which we call the Benedictus, and which the Church has been using for morning prayer for many centuries now. You will find it at Luke 1:68-79, and you could do a great deal worse than to sit with it and let it speak to you of its author.

Next Luke gives us another double picture, of Mary and Joseph, framed by the powerful (Caesar Augustus and Quirinius) on the one hand, and the weak (a bunch of disreputable shepherds) on the other. The contrast is very much grist to Luke's mill, for this is the Gospel of the poor. And Luke's Infancy Narrative ends with two very striking stories, artistically recounted to help us grasp more about who Jesus really is. Both of these stories are often painted, and as you read them you might ask yourself why this is.

The first (2:21-38) is the tale of the child and his parents fulfilling all that they are supposed to do in the Law: the baby is circumcised and (in accordance with Gabriel's instructions at 1:31) named 'Jesus'. Then Luke introduces the two great characters of Simeon and Hanna (2:22-38). What makes it possible is that those other two great characters, Mary and Joseph, are similarly observant Jews, and open to the new thing that God is doing. This is another unforgettable story, one that creates a thoroughly Old Testament atmosphere. Read it through carefully and get a feel of the picture that Luke is painting.

After that story Luke allows a breather, as they go back to Galilee and Nazareth, 'and the child grew, and became strong, being filled with wisdom – and God's grace was upon him' (2:39, 40). That, however, is only a pause before the final picture Luke paints in this particular gallery, that of the adolescent Jesus joining his parents on pilgrimage to Jerusalem, and making a break for freedom by staying on and interrogating the religious teachers, to the consternation of Mary and Joseph. This picture has a sadness to it, as we see the desperate parents, stunned by what Jesus has done to them. What perhaps makes it worse is that when his mother chides him for the agony he has inflicted on 'your father and me', he redefines the notion of who his father is: 'Did you not realise that I must be on my Father's mission?' So his 'father' is not Joseph, who in any event never appears again in Luke.

So the thing to do in chapters 1 and 2 of Luke is to walk up and down the picture gallery, inspecting all the pictures, with a view to drawing from them all that Luke might want you to pick up about Jesus before he starts on his version of what he has found in Mark. There is a good deal of material here, for not only is Luke the longest of the Gospels, but this Gospel is the first of two volumes, the second of which, as we shall see, is Acts of the Apostles. And watching the way Luke manages his material can be very instructive for our reading of it.

In another chapter we shall see how Luke does this with the idea of the Gospel as a journey, which gives an unusual shape to the story. However, at this point I should like you to look at another Lucan technique, which I call the 'disastrous dinner party'. There are, depending on how you count them, something like seven of them, and they are as follows. (Not all of them, you will see, are absolutely disastrous, and not all of them are dinner parties, but they may give you an idea of how this artist, whom we call 'Luke', operates.)

The first takes place at Levi's house (5:27-39). It is clearly the case that Jesus frequently went in for celebratory meals, and this is one of them, but one of the criticisms of him was that he used to eat with all the wrong sorts of people. Here there are two lots of criticism, all at the same dinner party, apparently. First there is the difficulty that he is eating with all his terrible friends, and second that his disciples do not fast. On top of that he tells a parable that indicates the newness of what he is doing.

The second setting is the house of Simon the Pharisee (7:36-50). Perhaps the most surprising thing about these dinner parties is the number of times Jesus is a guest of the Pharisees; though it must be said that they always turn disastrous. In this case, there is a woman involved. It looks (though not all scholars agree) as if Luke has taken over the story of the anointing of Jesus by a woman, which in Mark, followed by Matthew and, unusually, John, was the prelude to the Passion. Luke has placed this story rather early in Jesus' ministry and turned it instead into a beautiful story about love and forgiveness. Read it attentively, and notice how very shocking it is.

The third such affair takes place at the home of Martha and Mary (10:38-40). We shall be looking at this later under another heading, but it is worth reading as another party that (nearly) went wrong.

Then we find Jesus once again at the house of a Pharisee (11:37-54). Scarcely have we had time to digest the oddity of the invitation than once again disaster is looming, as the Pharisee host is pursing his lips in disapproval at Jesus' failure to observe the correct rituals. Jesus lets him have it with both barrels, we have to say, and the evening will not have gone down as a social success: 'Woe to you Pharisees' is the tune Jesus plays, and things get no better when a lawyer joins in to take some of the flak, for it is now, 'Woe to you lawyers . . .' as well. Luke's narrative does not suggest that they got as far as eating the meal.

The next disaster is also at a Pharisee's house, and when we hear that it takes place on the Sabbath, we just know that it is going to be catastrophic (14:1-24). And so it proves: almost in the first line we discover that 'they were watching him', which does not bode well. First Jesus cures a man with dropsy on the Sabbath, and argues the point; then he criticises the over-eagerness of the guests for the top places, and finally he attacks his host's criteria for inviting people. Last of all, in response to someone who seems to have been trying to restore calm, he tells the story of the great banquet. One cannot imagine that the Pharisee's wife will have been begging her husband to invite Jesus back.

The next incident is at Zacchaeus' house (19:1-10). This one actually works out quite well, despite the complaints of certain onlookers about Jesus' terrible choice of dining companions. So we can probably ignore this one. Our next meal, however, is something of a disaster, for it is Luke's version of the Last Supper. Luke makes it quite clear, with the addition of another cup to that which he found in Mark, that it is indeed a Passover meal (22:7-38). But it is not the joyful occasion that it ought to have been, with Jesus telling his disciples that one of them is a traitor. This is followed by some, possibly drink-fuelled, squabbling among the disciples about who is Mr Big, and then a prediction about Peter's imminent failure. Finally, one of the disciples brightly contributes, 'Lord – look; here are two swords' (22:38), to which Jesus (possibly in despair by now at their lack of comprehension) responds, 'It is enough.'

There are two more meals in the Gospel, both after the Resurrection. Neither is really disastrous, but they both contain an element of disarray and doubt. The first is at Emmaus (24:28-31), and the second is with the Eleven Plus Two (24:36-43), where the disciples are unable to cope with the return of Jesus from the dead, even though he has appeared to Simon and to the Emmaus Two. Eventually Jesus has to show them his wounds and eat a portion of grilled fish before their astonished gaze, in order to demonstrate his identity.

Luke's artistry is such as to weave all these disasters into a proclamation of the Gospel.

I would like to finish this chapter by drawing your attention to the opening four verses of the Gospel, where Luke, unlike Mark and Matthew, actually tells us what he is up to. He says that it is because 'Many people have attempted to draw up an orderly account of the things that have been fulfilled among us', and (we assume) Luke feels that they have not got it quite right, and so 'since I have followed it from the beginning, I have decided to write to you, accurately and in order'. He names his addressee: it is Theophilus, which could mean 'lover of God' or 'beloved by God', or it might be the name of Luke's patron, high up in Hellenistic/Roman

LUKE: THE SUPREME ARTIST

society. The purpose of the document that 'Theophilus' is just starting to read is 'so that you may know the infallibility of the things in which you were instructed'.

Is Luke's artistry, do you think, concerned with history or religion, or with something else?

Questions

1. What do you feel about the idea of Luke's first two chapters as a 'picture gallery'?

2. In what ways is it accurate (or inaccurate) to call Luke an 'artist'?

3. Does thinking about this Gospel as a work of art help us to grasp what Luke is about?

CHAPTER 17

The Lucan journey

One of the extraordinary things about Luke's Gospel is that it presents itself as a journey. You can see that quite clearly if you read Luke's two opening chapters, which (we must always remember) function like the overture to an opera, spelling out the themes that the Gospel is going to explore. You might like to check this out by opening the Gospel and seeing how it moves. After the opening address to Theophilus, which takes place nowhere in particular, we start at a particular time ('the days of Herod the King of Judea'). This also gives us the place, for it is in Judea that Zachary and his wife Elisabeth live, and it is in the 'Temple of the Lord' (1:9) that the angel of the Lord appears to him.

The next move is to Nazareth, and once again the angel Gabriel is involved, but we are also taken there to the virgin who is betrothed (1:26-38). After that the move is southwards once more, to 'the hill country, to a city of Judah', where Elisabeth and Zachary live (1:39-56). That episode concludes with Mary returning to her home in the North. Then the narrative returns to Judah, and Elisabeth produces her child, who is duly given the appropriate name; John is then sent off into the 'desert places until the day of his showing to Israel' (1:80). Do you see how the journey continues, even though we have not the slightest idea where John might be? He is parked in the desert to wait for his appearance in the area around the Jordan (3:2, 3); the reader's imagination is widened, and the setting of the story is taken even further, to the Jordanian desert.

Chapter 2 starts with a glimpse as far away as Rome, to the office of Caesar Augustus, who is sending out messages from his computer (2:1). And so the journeying continues, and Joseph and Mary make the weary trek from Nazareth to Judah, this time to Bethlehem, not very far from Judah. There the child is born, and feted by a cast of odd characters including shepherds (2:6-20); he is properly circumcised and named (though Luke does not take the opportunity to indicate a move back to Nazareth).

The next turn that the narrative takes is, presumably after 40 days, to Jerusalem and the Temple for that important encounter with Simeon and Hanna (2:22-38). When all that has been completed we are on the road again, once more to Jerusalem, where Jesus gets lost, so his parents have to cover a whole day's journey back to Jerusalem (2:41-50). Then we breathe a sigh of relief as we hear that the adolescent Jesus 'went down with them, and came to Nazareth, and was subjected to them'.

So Luke starts the story off with no fewer than 12 moves (depending on how you measure it), with the result that right from the beginning we are aware of being 'on the move'. We shall continue to be on the move all the way through both volumes: Acts of the Apostles, indeed, will bring us to Rome, where all roads lead, as the medieval proverb has it.

There is another way in which Luke presents the idea of journeying – what I call the 'ripple effect'. This is like dropping a pebble into a smooth pond and the ripple goes outwards. In the early part of Luke's Gospel, the message is frequently seen to spread outwards. Have a look at the following texts: 4:37 ('a report about him went out to every place of the region round about'); 7:17, after the healing of the widow's son at Nain we read, 'And the word went out in all Judea about him, and in all the area round about.' See if you can find any other texts like this, whereby the report enables Jesus' word to continue its journey.

Then there is the remarkable way in which Luke handles his Marcan source. Look at Mark 6:45–8:26, the long set of stories from the feeding of the 5000 to Caesarea Philippi, and a slightly shorter run from 9:41–10:12, and you will see that Luke omits them. Instead, at 9:51, Luke starts us on the journey that will lead us to Jesus' suffering and death in Jerusalem. As a matter of fact, Luke has signalled to us what is coming in his account of the Transfiguration, where he has Moses and Elijah talking about what they call Jesus' 'exodus' which he is going to accomplish in Jerusalem. But the journey proper starts, very formally, at 9:51 with, 'And it happened in the fulfilment of the days of his taking-up, and he set his face to journey to Jerusalem' (we shall come back in a moment to that word 'journey'). The journey immediately gets off to a bad start when a Samaritan village refuses them hospitality, 'because his face was journeying towards Jerusalem' (9:53). This, of course, brings out the worst in James and John, who offer to destroy the villagers.

Then, introduced by the phrase, 'As they were journeying on the way', we meet three potential disciples. The first offers to follow Jesus 'wherever you are going' (9:57), and receives a fairly discouraging response ('the Son of Man has nowhere to lay his head'). The second is invited to follow Jesus and asks, not unreasonably, for time to bury his father; he receives the chilling response, 'Let the corpses bury their corpses' (9:60). The third is willing to follow but first wants to say goodbye to those at home, and is sternly rebuked. This journey of discipleship is not, you see, for the faint-hearted. And Luke keeps us aware of the continuing journey, so that at 10:38 we read, 'As they were journeying, he himself went into a certain village.' Do you see how Luke just throws out the signals to keep us on the road? Similarly, at 13:22 we are told, 'And he was journeying through cities and villages, teaching and making a journey to

Jerusalem.' Then at 17:11 it is, 'It happened as he was journeying to Jerusalem, and he was travelling between Samaria and Galilee.'

There is one other thing Luke does to give us the feel of a journey, and it is the word that we have already translated as 'journey', both verb and noun. If you were to press the button on your computer (but it would have to be in Greek, because vernacular translations don't always bring this out), you would find that in Luke–Acts the author uses this word well over a hundred times, on its own or as a compound, such as 'journey into/journey with/journey from'. No other New Testament author gets much above single figures. One characteristic employment is at 4:30, when the inhabitants of Nazareth were determined to kill Jesus by throwing him down a cliff, and we read, 'But he went through the middle of them and was journeying.'

Another lovely example of the use of this word is in the Emmaus story (24:13-32), where Cleopas and his companion are trudging away from Jerusalem, 'journeying', says Luke, 'to a village that was 60 furlongs from Jerusalem'. Then we watch and discover that 'as they chatted and argued, Jesus himself drew near and was journeying with them'. That is close to the heart of the meaning of Luke's 'journey' word: at times you can almost translate it as 'pilgrimage'. And, of course, the whole of Acts of the Apostles is a journey, as we shall see; you will not be surprised to know that Luke uses the verb very frequently in his second volume.

Now the climax of this pilgrimage journey is Jerusalem; in Acts of the Apostles the story begins there and keeps coming back, until at 21:30 the Temple doors are slammed shut. In the Gospel, it is of a piece with the journeying theme that Luke offers us no fewer than four 'Jerusalem oracles'. So at 13:34 we hear Jesus responding to the Pharisees' warning against Herod with the words, 'Today and tomorrow and the next day, I must journey, because it is not permissible for a prophet to die outside Jerusalem. Jerusalem, Jerusalem, who kills the prophets and stones those who were sent to her.' And then he gives us the heart-rending picture of Jesus like a mother bird wanting to gather the chicks. Then at 21:20 there is the prediction of the siege of Jerusalem: 'When you see Jerusalem surrounded by armies, then know that her desertification has drawn near.' At 21:24 he speaks of 'Jerusalem trodden down by the Gentiles', and at 23:28 Jesus speaks to the mourning women as he goes to his execution: 'Daughters of Jerusalem, do not weep over me – instead, weep over yourselves and your children.'

Because this journeying story is the story of God, when finally we get to Jerusalem, that is not the end of the matter. We have known for several chapters that at Jerusalem Jesus is going to die, but we discover after Emmaus that it is not an ending but rather a new beginning. So when the risen Jesus is found among them, they clearly do not really believe it, and he has to show them his wounds and then eat some fish to prove that he is not a ghost. After that he gives a biblical lesson, about 'all the things written in the Law of Moses and in the Prophets and in the Psalms about me' (24:44). Jesus then offers a short sermon, indicating that this was all part of God's plan, that 'the Messiah should suffer and rise from the dead on the third day, and that repentance should be proclaimed in his name to all the Gentiles'. Then comes the key journeying phrase: 'beginning from Jerusalem. You are witnesses of this' (24:47, 48). And Jesus promises to send 'my Father's promise upon you – and you are to sit in the city until you are clothed with the power from on high'. Do you see what this means? It means that the journey is not under their control. They cannot start the journey until they have received the Spirit; it is their duty to continue Jesus' journey, and we shall watch them doing it in Acts, but it is not they who are in charge.

And for that reason, this is how the journeying Gospel ends, after the Ascension (so important to Luke that he tells the story twice). It says of the apostles: 'And they returned to Jerusalem with great joy – and they were all the time in the Temple blessing God.' At that moment we recall that the story started in that same Temple, with the annunciation to Zachary. Does that mean that it has all been a waste of time? That you begin in Jerusalem and end in Jerusalem, and we must now all go home? Clearly not, for something very important has happened during those 24 chapters, and now the infant Church is ready, once they are given the word, to get under way and to continue the Jesus journey.

And what of you? Are you, as they say, 'up for it'?

Questions

1. Is it helpful to regard Luke's Gospel, and its second volume, Acts of the Apostles, as a 'journey'?

2. What does the journeying tell us?

3. Where is the journey headed?

CHAPTER 18

Luke:
The Gospel of the Holy Spirit,
of prayer and of joy

Luke is very much the Gospel of the Holy Spirit, and this carries consequences. The idea runs all the way through both volumes of Luke's work, though sometimes we have to look hard for it.

Start with the opening lines of the Gospel, where the evangelist is, on the face of it, telling Theophilus that he proposes to give him an accurate account of Jesus' story: we think, 'Ah! He is writing history, then.' But we should pay careful attention here, for Luke talks of 'the things that have been fulfilled among us'. When you use words like 'fulfilled', you are thinking in terms of what God is doing, or, in Luke's terms, the work of the Holy Spirit.

It becomes more explicit at the Annunciation at Nazareth, when Mary asks, 'How can this be?' and Gabriel gives her the answer: 'The Holy Spirit will come upon you,' and then translates this as, 'the power of the Most High will overshadow you; therefore that which is being begotten shall be called Son of God.' So the Spirit is Luke's way of expressing that God is at work in this narrative.

In addition, there are people in the story who are described as 'filled with the Holy Spirit'. The first of these is Elisabeth at 1:41; then there is her husband Zachary at 1:67 as he intones the Benedictus. In chapter 2 we are told of the devout Simeon that 'the Holy Spirit was upon him', and that he had been 'warned by the Holy Spirit not to see death before he should see the Lord's Messiah' (2:25, 26). When Jesus is baptised, Luke adds to the mention of the Holy Spirit that he found in Mark that it was 'in bodily form', inviting the reader to pay a bit more attention to the phenomenon, and perhaps to ask what Luke understands by the Holy Spirit (3:22). Then all three of the Synoptic authors agree that the start of Jesus' mission, following immediately on from the baptism, was under the impulse of the Holy Spirit: Mark says that 'the Spirit drives him out into the desert' (1:12); Matthew says that Jesus was 'led up by the Spirit' (4:1). But Luke alone has Jesus 'full of the Spirit' (4:1), which emphasises slightly more Jesus' ability to make his own decisions.

It is only Luke who places the episode at Nazareth immediately after the baptism and temptations of Jesus; but here again we can feel the Spirit at work, for Luke has Jesus quote Isaiah 61, that 'the Spirit of the Lord is upon me', and then preach his sermon, the shortest in history: 'Today this Scripture is fulfilled in your hearing' (4:16-22). We have seen already how the word 'fulfil' is for Luke a sign of the Spirit of God at work. Then in the passage about 'Ask and you shall receive', which is also in Matthew (Matthew 7:7-11; Luke 11:9-13), Luke adds 'the Holy Spirit' to what the Heavenly Father will give to those who ask him.

When we come to look at Luke's second volume, Acts of the Apostles, we shall see how the Spirit drives the narrative; indeed, that work may safely be called the 'Gospel of the Holy Spirit', whereas in the Gospel of Luke in a sense the Holy Spirit goes underground for the rest of the Gospel: he will not be mentioned again, except as 'promise' (Luke 24:49) until the start of Acts, at 1:8.

There is, however, another aspect of the Spirit that is of immense importance in Luke's Gospel, namely prayer. Luke is very much the Gospel of prayer. Read slowly (again!) through chapters 1 and 2, which do so much to set the atmosphere for the Gospel, and notice the signs of prayer. The first scene presents us with Zachary doing his professional job of praying in the Temple (1:9-10), and 'the people [that is, Israel] praying outside'. Zachary is told, 'Your prayer has been heard' (though here we must hasten to add that this is a slightly different word for prayer, meaning 'asking for something' rather than speaking and listening to God, building a relationship). Still in those first two chapters, read carefully through Mary's Magnificat and Zachary's Benedictus, and taste the atmosphere. Look, too, at the prayerfulness of Mary, who 'kept all these things, comparing them in her heart' (2:19; 2:51). Likewise there is the prayerfulness of Simeon (2:25, 26), who is said to be 'waiting for the comfort of Israel', and of Hanna, who 'never left the Temple, worshipping day and night with fasting and intercession' (2:37).

It is somehow no surprise, therefore, that Luke has Jesus pray at every important moment of his life. Indeed, Luke sets the teaching of (his version of) the Lord's Prayer in a context where Jesus has been praying (see 11:1, and contrast what Matthew does at 6:9-13, which is the very different setting of the Sermon on the Mount).

Look now at the various episodes where Luke has Jesus pray. The first is at the baptism; unlike Mark or Matthew, in Luke it is when Jesus is praying that he sees the Spirit. Then there is a brief summary at 5:16. Luke often paints the picture by way of a summary of Jesus' activity, but here it is worth noticing that Jesus was 'going in the desert places and praying'.

Then Luke's Jesus prays before selecting his disciples: 'it happened in those days that he went out into the mountain to pray. And he was praying all night in his prayer to God' (6:12). Then the disciples are summoned and named. Do you see how Luke subtly alters the atmosphere by insisting on Jesus' prayerfulness?

Luke does it again before that moment which Mark places at Caesarea Philippi, when he asks the disciples, 'Whom do the crowds say I am?' and then the more important question, 'What about you – who do *you* say I am?' The setting is, once again, that Jesus is at prayer (9:18-20).

Then the next time it happens is later in the same chapter, at 9:28, 29, prior to his Transfiguration. The way Luke tells the story suggests that it is the fact of Jesus' prayer that enables the change in his features: 'It happened *while he was praying* that the appearance of his face became different, and his clothing flashing like lightning.'

The next time we learn of Jesus praying is at 22:32, at the Last Supper, when he turns to Simon and indicates that he has already prayed for him: 'Look! Satan sought to sift you like wheat,' he says, 'but I prayed for you that your faith should not fail. You are to turn and strengthen your brothers and sisters.' Neither Jesus nor his disciples can do their job, according to Luke, without prayerful assistance.

We next watch Jesus at prayer on the Mount of Olives (22:40-46), where all the disciples (not just Peter, James and John, as in Matthew and Mark) are instructed to 'pray not to enter into temptation'. Then we eavesdrop on his prayer to the Father: 'If you are willing, take this cup from me. But not my will but yours be done.' Then, but alas not in all manuscripts, we are allowed to see an answer to the prayer in the strengthening presence of an angel, and Jesus sweating drops of blood.

Then Jesus prays again as they crucify him (though once again this is not in all manuscripts), 'Father, forgive them, for they do not know what they are doing' (23:34), and, lastly, when he is at the point of death: 'crying out in a loud voice Jesus said, "Father, into your hands I commit my spirit"', which is quite different from Mark's 'My God, My God – why have you forsaken me?' and slightly changes the atmosphere.

In addition, Luke has four pieces of instruction on prayer:

- Parable about persistence (11:5-13, the friend who comes at night)

- The widow and the unjust judge (18:1-8)

- The Pharisee and the publican (18:9-14)

- Praying all the time (21:36); this is in the instructions about what to do when the end-time comes: 'Stay awake on every occasion, praying that you may have the strength to escape all these things that are going to happen, and to stand before the Son of Man.'

So this is a deeply prayerful Gospel, and one of the things that Luke thinks will happen if you pray, and if you are in touch with the Holy Spirit, is that there will be joy in the air.

Luke is also the Gospel of joy. There are at least two words for 'joy' in Luke. See how the idea threads through the entire Gospel. In chapters 1 and 2 you might look at the following passages:

The first is 1:14, where Zachary is told that 'there shall be joy for you, and exultation'.

Then 1:28, where the angel Gabriel tells Mary, 'Rejoice, graced lady' (or, possibly, 'Cheer up, you lucky thing'); and the dialogue between Elisabeth and Mary at 1:42-45, where it is a matter of the tone of Elisabeth's remarks, rather than the words that she uses.

Mary's Magnificat immediately follows this, which is indeed a joyous occasion (see especially 1:46, 47). Then we meet joy at 1:58, in the reaction of Elisabeth's neighbours and kinsfolk to the news of John's birth, not to mention the joy of Zachary (1:64, 68). In the same context, you might look at 2:10, 14, 20, where several different words are used to convey the joy of Jesus' birth announced to the shepherds: 'preach good news', 'glory', 'peace among human beings of good will', and the shepherds are said to 'glorify and praise God over all that they had heard and seen'. Joy is indeed the mood here, as it is in the case of Simeon and Hanna (2:28, 38), even though the word itself is not used.

And there is plenty of joy to find elsewhere in the Gospel. It is there at 4:18, 19, in the Isaiah reading in the synagogue at Nazareth; or in the Sermon on the Plain in 6:23. A different Lucan word, 'glorify', appears after the healing of the widow's son at Nain (7:16). Another word conveying joy, the idea of 'gospel' or 'good news' is to be found at 7:22. At 10:17, the 70 or 72 whom Jesus sent out at the beginning of the chapter 'returned with joy' because the demons had been subordinated to them. At 10:21 the link is made explicitly between the Holy Spirit and joy, when Luke says that Jesus 'rejoiced in the Holy Spirit'. Then, of course, there is the lovely chapter 15, where we have a series of stories about rejoicing over the finding of what had been lost: the lost sheep, the lost coin, and the lost son. In that chapter you might look at verses 6, 7, 9, 23, 24, 32 (and contrast the dreary lack of joy on the part of the elder brother in verse 29).

Also joyful is the story of the ten lepers (17:11-19), including the gratitude of the one who was a Samaritan. Or look at the blind man at Jericho, who 'followed Jesus, glorifying God' (18:43). See also 19:6 and 19:37, and a rather more sinister joy on the part of Herod at 23:8, as well as a rather curious reference at 24:41, where the disciples fail to believe that Jesus was indeed risen. Luke charitably interprets their incredulity as being 'out of joy'. Finally, at 24:52, 53, the Gospel ends on an appropriately unambiguous note of joy: 'When they had worshipped [Jesus], they returned to Jerusalem with great joy, and they were all the time in the Temple, blessing God.'

For Luke, there is a clear connection between joy and prayer and the accompanying presence of the Holy Spirit.

Questions

1. Is it accurate to call Luke the 'Gospel of the Holy Spirit'?

2. What are the signs that prayer is important in this Gospel?

3. Why does joy matter to Luke?

CHAPTER 19

Luke and Judaism

You often hear it said, though I am not sure that I know what the evidence is, that Luke was a Gentile, dealing with the problems of the Church coming to grips with the fact, bewildering to most of that first generation of Christians, that while this new movement based on Jesus took off in the most remarkable way among non-Jews, Jesus' fellow Jews for the most part were not attracted to it.

So the question arises: was Luke at all hostile to the Judaism from which Jesus emerged? Certainly when you come to Luke, the feeling from both volumes of his work, but perhaps most especially from Acts of the Apostles, is that Luke, like Paul, is more at home in the great Greek metropoleis like Rome, Athens, Ephesus, Corinth and Antioch, where Jews and Gentiles were rubbing shoulders every day. So some people argue that Luke is pro-Gentile and anti-Jewish. Certainly Luke's Greek is better than Mark's, and he omits the Aramaic terms that Mark often includes. But does that make him anti-Jewish?

Undeniably, there is one interesting thing that Luke does with regard to dating. At the beginning of each of his first three chapters he makes a reference to what sounds like a rather Gentile way of dating, but in each case he plays something of a trick on the reader and brings us to realise that what he is really talking about is the old story of God and the people of God. So, in fact, he turns out to be telling the story from a thoroughly Jewish point of view.

So the first 'date' is 'it happened in the days of Herod the King' (1:5). And we shudder appropriately, because anyone of that name (and this is Herod the Great, not his son, under whom Jesus died) is bad news. Yet before the pallor has risen to our cheeks, Luke rushes on to the people in whom he is really interested, namely Zachary and his wife Elisabeth, those exemplary Old Testament figures. So let us bow graciously in the direction of this very smart evangelist, who is reminding us of what really matters in life: not the heroes of the Gentile world but these thoroughly Jewish characters.

Luke plays the same trick on us at the beginning of the next chapter (2:1-4), when we read, 'It happened in those days that a decree went out from Caesar Augustus that the entire inhabited world should be registered. This first registration took place when Quirinius was procurator of Syria.' So we, priding ourselves on being alert readers, say to ourselves, 'Now Luke is making it quite clear that he is writing for the Gentile world.' But hardly have we breathed this sentiment when we read, 'Joseph also went up from the Galilee, from the city of Nazareth to Judea, to the city of David, which is called Bethlehem.' This is not the Gentile world but a thoroughly Jewish one, and we reflect with some astonishment on the fact that Luke is far more interested in the obscure couple, Mary and Joseph, and in the two wholly unknown towns of Nazareth and Bethlehem, than in the city of Rome, Augustus, who is the most powerful person in the entire world, and Quirinius, his local representative. This is clearly going to be a Gospel that will turn all our expectations upside down.

At 3:1, 2 Luke treats us to a very solemn-sounding date (the only date in the entire New Testament, as it happens), and even with the two previous reversals we find ourselves thinking, 'Surely he means it this time', as he intones:

> In the fifteenth year of the Imperium of Tiberius Caesar, when Pontius Pilatus was procurator of Judea, and Herod was tetrarch of the Galilee, and his brother Philip was tetrarch of Ituraea and the region of Trachonitis, and Lysanius was tetrarch of Abilene, in the high-priesthood of Annas and Caiaphas, the word of God came to . . .

That fifteenth year of Tiberius, by the way, takes us to roughly the year AD 29 or 30. Anyway, just as we were reflecting that this sounds like serious history and all about the Gentile world and the people who are really powerful in it (and perhaps we also found ourselves thinking that apart from their power, the list of names is distinguished by being as unwholesome a bunch of rogues as you could wish to meet on a dark night), Luke once more plays his three-card trick and reveals who he is really interested in, the person to whom 'the word of God came', and it was none of the above, but 'John, son of Zachary, in the desert'! This is, of course, the thoroughly Jewish figure of John the Baptist, who will later be executed by Herod the tetrarch, because the Baptist disapproved of his having married the wife of his brother Philip, both of whom were mentioned in that little list. John is a contemptible eccentric in the eyes of Luke's Gentile readership, but that is the person in whom God (and the evangelist) is really interested.

So we should not be too certain about Luke's audience. A better argument is to notice where the Gospel begins and ends. It starts, as we have seen in previous chapters, in the Temple in Jerusalem, Zachary performing his priestly duties, with the people of Israel waiting prayerfully outside (1:9, 10). And the Temple is where the Gospel ends, with the community at prayer: 'They were all the time in the Temple, blessing God' (24:53). You could not imagine a more Jewish setting than this.

And thoroughly Jewish are the three canticles that Luke inserts into his narrative. First, there is Mary's Magnificat:

And Mary said,
'My soul extols the Lord
And my spirit has exulted in God my Saviour
because he has looked [favourably] on the humble state of his slave-girl.
For look! From now on, all generations will congratulate me
because the Powerful One has done great things for me,
and holy is his name.
And his mercy is for generation after generation on those who fear him.
He has done a mighty deed with his arm.
He has scattered those who are haughty in the thoughts of their heart.
He has deposed rulers from their thrones
and raised up the humble.
The hungry he has filled with good things
and the wealthy he has sent away empty.
He has helped his servant Israel, remembering his mercy.
As he spoke to our ancestors,
to Abraham and his descendants for ever.'
Mary remained with her about three months, and she returned to her home.
(1:46-56)

This lovely poem can hardly be understood without reference to its Old Testament background. Many scholars regard it as based on the song of Hannah (1 Samuel 2:1-11), although it might simply be picking up on an ancient Jewish theme rather than being directly dependent on that other great poem.

Then there is Zachary's song, the Benedictus, sung, significantly enough, at the moment of his son's circumcision. Again this is a very Jewish prayer:

And Zachary his father was filled with the Holy Spirit, and prophesied,
    saying,
'Blessed is the Lord, the God of Israel,
for he has looked at his people, and brought about their release
and raised up a horn of salvation for us
in the house of David his servant,
as he spoke through the mouth of the holy ones of old, his prophets,
salvation from our enemies, and from the hands of all those who hate us,
to work mercy with our ancestors
and to remember his holy covenant,
an oath which he swore to Abraham our ancestor
to grant to us, once we had been fearlessly delivered from enemy hands,
to worship him in holiness and righteousness
before him all our days.

And you, little child, you shall be called a prophet of the Most High;
for you shall go before the Lord, to prepare his ways,
to give knowledge of salvation to his people, through forgiveness of their sins
through the compassionate heart of our God,
by which he will visit us, the risen sun from on high,
to appear to those who sit in darkness and in the shadow of death,
to straighten our feet into the way of peace.'
And the little child grew and was strengthened in the spirit; and he was in the
    desert until the day of his revelation to Israel.
(1:67-80)

Every word of these two poems is deeply Jewish in tone.

Likewise, it is a significant and important point that Jerusalem is of immense importance to Luke. Indeed, 60 per cent of all the Synoptic Gospel references to the city are in Luke, so that simply carries on the tone of the opening chapters, where, as we have seen, the narrative starts in the Temple and keeps coming back.

Now read this passage, where we are clearly meant to applaud Jesus' parents for doing what they do:

And when the eight days were fulfilled for him to be circumcised, and his name was called Jesus, which [he] had been called by the angel before he had been conceived in the womb.

And when the days of their purification were fulfilled according to the Law of Moses, they took him up to Jerusalem, to offer him to the Lord, as it is written in the Law of the Lord that 'every male that opens his mother's womb shall be called holy to the Lord', and to give sacrifice according to what is written in the Law of the Lord, 'a pair of turtle-doves, or two young doves'.

And look! There was a man in Jerusalem, whose name was Simeon, and this man was righteous and pious, and waiting for Israel's comfort; and the Holy Spirit was on him. And it had been revealed to him by the Holy Spirit [that he would not] see death before he saw Christ the Lord. And he came in the Spirit into the Temple; and as the parents brought in the child Jesus, for them to act in accordance with the Law about him, he himself took him into his arms and blessed God and said,

'Now you are letting your slave go, Master,
according to your word in peace;
because my eyes have seen your salvation
which you have prepared before the face of all the peoples,
a light for the revelation of the Gentiles
and the glory of your people Israel.'

And the child's father and mother were in a state of astonishment at the things being said about him; and Simeon blessed them, and said to Mary his mother: 'Look! This one is destined for the fall and rising of many in Israel, and as a sign of contradiction (and your own soul will be pierced by a sword) so that the thoughts of many hearts may be revealed.'

And there was Hanna, a prophetess, a daughter of Phanuel, of the tribe of Asher; she was advanced, with many days, having lived with her husband for seven years from her virginity, she was now a widow of as many as eighty-four years; she did not leave the Temple, worshipping with fasting and prayer, day and night. And at that hour, she stood and praised God and spoke of him to all those who were waiting for the redemption of Israel.

And when they had completed everything in accordance with the Law of the Lord, they returned to Galilee, to their own city of Nazareth. (2:21-39)

So Mary and Joseph are bringing the child 'to Jerusalem, to offer him to the Lord, as it is written in the Law of the Lord'. This sort of language is not that of one who thinks that Judaism has been superseded.

Similarly we should take seriously the next episode, something like Jesus' bar mitzvah:

And his parents used to journey each year to Jerusalem for the Passover festival. And when he was twelve years old, when they went up according to the custom of the feast, and when they had completed the days, as they returned, the boy Jesus stayed behind in Jerusalem; and his parents did not know. Thinking that he was in the caravan, they went a day's journey, and then started to hunt for him everywhere among their relatives and acquaintances; and when they couldn't find him, they returned to Jerusalem in their hunt for him; and so it was that after three days they found him sitting in the Temple in the middle of the teachers, and [he was] listening to them and asking them questions; and all those who heard him were astonished at his intellect and at his responses. And when they saw him they were overwhelmed; and his mother said to him, 'Child, why did you do this to us? Look – your father and I have been looking for you in agony.'

And he said to them, 'Why were you looking for me? Didn't you know that I had to be on my Father's business [or: 'in my Father's house']?' And they did not understand the word that he had spoken to them.

And he went down with them to Nazareth, and put himself under their authority. And his mother kept all these events ([or 'words']) in her heart.

And Jesus advanced in wisdom and stature and favour before God and human beings. (2:41-52)

This story of Jesus escaping his parents' vigilant attention is very striking from the point of view of Luke's attitude to Judaism. Notice what the family was doing: they were engaged upon the eminently Jewish business of journeying 'to Jerusalem, for the feast of Passover', and the 12-year old goes missing. Obviously they must have been in a panic; indeed, his mother says, 'Your father and I were in agony looking for you.'

But that is not the main point, nor Jesus' slightly over-sharp response: 'Why were you looking for me? Didn't you realise that I must inevitably be in my Father's place?' The deeper point is that they went straight back to Jerusalem, and to the Temple, which is almost a character in Luke's Gospel, so they knew that was where he had to be. The Gospel is permanently on the move towards Jerusalem, and even though we know that Jesus is to die there, that is not the main point that the evangelist is making. The main point is the return to Jerusalem, looking ahead to the end of the Gospel and the setting of the first seven chapters of Acts. Then, even after the death of Stephen, the story keeps returning there. This is a deeply Jewish Gospel.

So that is the mood created with regard to Jerusalem and Judaism by the first two chapters of the Gospel, and it is reinforced by the old-fashioned charm of the three couples, Zachary and Elisabeth in Judea, Simeon and Hanna in the Temple, and even Joseph and Mary, even though they are Galileans with strange accents, who keep coming back to Judea and to the Temple. We are clearly intended to approve of them, and indeed of Jerusalem, which is the pivot on which the whole narrative turns, and the destination of the Lucan journey. Luke makes this quite clear at 9:31, with its reference to Jesus' 'exodus' which he was going to 'fulfil [that word again] in Jerusalem'. It is also clear at 9:51, where Luke writes, 'It happened in the fulfilment of the days of his taking-up, and he had set his face to journey to Jerusalem . . .'

Jerusalem as a kind of climax in Luke also comes out in the story of the temptation of Jesus in the wilderness. Both Matthew and Luke report three temptations, building on the rather thin narrative found in Mark, but they tell them in a different order. This is the third temptation in Luke, which is presumably intended as a climax, like other Jerusalem references that we have looked at: '[The devil] took him to Jerusalem, and put him on the pinnacle of the Temple, and said to him, "If you *are* the Son of God, throw yourself down from here . . ."' (4:9). One cannot help feeling that Luke tells the temptation story in this order precisely because of the importance that the Temple holds for him.

So it does not really make sense to classify Luke as anti-Jewish, pro-Gentile.

Then there are the four 'Jerusalem' oracles in the Gospel, which we mentioned in a previous chapter, but in a different context. The first is at 13:31-35. The setting here is of a warning from some friendly Pharisees of Herod's lethal intentions for Jesus. Jesus' response has to do with the certainty that a prophet cannot die outside Jerusalem. Then we hear the oracle, 'Jerusalem, Jerusalem, you who kill the prophets and stone those who are sent to you, how often I longed to gather your children, like a mother bird gathers her offspring under her wings.' This seems like a very different attitude from the optimism of 2:49 and Jesus' certainty that he had to be 'in my Father's house'. Matthew also repeats this oracle (Matthew 23:37-39), but it may be worth noticing that Luke omits the reference in Matthew to Jerusalem becoming 'a desert'. Both Luke and Matthew are, of course, writing after AD 70, and that terrible event of the destruction of Jerusalem and its Temple.

In the next oracle (19:41-44), Jesus once more weeps over Jerusalem, saying, 'If only you also had known on this day the things that make for peace!' This is followed by a clear prediction of the Roman invasion: 'They shall not leave a stone upon a stone within you.' This is then given added effect by Jesus' very next action, the 'cleansing of the Temple', followed by Luke's revelation that 'the high priests and the scribes were seeking to destroy him, as well as the Number Ones of the people'. Here is the point: the religious authorities had lost sight of God since Jesus went there as a 12-year-old.

The sadness, that is to say, is a very Jewish sadness.

The third of these oracles is at 21:20-24, again a prediction of AD 70: 'When you see Jerusalem encircled by armies – then you will know that her desertification has arrived.' In a sense, there is nothing new about this: there is plenty of Old Testament precedent for the judgement of God on the city. You might look at Isaiah 29:2-4; Jeremiah 52:2-5; Ezekiel 4:1-3; 21:27, to take examples almost at random. That sort of oracle is a very Jewish thing to deliver.

The final oracle is at 23:27-31, when Jesus, on the way to Calvary, meets the women of Jerusalem: 'Do not weep for me, daughters of Jerusalem, but for yourselves and for your children.' Does this imply hostility on Luke's part towards Jerusalem? Not really: once again we are hearing an inner Jewish debate. Look, for example, at Jeremiah 9:16-21 and Hosea 10:8, which are both echoed here.

The fact is that Jerusalem is a problem for the whole of the New Testament. It was the centre of the Old Testament promises, but also the place where Jesus was rejected and where he died. And it is, we must never forget, a problem also for us Christians, after the Holocaust. Luke is writing, of course, from a particular point of view; he is trying to cope with the fact that on the whole Jews have resisted the appeal of Jesus and, unexpectedly, Gentiles have come flocking to the Church. But Jerusalem remains central to the plan of God, even when its Temple has been destroyed. It is simply misreading what Luke is about to think of him as pro-Gentile and anti-Jewish.

Questions

1. How 'Jewish' a Gospel do you think Luke is?

2. Does Luke strike you as a Gentile?

3. What is the importance of Jerusalem in Luke's Gospel?

CHAPTER 20

John's Gospel:
the prologue, and 'trying on hats'

The one part of John's Gospel that is known to everybody is its astonishing prologue. There was a time when it was fashionable to argue that the theology of the prologue was so sophisticated that it must have been written much later than the rest of the Gospel. Nowadays scholars are much more confident that the prologue belongs with it. What I am aiming to do in this chapter is to go through the prologue with you, and the rest of the first chapter of the Gospel, and invite you to see how it works, as it invites the reader to go deeper into the mystery of who Jesus is.

One of the things that the prologue does is to tell us, right at the beginning, that we are in a different world from that of the Synoptic Gospels. There is an old saying (now impossible to track down, alas) that John's Gospel is a 'magic pool, in which an elephant may swim and an infant paddle'. You might remember that over the course of the next few chapters.

It is an astonishing beginning, and I should really like you to make time to read it for yourself, and keep your Bible open as you read the rest of this chapter. In those first verses we hear a hymn to 'the Word', who is not identified at all, though we assume it to be Jesus. 'In the beginning was the Word, and the Word was towards God, and the Word was God.' You could spend a lifetime meditating on those words, but for the moment I just want you to see that they count as your rules for how you read this extraordinary Gospel.

Then, quite abruptly, from high poetry, up there with God, we land with a bump on the ground, with John the Baptist, and prose (verses 6-8); but it is still part of the same story, and deals with the central question of John's Gospel: 'Who is Jesus?' Notice the language used of John: 'a man', 'sent from God', 'witness' (both as verb and as noun), 'light', 'believe' (or 'come to faith'). This is all language that you will hear again and again in this fourth Gospel, and it is part of the journey into the mystery of Jesus on which we are engaged.

Then at verses 9-11 we are back in that upper world where the Word belongs, with the entry of light into the world. 'Light' is an idea that we shall come across again and again in this Gospel; indeed, chapter 9 can be seen as a dramatisation of what it means for Jesus to be the 'light of the world'. And 'world' is another word of considerable importance in this fourth Gospel: it stands for that which

God loves, and also for those forces arrayed against God's project that we encounter in Jesus. Every time that you meet it, try asking yourself whether it is the good or the bad meaning that you are dealing with.

Here too we should notice the theme of rejection, which we shall encounter quite frequently: 'He came *to his own*, but *his own* did not receive him.' But we should also remember what happens at the end of the Gospel, when the dying Jesus says to his mother, 'Woman, behold your son,' and to the Beloved Disciple, 'Behold your mother.' Then we hear that the Beloved Disciple 'took her *to his own*' (19:26, 27), and so founded the community that carried on the project of God's word. These are the ones described in 1:12, 13 as 'children of God': 'those who believe in his name, who were born, not of blood, nor of the will of flesh, nor of the will of a man, but were born of God'. That, among others, is you, the reader or hearer of John's words. You, the hearer, from now on will understand virtually everything Jesus says (with two exceptions, which I shall come to in a moment), and you will notice that you will often witness conversations between Jesus and other interlocutors, where they have no idea what Jesus is talking about, and we the reader complacently preen ourselves because *we* understand. There are good examples in the Nicodemus story in chapter 3 or the Samaritan woman in chapter 4, if you want to have a look. The name for the failure on the part of Jesus' interlocutors to understand while we, the reader, understand is 'Johannine irony'. We understand because we have read the prologue, and we know where Jesus comes from, and who he is.

Then, in 1:14 we come to the astonishing statement which is right at the heart of the Gospel and must stay with us in our reading. It is this: 'The Word' (which, you remember, was with God and close to God) 'was made flesh [*flesh???*] and pitched his tent among us. Stay with that sentence, and go deep into its mystery.

On, then, to verses 15-18, where once more we encounter John and his 'witness' (that word again, you see) of pointing to the *Logos*, or Word, and a contrast: 'Law came through Moses', and 'grace and truth came through Jesus Christ'. So now at last we know that the Word is indeed Jesus Christ, but do you see how slowly the mystery is revealed to us?

And the revelation continues in the rest of chapter 1, with the process that I call 'trying on hats': various titles are offered for Jesus, to see if they fit, and as we watch the process we go ever deeper into the mystery. It starts with John the Baptist once more, and here the process is negative, to confirm that John is not the Messiah, or Elijah or 'the Prophet'. Then they ask why he is baptising if he is none of the above. The answer is that his task is to point to Jesus, 'the One in your midst'.

Finally, at verse 29, we actually encounter Jesus. It is Day 2 of his mission, we gather, and now we start the serious business of trying on hats. The first hat is 'Lamb of God, who takes away the sin of the world'. The extraordinary thing is that this hat fits, for we repeat the phrase no fewer than four times every time we celebrate the Eucharist, whereas we never use 'Son of Man' except when reading the Gospels, a phrase that was frequently on Jesus' lips.

What does 'Lamb of God' mean? There are several possibilities, and perhaps we should go for all of them: there is the Passover Lamb, for one, and in John's Gospel Jesus dies at the time when the Passover Lamb is sacrificed. Then there is the scapegoat, who does not die, but symbolically carries Israel's sins out into the desert on the Day of Atonement. It may also represent a victorious lamb, and perhaps also it may be an Aramaic word for 'Messiah'. There are too many possibilities, and you will perhaps need to stay with all of them. But notice the 'of God' part of the phrase, which we shall find elsewhere in this remarkable Gospel in 'Son of God', 'Chosen One of God', 'Gift of God', 'Bread of God' and 'Word of God'. This Gospel is the story of God, freshly revealed in Jesus, and what we are calling the 'hats' are a part of this.

John the Baptist, we learn (1:31) 'did not know Jesus', but came to reveal him, which is what this extraordinary Gospel is all about, and he 'saw the Spirit descend upon him'.

So to hat 2, in verse 34, where Jesus is revealed as Son of God, with a curious legal formulation from John the Baptist: 'I have seen and I have borne witness.' Then to verses 35 and 36 and a repetition of hat 1, but notice that we are now at Day 3. At this point something shifts with John the Baptist, for two of his disciples become disciples of Jesus, one of them being Andrew from Bethsaida.

Then at last we hear the 'Word's' first words: in the story they are spoken to these two disciples of John the Baptist; but they leap off the page to us, the reader: 'What are you looking for?' (1:38). If you have your text open in front of you, go to almost the end of the Gospel, 20:15, when Jesus asks Mary Magdalene, who takes him to be a passing gardener, as she weeps for her beloved, 'Whom are you looking for?' There is a sense in which the whole journey of this extraordinary Gospel is from a 'what' to a 'who'.

Then listen to the response of these two former disciples of the Baptist: 'Where do you stay?' That word 'stay' can also mean 'dwell', 'abide' or 'remain', and it comes up quite frequently in the Gospel, so watch out for it. There is a connected noun, which carries the same idea, and can be translated as 'dwelling place' or 'mansion', as when Jesus says, 'In my Father's house there are many mansions' (14:2). Notice that these two disciples then 'saw where he stayed' and then 'stayed' with Jesus for the rest of that day. Something irrevocable has happened to them, and to us who read the words. And the reason it has happened is that Jesus has said something else to them that likewise leaps off the page at the reader: 'Come, and you will see.' That is what is going to happen to us as we read through the text.

Now it is time for another 'hat', the third of that ilk; and Andrew, who offers it to his brother Simon, fits it upon Jesus. This provides the first of several examples where Jesus shows unexpected knowledge (and which many scholars dismiss as 'supernatural', by which they mean, I suppose, that it could not possibly happen), when he addresses Peter by his full title: 'Simon, son of John', and offers him a nickname of 'Rock', possibly because he is not all that 'Rocky'.

Then we are on to Day 4, which starts with a slight awkwardness that you will find to be typical of this Gospel, about Jesus going to Galilee (the feast at Cana is the next event) and needing to find Philip. This turns out to be an excuse to produce hat number 4, as Philip introduces Jesus to Nathanael (whom we have not met before and whom we shall see only once more, at 21:2), with the title 'the One whom Moses and the prophets wrote about', and specifies him as 'Jesus, Son of Joseph, the one from Nazareth' (1:45). There is barely time for Nathanael to issue his contemptuous dismissal: 'Nazareth??' before we are into another piece of supernatural knowledge on Jesus' part: 'an Israelite without guile'. Then when Nathanael asks, 'From where do you know me?' we are suddenly presented with three more hats: 'Rabbi, Son of God, King of Israel', the last of which makes the seventh in all. And why? Because Jesus has said, 'I saw you under the fig tree.' Now there is a whole learned library of suggestions about what this might mean, none of them compatible; the fact is that the evangelist does not tell us, and perhaps we should be content with that.

The point to grasp here, however, is that what follows is an example of the 'Johannine irony' that I mentioned above. You will remember that I applied this term to situations where someone to whom Jesus is talking completely fails to understand him, while we know perfectly well what is going on. Here, at 1:48, and in the very next episode, the wedding feast at Cana when Jesus' mother (2:5), having apparently been abruptly turned away, says to the servants, 'Whatever he says to you, do.' At these two points, the irony is on us, and we do not know what is going on, though there is no shortage of scholarly suggestions.

And this little episode leads us to the last hat in this extraordinary first chapter, as Nathanael has to be told about 'angels of God ascending and descending on the Son of Man'. You and I have read the prologue, so we (at least dimly) understand what is going on; the evangelist does not reveal what Nathanael made of this final hat, but we move into chapter 2 quite ready to go deeper into the mystery of who Jesus is.

Questions

1. Who is the 'Word'? Does the text of the Gospel tell us?

2. Is it helpful to think of the evangelist as inviting us to 'try on hats', to work out who Jesus is?

3. What is meant by 'Johannine irony'?

CHAPTER 21

John's Gospel:
who is Jesus?

The question that most matters in this extraordinary Gospel is that of 'Who is Jesus?' From the very beginning we know that we are to understand him as part of the old story of God and the people of God; and in those astonishing opening lines of the Gospel, we hear that the Word 'was in the beginning near to God – and the Word was God'. So we more or less come to assume that Jesus is the Word, though the Gospel never quite tells us as much.

But now here is a problem, for the author of our fourth Gospel, and the people he was writing for, and indeed Jesus himself, are all good Jews. And one of the things that all good Jews know is that there is one and only one God; indeed, twice a day they will say the Shema: 'Hear O Israel – the Lord your God is one God.' One thing that good Jews simply cannot do is to run around the place saying that human beings are gods, because that is pagan, and we don't want to do what those pagans do.

That is why again and again in John's Gospel we hear accusations of blasphemy against Jesus. It is not just a problem for the fourth Gospel: all of our New Testament authors recognise that if they are to get Jesus right, they have to use language of him that has been hitherto reserved for God; and they did not come easily to that, good Jews as they were. It was simply that they discovered that they could not do justice to their experience of Jesus unless they did use that sort of language for him.

It did not come easily to them, but they knew they had to speak of this newly discovered richness of God; but they also had to face the difficulty that this posed for their beliefs about the oneness of God. That is why we encounter all those accusations of blasphemy against Jesus in the fourth Gospel. At 5:18 we read, 'The Judeans sought all the more to kill him, because not only did he undo the Sabbath – but he also made God his own Father, making himself equal to God.'

This is Jesus' response:

So Jesus answered and said to them, 'Amen, Amen, I am telling you: the Son cannot do anything at all on his own account unless he sees the Father doing something. For whatever That One does, the Son likewise does the same. For the Father loves the Son, and shows him everything that he does. And he will show him greater works than this, that you may be amazed. For

as the Father raises up the dead and gives them life, so the Son gives life to those whom he wishes. For neither does the Father judge anybody – no: he has given all judgement over to the Son, in order that all may honour the Son just as they honour the Father. The one who does not honour the Son does not honour the Father who sent him.
(5:19-23)

You can feel those Jews, and those early Christians, wrestling with the mystery. Listen to this, from chapter 7 of the Gospel:

On the last day, the great one, of the Feast, Jesus stood up and cried out, saying: 'If anyone is thirsty, let them come to me and drink. The one who believes in me, as the Scripture said, rivers shall flow from his belly, of living water.' He said this about the Spirit which those who came to faith in him were going to receive. For there was as yet no Spirit, because Jesus was not yet glorified.
(7:37-39)

We who have read the prologue understand what is meant, but we are also aware that we are on dangerous ground.

And the Gospel is well aware that this is a life and death question: at 10:30 Jesus says, 'The Father and I are one' (when they only asked him if he was the Messiah), and 'the Judeans picked up stones to stone him'. When asked the reason for this aggression, they simply respond that 'it is for blasphemy – because you who are a human being are making yourself God'. Now that cannot be quite true; no one can make themselves God: you either are or are not, but the point is that you and I as we read John's Gospel have to decide who Jesus is. And it does not stop there, because it also says something about who human beings are, if human nature is so constructed that we can reveal God. Jesus simply challenges his opponents to decide, 'If I am not doing the works of my Father, then don't believe me.'

See the mystery of who Jesus is:

Jesus replied, 'If I glorify myself, my glory is nothing. It is my Father who glorifies me, the One of whom you say, "He is our God." And [yet] you do not know him; but I know him. And if I were to say "I do not know him", then I shall be like you people, a liar. No – I know him, and I keep his word. Abraham your father rejoiced that he might see my day. And he saw it; and he rejoiced.' And so the Judeans said to him, 'You are not yet 50 years old, and you have seen Abraham?!' Jesus said to them, 'Amen, Amen, I am telling you: before Abraham was, I AM.' So they took up stones, to throw at him. But Jesus was hidden, and he went out of the Temple.
(8:54-59)

Likewise, in that strange trial before Pilate, the Judeans terrify Pilate by insisting on death: 'We have a Law, and according to the Law, he has to die, because he made himself Son of God' (19:7). Now at this point you and I have to decide: are we going to abandon the struggle, as Jesus' opponents do, or are we going to allow the puzzle to do what the fourth Gospel wants and go deeper into the mystery?

We do, it is true, have an advantage over those people who are talking to Jesus, most of the time, because we have read the prologue, and they haven't; but that does not make it easy, and we cannot run away from the challenge; instead, we must look for a deeper clarity about who Jesus is.

The prologue does give us a few clues: it says that the Word 'was towards God' and that he 'was God', and that he was involved in creation. What it is doing here is hinting at the richness of God, for our monotheism is not to be a matter of a somewhat clinical austerity. The heart of the matter for Jews, and for Christians, is that God is love, and that means a certain untidiness that holds the mystery open for human beings. There is one and only one God, but the mix is very rich; Jewish thinkers were already starting to think of 'Wisdom' as a kind of personification that was and also was not God, present to God in creation. There is a real tension here in Judaism, and a tension too in Christianity, for both very much wish to affirm the oneness of God.

And you can feel the tension in John's Gospel also. For on the one hand we hear Jesus say things like, 'The one who sees me sees the One who sent me' (12:45), which asserts his identity with the Father, or, 'The one who has seen me has seen the Father' (14:9). On the other hand, we hear him say, 'the Father is greater than I' (14:28). What we have to do, therefore, is sit with the tension, and allow it to point us to the identity of Jesus.

Very important here is the basic insight, the sound Jewish view, that 'no one has ever seen God'. You will find that in the prologue, at 1:18, and the important next step in the Gospel: 'The one and only God, the one who is in the bosom of the Father, is the one who has explained God.' It is all right, by the way, for you to clutch your hands to your head and say, 'Well, I really don't understand that.' You are invited to sit with it as you go through the Gospel and go deeper into the mystery. The essential thing is not to pick out one phrase or another, but to allow the Gospel to form in us the picture of Jesus, and to hold several phrases together, even if on the face of it they seem to be contradictory. So it is important for us to sit with what we find at 5:37: 'The Father who sent me is the One who has borne witness about me; and you have never heard his voice or seen his appearance.' One way of expressing this might be in the words of an old teacher of mine: 'If you want to know what God looks like, look at Jesus.' And what Jesus does is what God does.

So the important question is the one that the representatives from Jerusalem put to John the Baptist at 1:19: 'Who are you?' And the invitation to face that question also helps us to face the real question, 'Who is Jesus?', as well as that other related question, 'Where is he from?' There is a tiny little Greek word, of just two syllables, that appears again and again in this Gospel, and we do not always notice it. It means 'where from?' And it is really important. So Nathanael (1:48), when Jesus addresses him as 'an Israelite without guile', says to him, 'Where do you know me from?' Or at Cana (2:9) we are told that the head waiter did not know where the water-become-wine was 'from', but *we* know, because we have been watching, and we have read the prologue. At 3:8 Nicodemus has to be told about the wind (and the word can also mean 'Spirit'), that 'you do not know where it comes from or where it is going'. That is the important question, and Pilate asks it of Jesus at 19:9, when the Judeans demand death for someone who calls himself 'Son of God': 'Where are you from?' And that is the only time that Pilate comes anywhere near to asking the right question.

What this Gospel is about, therefore, is 'revealing the mystery'. So at 1:31 we listen to John the Baptist telling his disciples, 'I did not know him, but in order that he might be revealed to Israel, that is why I came.' If you go carefully through chapter 1 you will see that revelation is indeed John's function. The revelation, though, is always about Jesus, and so at 2:11 after Cana, we read, 'This Jesus did as the beginning/first of his signs; and he revealed his glory, and his disciples believed in him.' To 'believe' is what you and I are also invited to do as we read and marvel.

The 'glory' mentioned there is all about Jesus' relationship – obscure, perhaps, but unmistakable – to God. The revelation also has to do with us, though, because at 3:21 we are warned that 'those who do the Truth come to the Light, that their works may be revealed, because they are done in the light'. Similarly, we are told of the man born blind, that his blindness, oddly enough, was not because of sin, but 'in order that the works of God might be revealed in him' (9:3). (See also 21:1 (twice), 14.) This revelation is right at the heart of the Gospel: as we go deeper into its mystery, we come more and more to grips with the baffling truth about Jesus.

A good example of this comes in chapter 4, the story of the Samaritan woman. As we read this remarkable chapter and the spirited dialogue that it provides, every step on the woman's journey is also a step on our journey. First she asks, 'From where do you have this living water?' (4:11); then, hesitantly, 'Are you – can you be – greater than our father Jacob?' Well, yes, actually, is the correct answer. Next (4:19) she goes a bit further: 'Lord, I see you are a prophet.' Her next move is to raise the Messiah question: 'I know that Messiah is coming, the so-called Christ' (4:25). Now, because of her openness, the revelation comes loud and clear: 'I AM, the one who is speaking to you.' 'I AM' is spoken in capitals: at one level it simply means, 'Yes – that's me.' At another level it asserts Jesus' identity with the God of Israel (4:26). In the end, and rather unexpectedly, the quest goes even deeper, and this time it is not the Samaritan woman but her compatriots who are able to say, 'We know that this one is truly the Saviour of the World,' and we then sit back and applaud.

There are many examples of going deeper into the mystery in John's Gospel. Another is 6:20, when Jesus is walking on the water as the disciples make heavy weather of their rowing, and 'they were afraid'. He says to them, 'Don't be afraid, I AM.' Once again that could just mean, 'It's me', but when we hear 'I AM', we know that there is something deeper going on. He does this in several places, of course: I am the Bread of Life, I am the Good Shepherd, I am the True Vine and, just occasionally, extraordinary expressions such as, 'Before Abraham was, I AM' (8:58). Here we really feel that we are getting close to the heart of the mystery, and so do those who are listening to him, because 'they lifted up stones to throw at him'.

So what is our way into the mystery of who Jesus is? I should like to end with just two observations from this extraordinary Gospel.

The first is that we are not alone in our journey into the mystery, for Jesus leaves us what in the fourth Gospel is called the *Paraclete*, which means something like a counsel for the defence. If you turn to what is called the 'Last Supper Discourse', which you will find in chapters 13–17, you will find this character, possibly the fourth evangelist's greatest gift to us, at 14:15-17, 26; 15:26, 27; 16:7-15. Just stay with those four passages and ask to be led deeper into the mystery.

And where does our journey end? In a sense it never does, but it does reach a sort of climax at the end of the story, at 20:28. You remember the story: an appearance of Jesus to all of them except Thomas on that first Easter Sunday night, then the rest of them gloating over Thomas, and his crude refusal to believe unless he can physically touch Jesus' wounds. A week later comes Jesus' reappearance and invitation to Thomas to do just that, and the astonished cry of faith, deep into the mystery, that is wrung out of Thomas at that point, as we stand and listen and applaud: 'My Lord and my God!' That is the end of the journey, but we shall not have grasped it unless we have been into the darkness and the puzzlement of Thomas and all those others who meet Jesus on the way.

Questions

1. Why is the question of who Jesus is in the fourth Gospel so difficult?

2. What is the best answer that John's Gospel gives to the question?

3. What is *your* answer to the question?

CHAPTER 22

John's Gospel: the Passion Narrative

The Passion Narrative in John's Gospel, like every other part of the Gospel, as we have seen, takes us deeper into the mystery. Here in chapters 18 and 19 the fourth Gospel reaches its climax. It does so in a way quite different from that of Mark and Matthew (and Luke, too, though he comes from another stable). Where Mark's story of Jesus' suffering and death is bleak, John offers a Jesus who is very much in charge, and a cross that is a royal throne.

For one thing, before his account of Jesus' Passion, John places those four remarkable chapters, 13-17, that we call his 'Last Supper Discourse'. This is an extraordinary piece of writing, and what it does above all is to set Jesus' death in context, as an act of love. So the Last Supper begins and ends with the mention of love: 'Having loved those who were his own in the world, he loved them to the end' (13:1); and then at the end we hear him pray to the Father that 'the love with which you loved me may be in them, and I may be in them' (17:26). Indeed, love threads its way through Jesus' discourse, including that powerful saying (15:13) that 'no one has greater love than this, than to lay down their life for their friends'. Most dramatically of all, of course, John chooses to begin the supper with the enacted parable of Jesus washing his disciples' feet, doing a job for them that not even a slave should be asked to do. It is no wonder that Peter impetuously protests against it, and has to be persuaded by Jesus.

We shall not understand the Passion Narrative that follows unless we remember that example of love. We are to keep it in mind in the course of the story that now unfolds.

Now see how John starts the story: (18:1-11)

When he had said this, Jesus went out with his disciples across the Wadi Kedron, where there was a garden, into which he and his disciples went.

Now Judas, who was betraying him, also knew the place, because Jesus often gathered there with his disciples. So Judas took a cohort, along with servants from the High Priests and from the Pharisees. And he comes there with lamps and torches and guns.

So Jesus, knowing everything that was coming upon him, went out and said to them, 'Whom are you looking for?' They answered him, 'Jesus the Nazarene.' He says to them, 'I AM.'

Now Judas, who was betraying him, was standing with them. And so when he said to them, 'I AM,' they went backwards, and fell to the ground.

So again Jesus interrogated them: 'Whom are you looking for?' and they said, 'Jesus the Nazarene.' Jesus replied, 'I have told you that I AM. If it is me you are looking for, let these people go' (this was so that the word he had spoken might be fulfilled: 'The ones you gave me, I have not lost one of them').

So Simon Peter, who had a sword [and what on earth was he doing with one of those?!], drew it, and struck the High Priest's slave, and cut off his earlobe, the right-hand one. The slave's name was Malchus. So Jesus said to Peter, 'Put your sword back into its scabbard. The cup that the Father gave me – am I not going to drink it?'

At 18:2 you will see that Judas '*knew*' the garden across the Wadi Kedron where the arrest takes place, and takes a cohort with lamps and torches (because he has gone out into the dark (13:30), and is arresting the Light of the World). Judas, you see, knows the trivial things, the things that do not really matter; no doubt he has frequently visited the place with Jesus and the rest of them.

Talking of the 'garden', of course, reminds us of that other Garden, the Garden of Eden, where it all began. John may be offering us a hint that Jesus is now putting everything right in God's project that human beings have so badly messed up.

So Judas is not really in charge; his knowledge is not up to much. Jesus, by contrast, **knows** something much more important, namely what is coming (18:4), and does not need any light or any show of force, for he is 'the Light of the World'. Jesus is utterly in charge, and runs the whole show. He interrogates the arresting party, for example: 'Whom are you looking for?' When they tell him, 'Jesus of Nazareth,' he says *Ego Eimi* ('I AM'), and his authoritative statement simply knocks them over, and they fall backwards (18:6). It is Jesus who gives the orders round here: 'If it is me you are looking for – let these people go' (18:8), and the evangelist notes that this is so that Scripture may be fulfilled. So it is not just Jesus but also God who is in charge.

This contrasts with the inept attempt by Simon Peter, using his sword on the unfortunate servant of the High Priest (18:10 – and John even gives us his name and function), cutting off, absurdly, 'his earlobe, the right-hand one'. Jesus, who remains in charge, smartly rebukes this useless gesture.

In his favour, however, we should notice that Simon Peter is still there, in company with another disciple, who is known to the High Priest, but this is the start of the all too sad story of Simon's denial of Jesus. John tells this slightly differently from the three Synoptic accounts, but still shows Jesus as very much in charge. John manages this by careful storytelling, so that where Jesus is inclined to say 'I AM', telling the truth, Simon Peter (18:17) lies when asked if he is a disciple of this man, and says, abjectly, 'I am not.'

Then the narrative pauses to allow John's camera to switch (18:19) to Jesus again, while Simon warms himself (against the chill of cowardice). When Jesus is interrogated, it is clearly he who takes charge: 'I spoke openly to the world; I always taught in synagogue and in the Temple . . . and I said nothing in secret. Why ask me? Ask those who heard what I said to them.' That earns him a slap, to which Jesus responds, regally, 'If I have spoken badly, give evidence of the badness; if I have spoken well, why strike me?'

The authorities cannot cope with this figure, and Jesus is despatched to Caiaphas, just in time for another contrasting picture of Simon Peter, again warming himself, who once more says, 'I am not,' even when confronted with evidence. Then, of course, the cock crows. And we remember what that means . . . See the contrast in the beautifully constructed story:

> So the High Priest interrogated Jesus about his disciples, and about his teaching. Jesus answered him: 'I have spoken openly to the world. I always taught in a synagogue and in the Temple, where all the Judeans come together. Why are you asking me? Interrogate those who heard what I said to them. Look – these people know what I said.' When he said this, one of the servants who were standing by gave Jesus a slap, and said, 'Is that how you answer the High Priest?'
>
> Jesus replied to him, 'If I have spoken badly, give evidence of the badness. But if I have spoken well, why are you striking me?'
>
> So Annas sent him in chains to the High Priest Caiaphas.
>
> Now Simon Peter was standing and warming himself. So they said to him, 'Aren't you also one of his disciples?' He denied it and said, 'I AM NOT.' One of the High Priest's slaves, a cousin of the one whose earlobe Peter had chopped off, said, 'Didn't I see you in the garden with him?' And again Peter denied. And immediately a cock crowed . . .
> (18:19-27)

Caiaphas evidently cannot cope with Jesus for very long, and he comes to the Praetorium and the interrogation before Pilate. The authorities are reluctant to enter because they might be defiled and be unable to eat the Passover (as though a murder plot were not sufficient defilement for them!).

Then John does something quite interesting: he creates two stages, by his careful use of the words 'inside' and 'outside'. Have a look for yourself at how he does it, and you will see the alternation of these two stages in 18:28, 29, 33, 38;

then comes the mid-point, when Jesus is flogged, at 19:1, which we presume takes place inside, before the pattern continues at 19:4, 5, 9, 12, 13. What is going on here? Have a look at the text, but I would like to suggest that by setting the next episode on these two stages, outside and inside, dividing the episode into seven scenes, the evangelist invites us to go deeper into the mystery of Jesus and to grasp his quiet but unmistakable authority.

Outside there is a crowd, egged on by the authorities, who are closed to all reason and are noisily demanding Jesus' death; inside there is Jesus, who speaks when he chooses to and conducts a quiet and civilised debate with Pilate, largely about the nature of kingship (which is about the only thing that Pontius Pilate can seriously grasp). By contrast, Pilate, who does not appear here as a figure of immense stature, scurries like a frightened rabbit between the two stages, trying to keep peace outside, while inside he endeavours to make out this quietly authoritative figure that is Jesus, and to conduct a debate on kingship with him.

It may be worth pausing to listen to this debate. When the Judeans are offered the possibility of executing justice themselves (18:31), they respond, significantly, 'We're not allowed to kill anybody,' which reveals their agenda.

At this, Pilate goes back inside and addresses Jesus, 'Are you the King of the Jews?'

Jesus answers a question with a question: 'Do you say this on your own account or did others say it to you about me?'

Pilate is not used to this kind of interrogation, and asks, 'What have you done?' which is not a normal enquiry on the part of a presiding magistrate.

Then Jesus gives him the answer he was looking for: 'My kingdom is not of this world; if my kingdom were of this world, my servants would have fought for me. But as it is, my kingdom is not from here' (18:36).

Pilate hangs on gamely: 'So you are a king, then?'

He receives an answer which might not satisfy him, but which speaks regally down the centuries: 'You say I am a king. It was for this that I was born and for this that I came into the world, to bear witness to the truth. Everyone who is of the truth listens to my voice.'

Pilate simply cannot cope, and comes back with yet another question, to evade the challenge: 'What is truth?' However, we notice that he then rushes outside and proclaims Jesus 'Not Guilty'.

Then see how John presents the regal appearance of Jesus here:

> Then Pilate took Jesus and flogged him. And the soldiers wove a crown out of thorns, and put it on his head; and they clothed him with a purple cloak; and they kept coming to him and saying, 'Hail, Your Majesty of the Jews.' And they gave him slaps.

Jesus is now ironically mocked, precisely as a king, with a flogging (instead of sycophancy) and a crown (but of thorns, not jewels), and an appropriate purple robe (such as an emperor would wear) and homage ('Hail, King of the Jews') and slaps, instead of royal gifts. He is then presented, in his royal garb, to the stage outside, with the entry cue: 'Behold the man.' This produces such anger that Pilate has to rush once more inside, where he asks, for once, absolutely the right question, 'Where are you from?' (19:9). To his astonishment, Jesus refuses to respond. Pilate then turns petulant, and squeaks, 'Aren't you talking to me? Don't you realise that I have authority to set you free and authority to crucify you?'

Jesus responds regally, 'You would have no authority unless it were given you from above.'

Pilate is definitely struggling now; he is not in charge, either of Jesus or of the noisy crowd, who threaten his status, accusing him of being 'no friend of Caesar; everyone who makes himself a king is contradicting Caesar'.

Of course, though Jesus is every inch a king, he never says so, nor does he claim to rule. Instead, Pilate proclaims him king: 'Look! Your king!' And when he tries to quieten the bellowing with, 'Is it your king you want me to crucify?' they come back with the appalling betrayal of their nation's history: 'We have no king but Caesar.'

And so to Golgotha. 'Carrying his cross for himself' (you see, there is no need for Simon of Cyrene in John's version of the Passion), he goes out and is enthroned (there is no other word for it) on the cross, with co-rulers to left and right, and Jesus royally in the middle (19:18). Remarkably, Pilate's verdict is now given in writing, and to make sure that there can be no mistake at all about it, Pilate himself (that is what the text seems to mean) writes in three languages, so that there can be no doubt about the verdict: in Aramaic (the common language of Judea and Galilee), in Latin (the imperial language – so it is the Emperor's verdict also), and finally in Greek, the language of economics and politics, the language that united the Mediterranean basin. John comments (19:20) that 'many of the Judeans read this verdict, since the place where Jesus was crucified was near the city'. The authorities want Pilate to change the verdict and to turn it into a statement of Jesus' preposterous claims, and at the last, Pilate finds the courage to stand firm (only it is too late): 'What I have written, I have written.' And that is it: Jesus is King.

Not only that, but Jesus founds a dynasty, once he is 'lifted up', as he predicted back in chapter 3:13-14. For after royally bequeathing his undivided robes to the accompanying soldiers (19:23-24), he addresses his royal mother, in the calmest of tones. This is how the evangelist tells the story: 'There were standing by the cross of Jesus his mother [whom we last saw at Cana, setting him off on the first of his 'signs'], and Mary of Clopas, and Mary the Magdalene.'

Having thus attracted our attention (for we were not expecting these ladies), he now invites us to hear what Jesus says: 'When he saw his mother – and the disciple whom he loved standing there [we were certainly not expecting *him*], he says to his mother, "Woman, look – your son."' There is nothing impolite about the address 'Woman'. He used it to the Samaritan woman back in chapter 4 and will use it again to Mary Magdalene at the opened tomb. Nor does it stop there, for Jesus continues, turning to the Beloved Disciple, 'Look! Your mother.' And that has a powerful effect, for we are told that 'from that hour' [and the word 'hour' is an important idea in John's Gospel, standing for Jesus' Passion and for God's time] 'he took her to *his own*'. We remember how back in the prologue we were told that the incarnate Word 'came to *his own*; and his own did not receive him'. Here, on the royal throne that is his cross, his own courtiers are indeed receiving Jesus.

But the royal story does not end there. For see how John describes Jesus' death:

> After this, Jesus, knowing that already everything was accomplished, in order that Scripture might be fulfilled, said 'I am thirsty.' Now a jar lay there, full of vinegar. So they put a sponge full of the vinegar, wrapping round a piece of hyssop, and offered it to his mouth. So when Jesus had accepted the vinegar, Jesus said, 'It is accomplished.'
>
> And he bowed his head. And he handed over the Spirit. [Or: he gave up the ghost.]
> (19:28-30)

'After this', as John tells the story, there is no sense of urgency or brutality, 'Jesus, knowing that already everything was accomplished'. We have seen all the way through the entire Gospel that Jesus had knowledge, including right at the beginning of this Passion story. What does this mean? It means nothing less than that the story of God has run its powerful course. Then the evangelist makes an important point to support this idea, that Jesus, 'in order that the Scripture might be fulfilled' (so, once again, this is the story of God), said, 'I thirst', citing Psalm 22. This provokes a misunderstanding, in the shape of a sponge filled with vinegar, which might revivify him but would certainly not quench his thirst. As they make this unsatisfactory gesture, we might remember another day when Jesus asked for a drink (4:7); and he did not get that drink either! Graciously, Jesus accepts the vinegar, and proclaims, 'It is accomplished.' Then, in a regal gesture, 'he bowed his head', giving acquiescence to what is taking place, 'and died'.

Or rather, that is not quite what it says: what the evangelist wrote was, 'he gave up his breath', or 'breathed his last', or 'he expired', or, in the language of the King James Version, 'he gave up the ghost'. However, the phrase can also mean – and this point would not have been lost on John's first listeners – 'he handed over the Spirit'. So this moment of crucifixion is also Pentecost for the fourth Gospel. We think back to 7:37-39, and particularly the last of these verses, where Jesus says, in the Temple, 'If anyone is thirsty, let them come to me and drink; but the one who believes in me, as Scripture says, rivers shall flow from his belly, of living water.' Then the evangelist offers a gloss on this: 'He said this about the Spirit, which those who believed in him were about to receive. For there was not yet the Spirit – because Jesus had not yet been glorified.' And 'glory' in John's Gospel refers primarily to Jesus' royal crucifixion.

After this, it is no surprise to the reader that the Scripture is fulfilled with the flow of blood and water, and that Joseph of Arimathea and Nicodemus spring up from nowhere and give him a royal funeral, with no less than 100 litres of an alloy of myrrh and aloes.

This Passion story of Jesus is indeed a royal road.

Questions

1. Is it accurate to call the Passion Narrative in John's Gospel an exaltation?

2. Is it true to say that for the fourth Gospel, Good Friday is also Easter Sunday and Pentecost?

3. What is the function of the Beloved Disciple and the Mother of Jesus in John's Gospel?

CHAPTER 23

The Resurrection in John's Gospel

So we come to the end of the mystery. And to some extent it remains a mystery, for in this resolution of what has been an extraordinary story, we are given no fewer than four possible endings in chapter 20, with a concluding summary, and three further episodes in chapter 21, again with a concluding summary. In a way, the stories can be read separately (indeed, they generally are); but taken together they put the cap on the mystery that we have been following all this time.

The first story (20:1-10) has Mary Magdalene at Jesus' tomb:

> On the first day of the week, Mary the Magdalene comes early in the morning, while it was still dark; and she sees the stone taken away from the tomb. So she runs; and she comes to Simon Peter, and to the other disciple, the one whom Jesus loved. And she says to them, 'They have taken the Lord out of the tomb; and we don't know where they have put him!' So Peter and the other disciple came out and started going to the tomb. And the two were running together. And the other disciple ran quicker than Peter; and he got to the tomb first. And he stooped down and sees the wrapping-cloths lying [there]; but he didn't go in . . .
>
>   Then Simon Peter comes, following him – and he went into the tomb. And he sees the wrapping-cloths lying [there], and the sweat-cloth, which had been on his head, not lying with the wrapping-cloths, but rolled up, apart in a single place.
>
>   And so then the other disciple also went in, the one who had come first to the tomb. And he saw – and he believed. (You see, they did not yet know the Scripture, that he *had* to rise from the dead.)

And so the disciples went back home . . .

Unlike in the Synoptic Gospels, Mary Magdalene is on her own, and she finds the stone rolled away. This causes her to 'run' (and indeed this is not the last such extravagance) to Simon Peter and the Beloved Disciple and give them the news, not that Jesus is risen, but that 'they [?] have taken the Lord from the tomb, and we do not know where they have put him'. This sets Peter and the Beloved Disciple on another jog to the tomb, but 'the other disciple ran quicker than Peter, and got to the tomb first'.

We should notice that those who were closest to him are continuing here the mystery of Jesus, even after his death: Mary Magdalene, powerfully attached to him;

Simon Peter who had said, 'Lord, to whom shall we go?'; and the 'one whom Jesus loved'. Only those who share this attitude of love can really grasp the mystery. And that is what happens: the Beloved Disciple stoops down and sees the grave-cloths lying there, but courteously allows Simon Peter to go in first. Then he follows, and sees a bit more: 'the sweat-cloth, which had been on [Jesus'] head, not lying with the grave-cloths but was separate, wrapped up in one place'. The Beloved Disciple, that is to say, has grasped that we are not dealing here with grave robbers, for they would have taken everything. 'He saw and he believed' is an invitation to us to accept the mystery. The evangelist makes the point that they had not hitherto grasped what had happened, 'for they had not yet come to know the Scripture that he had to rise from the dead'.

That more or less ends the first episode, as the male disciples, rather oddly, just go home. Mary Magdalene, however, does not. She 'stood by the tomb weeping', having apparently not yet gone in, and certainly having not yet come to a view about the Resurrection of Jesus. Still weeping, she looks inside, and sees not the grave-cloths that were visible to the other two but, quite unexpectedly, 'two angels, sitting in white'. It is slightly surreal, and when we are told that 'one was at the head and one at the feet', we briefly suppose that perhaps Jesus was there after all. Jesus is not present, however; only two angels, and they address her, not unkindly, 'Woman, why are you weeping?'

She makes it quite clear that she has certainly not reached Resurrection faith, by replying, 'They have taken away my Lord' (she has that bit of the mystery right, at all events), 'and I don't know where they have put him.' Once again, there is no indication about who 'they' might be. However, that now becomes irrelevant as someone else appears on the scene. It is, of course, Jesus, though Mary does not know it: 'she turned round backwards (it is as clumsy as that) and saw Jesus standing there', and (oddly again – but this is part of the mystery into which we are moving) 'she did not know that it was Jesus'.

Jesus then repeats the angels' question, 'Whom are you looking for?' (And we may dimly recall that back in chapter 1 he asked the two disciples of John the Baptist, '*What* are you looking for?' so the story has moved on since then.)

The evangelist then tells us that Mary thinks that this is a passing gardener, who might have stolen the missing body. However, we should notice that she gets him right in one respect, since she addresses him as 'Lord' (though often it is translated as 'Sir') and asks to know where he has put Jesus. Then comes a beautiful moment when she gets very close to the heart of the mystery, in the only way that is possible – not by an intellectual grasp but by that deeper inner journey that is love, when he addresses her by name, and she in return responds in astonishment: 'Rabbouni!'

Mary is then given a job to do, which is not to carry on touching him, but to tell the brothers that 'I am going to my Father and your Father, and my God and your God'; in other words, taking us right back to the prologue in which we first encountered the mystery.

So Mary carries the message, and that brings us to the third episode:

> When it was late on that day, the first day of the week, and the doors were locked where the disciples were, because of their fear of the Judeans, Jesus came and stood in the middle; and he says to them, 'Peace be with you' [or: 'Peace is with you']. And when he had said this, he showed them his hands and his side.
>
> And so the disciples rejoiced, having seen the Lord. Then Jesus said to them again, 'Peace be with you. As the Father has sent me, so I am sending you.' And when he had said this, he breathed on them, and says to them, 'Receive the Holy Spirit. If you let go anyone's sins, they are let go for them; if you hold them bound, they are held bound.'
> (20:19-23)

This episode takes place almost as though neither of the others has happened (for we are dealing with mystery here). It starts with the doors closed 'for fear of the Judeans'. So the mystery has not yet fully dawned upon them; they clearly do not believe in the Resurrection. Effortlessly, Jesus walks through the locked doors, arrives in their midst and offers them the ancient Hebrew greeting of 'Peace'/*Shalom*. Then he shows them his hands and his side; presumably this is meant to indicate that, as in Luke's Gospel, they require proof of some kind, that it really is the Jesus who died. After that, they finally consent to rejoice. But then, as in all Resurrection narratives, they are given a job to do. For Jesus 'breathed on them, and says to them, "Receive the Holy Spirit. Whoever's sins you let go, they are let go; and whoever's you hold fast, they are held fast."'

This mission that they now have is not perhaps absolutely clear, but is often taken to indicate that they are given the power of exercising God's reconciling ministry. We may remember that, back in chapter 1, Jesus was identified as 'the Lamb of God, who takes away the sins of the world'. Now the disciples are seen as taking over his role.

It seems, however, when we get to episode 4, that episode 3 has not really made its full impact upon them. For one thing, they gloat over Thomas, like schoolboys in the playground: 'We've seen the Lord.' And for another thing, they are still frightened enough to lock the doors again. Thomas is not much better, of course, for when they tell him of the privilege that they have been given, he makes an astonishingly crude demand: 'Unless I see in his hands the mark of the nails, and thrust my finger into the place of the nails, and thrust my hand into his side, no way am I going to believe.' Clearly Thomas has been told at least some details of the crucifixion (the evangelist does not suggest that he was actually present).

A week later, the inevitable happens:

> Eight days later, again the disciples were inside; and Thomas was with them. Jesus comes, although the doors were [still!] locked and stood in the middle and said, 'Peace be with you.'
>
> Then he says to Thomas, 'Bring your finger here, and look at my hands, and bring your hand, and thrust it into my side. And don't be an unbeliever but a believer.'
>
> Thomas replied and said, 'My Lord – and my God!'
>
> Jesus says to him, 'Because you have seen me, have you come to faith? Congratulations to those who did not see, and yet came to faith.'
> (20:26-29)

Jesus is once again in their midst and greeting them with 'Peace'. Then, however, his attention is all on Thomas, who is told, very possibly to his immense embarrassment, 'Bring your finger here, and see my hands; and bring your hand and thrust it into my side. And don't be an unbeliever but a believer.' We wait with some interest for the sceptic's response, and when it comes, it goes far beyond what we should have predicted: 'My Lord and my God!' We stand back and applaud, for at this point we recognise that Thomas has gone right to the climax of the mystery. But there is more, for Thomas is given a mild rebuke: 'Because you have seen me, have you come to faith? Happy are those who have not seen but have believed.' That, we presume, refers to you and to me who have read the Gospel.

We are still not finished, however, for now the evangelist gives us what sometimes sounds like an ending of the Gospel, with a frank admission that he has not told us everything, only sufficient to take us into the heart of the mystery: 'Jesus performed many other signs in the presence of his disciples, which are not written on this scroll.' Then he explains why he has written anything at all: 'that you may come to faith that Jesus is the Messiah, the Son of God, and that believing you may have life in his name'. At this point we are near to the heart of the mystery.

Then, however, we discover that after all we have not come to the end, for there is another chapter to come. Most scholars are inclined to suppose that this chapter was written later, perhaps after the death of the Beloved Disciple and by someone else; but in a way that does not matter, for it is written in very much the same style and language as the rest of the Gospel. In any event, we should certainly be the poorer without it.

So let us look at this chapter also, and see what it says to us about the mystery into which we have been journeying all this time. It comes in three episodes. The first goes from 21:1-14 and constitutes the bulk of the chapter. The other two are reflections on the implications of the main episode, and have to do with the status of two of the most significant disciples in the post-Resurrection community. And, of course, the function of this community is to continue presenting the mystery.

After this, Jesus revealed himself again to the disciples, on the Sea of Tiberias. This is how he revealed himself.

They were together: Simon Peter, and Thomas (the one known as 'Twin'); and Nathanael (the one from Cana of Galilee), and the sons of Zebedee; and two others of his disciples. Simon says to them, 'I'm going fishing.' They say to him, 'We're coming with you as well.' They went out, and they went on board the boat. And on that night, they caught – nothing! When it was morning, Jesus stood on the shore (but the disciples didn't know that it **was** Jesus).

So Jesus says to them, 'Children, you don't have any fish to eat, do you?' And they answered back, 'No!' And he said to them, 'Throw the nets out onto the starboard side of the boat – and you'll find [something].' So they did that: and they were no longer powerful enough to drag it, because of the number of fish!

So that disciple (the one whom Jesus loved) said to Peter, 'It's the Lord!!'

So when Simon Peter heard 'It's the Lord', he put on his outer garment (because he was naked) – and he flung himself into the water! The rest of the disciples came in the boat (for they were not far from the land, only about two hundred cubits), dragging the net with the fish.

And when they disembarked on shore, they see a charcoal fire placed there, and fish put on it, and some bread. Jesus says to them, 'Bring some of the fish that you have just caught.' Simon Peter came up and dragged the net on land, full of huge fish; a hundred and fifty-three of them! And even though there were so many, the net was not split.

Jesus says to them, 'Come and have breakfast'. None of the disciples dared to interrogate him: 'Who are you?' (They knew it was the Lord.)

Jesus comes and takes the bread and gives it to them, and similarly with the fish.

This was now the third time that Jesus appeared to the disciples after he had been raised from the dead.

The episode takes the form of another post-Resurrection appearance – the third, according to verse 14. It takes place on the Sea of Tiberias (which is what the Gospel of John tends to call the Sea of Galilee), and six of the disciples go off fishing with Peter. Some readers tend to assume that this is rather a depressed gathering, returning to familiar work to cope with Jesus' absence, but the evangelist does not actually say so. They are an odd lot, with Thomas (who features more prominently in the fourth Gospel than in the Synoptics), Nathanael, the sons of Zebedee, who have not previously been mentioned, and two others, one of whom turns out to be the Beloved Disciple. It is a very familiar story, an all-night failure at fishing, with Jesus on the shore at dawn, although, very importantly, the writer suggests that 'they did not *know* it was Jesus' (so they had not yet penetrated to the heart of the mystery).

Then there is a (presumably) playful question from Jesus: 'Do you have anything to eat?' and a gloomy denial from the seven. This is followed by some advice about fishing from Jesus (a carpenter, you may recall), which yields spectacular results, so that they could hardly drag the net.

At this point the Beloved Disciple appears and interprets the mystery: 'It is the Lord!' Not to be outdone, Peter behaves quite absurdly: in order to dive into the sea, he puts his clothes on! The other disciples follow him by a more conventional means, and then we discover that Peter's gesture was irrelevant, since the boat was actually quite close to the shore!

Jesus turns out to have cooked some breakfast for them, with fish and a loaf of bread. Nevertheless, he invites them to supply some of their own food. Simon returns to the water and drags the boat in, with its prodigious catch (which, we learn, did not break the nets). Then we are told that there were 153 fish, and you will not believe the number of books that have been written about the meaning of this number.

Finally they are invited to breakfast, and we learn that 'none of the disciples dared to ask, "Who are you?"'. They knew that it was the Lord.' We notice that even now the risen Jesus retains an air of mystery. Then Jesus does something that sounds very much like a Eucharist: he takes the bread and gives it to them.

Nor does it end there. Simon Peter has to have a conversation with the Lord that he may have been dreading, for the last time we heard him saying anything he three times denied that he had ever heard of Jesus.

This is how the evangelist tells the tale:

So when they had had breakfast, Jesus says to Simon Peter, 'Simon, son of John, do you love me more than these?'

He says to him, 'Yes, Lord; you know I love you.' He says to him, 'Feed my sheep.'

He says to him a second time, 'Simon, Son of John, do you love me?' He says to him, 'Yes, Lord, you know I love you.' He says to him, 'Shepherd my sheep.'

He says to him a third time, 'Do you love me?' Simon was grieved that he had asked him a third time, 'Do you love me?' and says to him, 'Lord, you know everything; you *know* I love you.' Jesus says to him, 'Feed my sheep. Amen, Amen, I am telling you, when you were younger you used to clothe yourself and walk wherever you wanted. But when you get older, you are going to stretch out your hands and someone else is going to clothe you, and is going to take you where you do not want to go.' He said this, giving a signal by what kind of a death he was going to glorify God. And when he had said this, he said, 'Follow me.'

There are many explanations of the conversation, but clearly it has to do with Simon's treachery and with Jesus bringing him back to a place in the story of the community that is charged with the mystery. Three times he is asked if he loves the Lord, and three times given a mission to shepherd or feed them. This concludes with a prediction of Simon's death, but we notice that at the end of it Jesus says, 'Follow me,' so he is in there as a disciple.

And then there is the Beloved Disciple, and Peter's question:

Peter turns and sees the disciple whom Jesus loved, who had laid on his breast at the Supper, and said, 'Lord – who's the one who's betraying you?' So when Peter saw him, he said, 'Lord, what about this one?'

Peter has a question about the Beloved Disciple, from which scholars deduce that Peter has indeed gone to his reward by the time this chapter is written, and that this may have been a problem for the community. The main point, however, may be that the community of the Beloved Disciple and the mainstream community represented by Peter are depicted as coming back together.

Finally we arrive at the end of our journey into the mystery, and we hear the final lines: reflect on them, and ask, 'What do we now understand of the mystery?'

This is the disciple who bears witness about these things and who has written these things, and we know that his witness is true. There are many other things that Jesus did, which if they were written down one by one I don't think that the whole world would hold the books that were written.

It is a powerful ending to an extraordinary story.

Questions

1. Do you think it is true to say that John's Gospel gives us four alternative endings, after the Resurrection?

2. In what ways does the ending of the Gospel bring the mystery to its climax?

3. Do you think chapter 21 was originally intended to be part of the Gospel?

CHAPTER 24

The first, second and third letters of John

These three very charming 'letters' are dealt with quite naturally after the Gospel of John. Many people think that they come from the same author, and certainly they breathe the same air as the fourth Gospel. One possible explanation is that 1 John came after the Gospel, and was meant to exclude certain readings of it, particularly anything that might suggest that Jesus only *seemed* to be human, the heresy that is technically known as 'Docetism'. And some people think that 2 John may have been an accompanying note for 1 John, but the evidence is a bit vague, and we might just admit that we really don't know.

It may be best to start with 2 and 3 John, which are definitely letters, in a way that 1 John is not. They are good examples of the kind of thing that the ancients sent to each other, with the usual format of opening greetings, grounds for rejoicing, then the main body and finally concluding greetings. 2 John is addressed to 'the elect lady and her children (verse 1)', which some scholars think may have been a code of some kind, possibly to steer clear of imperial examination of the correspondence (some things never change, of course), so that the Roman secret police might not identify the recipient, possibly a church somewhere. 3 John is addressed to 'Gaius'. This name belonged, of course, to the person who had the biggest house in Corinth, where the Christians in that city used to meet. However, it is a very common Roman name, and it need not have been the same person.

In both letters, the problem being addressed appears to be that there are divisions in the Church (as I say, some things never change). But it is not only that: 'deceivers have come in the world', and their particular offence is that 'they do not admit that Jesus Christ is coming in the flesh – that one is the deceiver and the anti-Christ' (2 John 7). They are also described as 'going ahead and not remaining in the teaching of Christ' (2 John 9). And sanctions are invoked, so that if anyone comes 'and does not carry this teaching', then the 'elect lady' is not to greet them (2 John 10, 11).

There is also a certain reluctance, possibly because letters are insecure, on the writer's part to commit himself (or, just possibly, herself) to paper, 'but I am hoping to come to you and speak face to face, so that our joy may be fulfilled' (2 John 12). One rather suspects that in order to understand what is going on, we would need to be the 'elect lady' ourselves. As is sometimes said of the letters of St Paul, we are hearing only one side of the telephone conversation.

3 John is perhaps a little less encrypted, assuming that 'Gaius' is not also a coded symbol. Here the problem seems to be the very unchristian one of refusal of hospitality (verse 10), although it is not too churlish, I hope, to observe that 2 John was not enormously open to the possibility of exchanging greetings with those who get their doctrine wrong. There is someone called Diotrephes (of whom we know only what little we can glean from the text), who 'likes being Number 1', and who refuses to acknowledge the author's authority. Someone called Demetrius, on the other hand, who is likewise unknown to us, has credentials from 'everybody, and from Truth itself', and, indeed, from our author.

We should love to know more about all this, but one thing at least we can take away from our reading of these two charming letters is that divisions are not a recent invention in the Church. We may also reflect, after the mind of our author, that it is not always a good idea to put absolutely everything on paper.

And so to 1 John, which is a beautiful letter, and clearly from the same stable as the fourth Gospel. It is not a letter, and it is very hard to see who the addressees might be, except that they are clearly a community, with 'young men . . . fathers . . . children' (2:12, 13). As with 2 and 3 John there are opponents in view, and they are categorised as 'liars', but also as those who fail to keep Jesus' commandments: 'Anyone who says, "I know him" and fails to keep his commandments is a liar; and the Truth is not in that person' (2:4). In 2:22 it becomes a little bit more specific:

> Who is the liar, except the one who denies that Jesus is the Messiah? Such a person is 'antichrist', who denies both Father and Son. Anyone who denies the Son does not have the Father either; the one who confesses the Son has the Father also.

So it is a theological question, and certainly there can be no doubt that this absolutely belongs with the Gospel of John, for whom Jesus is the definitive revelation of God, the Son who points to the Father.

There is another feature of these 'liars', and that concerns the attitude to fellow Christians: 'Anyone who says "I love God" and hates their fellow Christian is a liar; for anyone who does not love their fellow Christian whom they have seen, is quite unable to love the God whom they have not seen' (4:20). So not only the Son, but also fellow Christians (the Greek word actually means 'brothers', but we assume that the sisters are not excluded) are revelations of God, if properly understood. The opponents are described (as indeed is the case occasionally in John's Gospel) as 'people who lead others astray' (2:26; cf. 3:7; 1:8).

If you read through the letter, you will observe that it is not always easy to find the structure; it seems at times to wander all over the place. Certainly, however, the author stresses the importance of love (because things are breaking up), the importance of faith (you have to keep your eyes on Jesus, as the author announces in its breathtaking beginning – 1:1), and the humanity of Jesus (1:7; 2:2).

With all that in mind, let us go through this document (and try to work out whether it is indeed a letter, as your Bible may suggest). Look at the opening lines:

> What was from the beginning,
> what we have heard,
> what we have seen with our eyes,
> what we have beheld,
> and our hands have touched
> with regard to the Word of Life.
> And the life was revealed,
> and we have seen and we bear witness and we announce to you
> the eternal life which was towards the Father and has been revealed to us.
> What we have seen and heard we announce also to you, that you may have
>   fellowship with us.
> And our fellowship is with the Father and with his Son Jesus Christ.
> And we are writing this to you, that your joy may be fulfilled.
> (1:1-4)

In a sense, this electric introduction gives you the whole of the document. One thing you cannot miss is that it echoes the Gospel, with the phrase 'from the beginning', which takes us back to the prologue of the fourth Gospel, and also of course to Genesis 1, with this difference: Genesis took the story back to the beginning of Creation; the opening lines of the Gospel went a bit further even than that, and to the richness of God that Jesus has always had. For 1 John, the 'beginning' refers to Jesus' first appearance on earth.

Many of the other words in these verses are familiar in the Gospel: 'hear', 'see', 'life', 'reveal', 'witness' and 'announce'. It also offers a sequence that may explain what our document (which I shall occasionally call a letter, even if it is not!) thinks it is doing, and which also echoes what the fourth Gospel thinks it is doing. First, 'reveal', then 'see', then 'bear witness', and finally 'announce to you', indicating a process that never stops, until the last person reads the last word of the text.

So far, so good; but I have to tell you that after that bright beginning, things are not all that easy. Once you start to look for the basic structure of the letter (I told you I would use the word!), it rather falls apart; and if you look at the various scholarly writings on the subject, you will find many different structures confidently indicated in the literature. So I don't want to be too dogmatic about it, but this is one way I suggest that you might like to look at it. The only thing that really matters is that you should read the text, and if you find my outline unhelpful, then ignore it, as long as you do not ignore 1 John.

After that remarkable beginning, the author starts to work out the implications of the revelation that we are talking about. So in 1:5-10, the revelation is expressed, in language that we recognise from the fourth Gospel, as 'light' not 'darkness', and also the reality of sin and the importance of Jesus' blood. That is why some people suggest that 1 John comes by way of warning against misreading the Gospel. It is possible, you see, that some people went for a 'docetic' interpretation, that Jesus only appeared to be human, given that the Gospel so powerfully asserts the identity of Father and Son. Christians have always, from this moment onwards, insisted on the full humanity of Jesus, and it is an excellent instinct that leads us to do so.

In the next section (2:1-8), the author picks up another important theme from the Gospel, namely that of the Paraclete, although here it is Jesus, not the Spirit, who is the Paraclete. Then we are told what is our task, namely to keep his commandments or 'word': this is the new commandment (echoing the Last Supper Discourse in the Gospel), which is also old, that we love the 'brothers and sisters'. The following two verses clarify this a little, elucidating the impossibility of living in the light and hating the brothers and sisters. The counterpoint of 'light' and 'darkness', so familiar from the fourth Gospel, is being played again here.

Then at 2:12-14 there is a lovely address to all the members of the community, though it is a little vague: children, fathers, young men (and presumably young women also), then children again (though a different Greek word this time), fathers and young men, which presumably is intended to cover the entire community.

In the following verses, 15-17, we pick up another theme from the Gospel, namely the 'world', which stands in enmity to God's project. This is then followed by warnings about 'antichrists', apparently ex-members of the community, who denied that Jesus is the Messiah.

From now on there is a certain shapelessness to the letter, with exhortations to 'remain in him', to be children of God, to avoid sin and lawlessness (2:28–3:10), before we reach the deepest message of this text, which is to 'love one another', and the corollary, that we should expect the world's hatred.

After that, at 3:19-24 we are exhorted to another Johannine value, that of Truth, to make sure that our hearts do not condemn us. But that cannot be done unless we are open to spiritual influences, and recognise that they are ambiguous. The test is this: do they confess that Jesus came in the flesh?

Do they lead us to love one another? Are they signs of the presence of God? And God's essence is love (4:17-21), which means that we have to love the brothers and sisters.

So we near the end (5:1-12) with the assertion that Jesus is Messiah, so that, once again, we are to love God and the children of God, so as to win victory over the world. Then we have the slightly baffling reference to the evidence – Spirit, water and blood (you will have to read a library of books to examine the theories of what this might mean, but it has something to do with the story of God and resisting Docetism).

Then, finally, we are at the end (5:13-21), and we meet the very Johannine themes of eternal life, and concern for the brothers and sisters. The last words of the 'letter' are, 'Children – steer clear of the idols.' And what are the idols? They are any of those unrealities with which we attempt to distract ourselves from our deepest reality, which is God.

This is a document to read and read again in our day.

Questions

1. Do you think that 1, 2 and 3 John breathe the same atmosphere as the fourth Gospel?

2. What is 1 John aiming to do, in your view?

3. Do you agree that 2 and 3 John are proper letters?

CHAPTER 25

Hebrews:
a great theologian talks about Jesus

Now it is only fair to warn you that the letter to the Hebrews is probably the most difficult document of the entire New Testament. It is important not to get put off by this, however, because it really is worth reading. So I shall try to thread a way through the maze, and not make it too repellently obscure.

There is an awful lot that we simply do not know about this remarkable document – the author, for example. Long ago, Origen, that great theologian of the third century, said, 'Who wrote it – only God knows,' and that might suffice for us. Many people have thought it was Paul; other names suggested, of those we know in the New Testament, have included Apollos, Barnabas, Silvanus and Priscilla. So it is anyone's guess.

Nor, I am sorry to say, do we know *when* it was written: the key date is that of AD 70, when the Temple in Jerusalem was destroyed. Was it written before or after this catastrophe? Perfectly good and competent scholars have taken different sides on the question. As you will see, Hebrews (that is what I am generally going to call it) speaks a good deal about the liturgical activity of the Temple, and scholars differ as to whether the author assumes that the services are still continuing (in which case it was written before 70) or whether the Temple has ceased to exist (after 70).

Nor do we know *to whom* it was addressed. It was given the title 'To the Hebrews' probably sometime in the second century, and that may simply have been a guess, based on the kind of material that we find in it and the fact that it talks about the Temple liturgy. Some people argue that the intended audience was pagan rather than Jewish, because 'Hebrews' are never mentioned in the text, and because at 6:1, 2 it tells the hearers to have 'faith in God . . . in the resurrection of the dead, and eternal judgement', which you would probably not need to say to a Jewish audience.

Nor, finally, do we know *where* the letter was written. There is a reference at 13:24 to 'those from Italy', which might mean that the letter was written in that country. Equally, it might mean that it was written somewhere else where there were émigrés from Italy, which could be anywhere in the entire Roman Empire.

So what can we know? I want to suggest to you that the main message of this remarkable document is simply that 'Jesus Christ is the real thing', and that

Christianity is the only serious option for an intelligent person. That is a message that we need to hear today, and which, if you keep calm in the face of the rather heavy argumentation of Hebrews, comes loud and clear out of the text.

What I want to do now is to go through the text with you, to see how it works.

The place to start is certainly the majestic beginning; and I would suggest that you simply sit with it, and let it speak to you:

> In many and various different ways God spoke long ago
> to our ancestors through the prophets;
> and now, at this end of time,
> he has spoken to us in a Son,
> whom he appointed heir of everything,
> through whom also he created the ages/worlds.
> He [that is, the Son] is the reflection of God's glory
> And the stamp of God's substance . . .
> (Hebrews 1:1-3)

There are two words in particular that you might like to think about: 'reflection' and 'stamp'. The first of these deals with the awkward problem of how any of us can know God. The reality is too dazzlingly bright for us to manage, so a 'reflection' makes it easier; but it is still possible to say that if you want to know what God is like, then look at Jesus.

The next thing that our gifted theologian does is to try to offer various ways of thinking about Jesus. You can imagine a Jewish theologian (and our author is certainly a Jewish theologian, whatever the people he is writing to) saying to him, 'Ah! So you mean Jesus is like an angel, then?' That is the argument that takes him from 1:4–2:9, and he does it with some skill, making use of scriptural texts to distinguish and show that Jesus is different from angels: '[God] makes his angels spirits/winds [the word is the same in Greek, and in Hebrew], and his servants flames of fire' (1:7). We should be aware that the word 'servants' also has a hint of the liturgical services in the Temple, and the first readers would not have missed this (see the same word at 8:2, for example).

So that is the angels; and to make it clear that they are inferior to Jesus, the author quotes Psalm 45 and says that it is addressed to Jesus: 'To the Son [he says], "Your throne, O God, is for ever and ever."' It is a neat argument for a scholar of his distinction, even if it leaves us today slightly scratching our heads as we try to keep up.

Then, still trying to prove that Jesus is superior to the angels, he does something rather daring: he quotes Psalm 8 (remember, 'What is mortal man that you should think of him, and the son of man that you consider him?'), and argues that 'son of man' here must refer to Jesus. Then he continues the quotation; 'You made him for a short time lower than the angels.' So we are talking here about what John's Gospel refers to as 'incarnation', 'the Word made flesh and pitched its tent among us' (John 1:14), and Jesus being up there with God and briefly coming down to us. Then, triumphantly, he finishes the quotation: 'With glory and honour you crowned him; you put everything under his feet.' We must imagine his audience applauding at that point, for two reasons. One is that the writer has been able to show that Jesus started off higher than the angels, took on the lower, human existence, and then once more resumed his more exalted status. The other reason is that this argument makes it clear that he (Jesus, God, and the author of Hebrews) is interested in us who are human beings.

And that argument allows our author to start another theme – or actually two other themes. For at the climax of his argument about the Son being superior to the angels, he does two things, as he says:

> He had to be like his brothers and sisters in every respect, that he might become a merciful and faithful High Priest for the things that lead to God, because insofar as he himself suffered by being tested [or tempted], he is able to be of assistance to those who are being tempted [or tested].
> (2:17, 18)

That is to say, first, that Jesus is very much, and very importantly, a human being, whatever else we might like to say about him, and utterly identifies with the 'brothers and sisters'. Secondly, the author has now introduced what in some ways is his most important category for Jesus: that of High Priest.

Now I don't want to confuse you even further, but we have to say that Jesus both is and is not a high priest, according to Hebrews. If he is, it is because he makes a link between God and humanity, but if he is not, that is because the all-too-human high priests in the Temple could not do for worshippers what Jesus has been able to do.

Now our author parks that issue for the moment and turns to another question, that of Moses. Moses is something of a test for religious figures within Judaism, and in Matthew's and John's Gospels Jesus is often compared with Moses. So it is not surprising that Hebrews considers the question: if Jesus is superior to the angels, how does he stand with regard to Moses? The answer, once again by way of skilfully selected quotations from Scripture, is that Moses is a 'servant', or perhaps a 'slave', in his house, whereas Christ is a 'Son' over the house that God created. (You will find all that argued at 3:1-6, if you would like to cast your eye over it.)

Now I hope that this barrage of theological and scriptural arguments is not causing you to nod off, but if you find that is happening, you may like to know that our author was aware that something of the sort might take place, for the next stage of his argument uses Psalm 95, which will run through a good deal of chapters 3 and 4. Here it seems the author is using it to make sure his audience are paying *good attention*: 'Today, if you listen to his voice, don't harden your hearts.' The point here is that the children of Israel did precisely that in the desert, and we are being warned not to repeat their failure. But our author is a very sophisticated operator, and he is doing more than just telling us to stay awake, for the psalm goes on to say that the Israelites 'shall never enter his rest', for which they and we are destined, and to which the Son is leading us.

In addition, however, in a brilliant theological coup, he links that 'rest' with the same word that is used at Genesis 2:2, which speaks about God 'resting on the seventh day, from all his works'. That is the rest to which we are invited, the rest to which Moses was unable to lead them. Yet it was not just Moses, but also his appointed successor, who was unable to lead them into their rest, when they reached the Promised Land. And who was this successor? We call him 'Joshua', but in Greek and Hebrew it is the same word as we use for the 'Son', namely 'Jesus'. You see that we have to watch our author every step of the way.

Now we come to the theological *coup de grâce*. For in a stroke of theological genius, our author continues his meditation on the idea of Jesus the High Priest, which he started back in 2:17. The point of a priest, of course, is the link between humanity and our utterly remote and transcendent God, and this theme is developed at 3:1, where Jesus is described as the 'Apostle and High Priest of our profession'. Then at the end of chapter 4 he gets really down to business, and in verse 14 Jesus is described as 'the great High Priest who has gone through the heavens'. This points to another important aspect of what our author is saying about Jesus, namely that Jesus represents our point of entry into the inaccessible. Secondly, however, this is not a high priest who demands perfection of us, but who is 'able to feel for our weaknesses, because he has been tempted in exactly the same way, but without sinning' (4:15).

Then he makes the point that you have to be called to priesthood; one does not 'take the honour for oneself . . . so it was not Christ who glorified himself to become a High Priest – no, it was the One who said to him, "You are my son; it is I who have begotten you today"' quoting Psalm 2 (5:4, 5). Then he quotes another psalm (Psalm 110) with the slightly mysterious remark, 'You are a priest for ever, according to the order of Melchisedek', which starts another theme that is intended to take us deeper into the mystery of Jesus ('the Real Thing', remember). We shall pick this up when we get to chapter 7 and another baffling reference to Melchisedek. For the moment, just sit with it and let it speak to you, and see how it reappears at 5:10 and 6:20. One of the problems with ordinary high priests is that, unlike Jesus, they are sinners, and they have to offer sacrifice for their own sinfulness (5:3); another problem is that they die. And at 7:26-28, our author shows how Jesus triumphs over them in these two respects: 'We needed a High Priest like this: holy, un-bad, stainless, separated from sinners, and one who became higher than the heavens.' Unlike other high priests, his offering was 'once and for all' (a very important idea in Hebrews, which comes three times (9:12; 10:10 are the two other occasions) to indicate how Jesus is utterly unique (or, as I keep saying, the 'Real Thing'). This High Priest is one who has, remarkably, we read in the next verse (8:1), 'sat down on the right hand of the Throne of the Majesty in the heavens'.

There are two more important points about the idea of Jesus as High Priest, which we shall do well to reflect upon. The first is the question of what Jesus has done for us, and the answer Hebrews offers is that he has given us *access* into the sanctuary. This idea has already been expressed at 4:14 and 6:20, where Jesus is described as a 'forerunner High Priest'.

And that is quite something, for God and the house of God are utterly remote from us, you see; but listen to what this great theologian says to us about the access that Jesus has gained for us as High Priest. He is contrasted at 9:7 with the ordinary high priest, who goes into the Holy of Holies once a year. This means, our author points out, that 'the way into the Holy of Holies had not yet appeared while the original tent was still standing' (9:8), whereas 'Christ appeared as High Priest of the good things, through the greater and more perfect tent, the one not made by hands, i.e. not belonging to this creation . . . he went into the Holy of Holies, once and for all, through his own blood' (9:11, 12).

At 10:19, the effect of this remarkable High Priest is described as giving us 'confidence' to enter the Holy of Holies. Here the writer uses a word that the early Christians often employed to describe what God in Christ had given them. Literally it means the 'ability to say anything', and perhaps the nearest equivalent is the Yiddish word 'hutzpah'. That is what Jesus the High Priest has done for us.

The second aspect of Jesus' priesthood has already been hinted at, namely his sympathy with the weak, which we saw at 4:15 and 5:2, where Jesus is described as able to 'sympathise with our weakness' and to 'deal gently with those who know nothing and are wandering astray'. This 'fellow feeling', as we might call it, is dramatically expressed at 13:11-13, where the argument goes in three stages: first, the author reminds us that the corpses of animals sacrificed for sin offerings were to be 'burnt outside the camp', according to Leviticus. Secondly, and because of this, 'Jesus dies outside the gate, in order to make the people holy through his own blood'. Thirdly, therefore, we are invited to 'go out to Jesus, bearing his reproach, for we have no abiding city here, but are looking for the one that is to come'. In those three steps, our author has brilliantly captured what it is Jesus has done for us, and what we should do about it. So the high priest idea has turned out to be a fertile theological field, explaining to us why Jesus is indeed the 'Real Thing', and why it matters.

This leads us to one other point, which is that good theology is not, ever, meant to be a wonderful creation that we admire like a work of art. Instead, it is something that is supposed to make a difference. That is the reason why in the letter to the Hebrews we find not just 'theological argument' but also what scholars call 'exhortation', encouraging us to live in a particular way. And, unlike most preachers, the writer talks to himself quite as much as to the objects of his preaching: 'We should pay attention to what has been heard, lest we drift away,' he says at 2:1, and you will see something of the same at 4:11 and at 6:1, where we are encouraged, 'Let us leave behind the basic Christ message, and be carried on to perfection.' At 6:11 he encourages them again: 'We desire each of you to show the same enthusiasm in getting to the fullness of hope, right to the end.'

Or look at the passage in 10:23-25:

> Let us hold on to the unbending confession of hope; for the One who gave the promise is reliable; and let us think about how to drive each other in the direction of love and good works, not leaving the get-together, as some people habitually do.

And there is more as we approach the end of the letter: after chapter 11 has listed many examples of faith among those who have gone before us, the writer continues in 12:1, 2:

> So since we have such a cloud of witnesses around us, let us put down every burden, including the sin that clings closely to us, and run the race that has been put before us, with our eyes on Jesus, who is the Leader and Perfecter of our faith, who despised the shame of the Cross because of the joy that lay before him.

Then there is a metaphor from athletics, at 12:12-15:

> So straighten your drooping hands and your wobbly knees, and run straight ahead on your feet, so that what is lame may not be dislocated, but rather healed. Seek peace with everybody, and holiness, without which no one is going to see the Lord, watching out that no one falls short of the grace of God, that no root of bitterness springs up and causes trouble, and so the majority get defiled.

We get the strong sense here of the urgency of our author's appeal. In the final chapter the Hebrews are exhorted to stick to love of the brothers and sisters, offer hospitality to strangers, look after prisoners and those who are abused, and are given a strict view of the sanctity of marriage (13:1-5). Not only that, but 'the way of going on must not be money-grubbing, but be content with what we have'; and they have to pay attention to their leaders (13:7-9) and 'not get carried away by sophisticated external teachings'. And, finally, they are told, 'pray for us, for we are convinced that we have a clean conscience, wanting to live morally in every respect' (3:18). So we are all in it together, and this difficult teaching is profoundly relevant to living in the contemporary world.

One last thing. Chapter 11 is a really charming list of various Old Testament characters who exemplified the virtue of faith, 'the solidity of things hoped for, the conviction of things that have not been seen'. I suggest you sit down with this chapter and look through the list of people, possibly looking up their Old Testament stories, and ask our author: why did you give us these people to imitate?

Questions

1. Do you find Hebrews rather difficult to understand?

2. Does it help if you think of the message of the book as 'Jesus, the Real Thing'?

3. Does the author of Hebrews do enough to show how his message is relevant to our time?

CHAPTER 26

The first and second letters of Peter

Welcome now to two documents attributed to Peter, who appears to have exercised leadership in the early Church. Now it must be admitted that many scholars are doubtful about the possibility of a Galilean fisherman writing either letter, especially the first one. The arguments are endless, and you will find plenty of people arguing, for example, that Greek was spoken in Bethsaida, Simon Peter's home town, and others pointing to the possibility of Silvanus (1 Peter 5:12) polishing up the letter that Peter had instructed him to write. I propose to leave all that; you can read the scholarship on the issue for yourself. In this chapter I should simply like to indicate to you what you might enjoy in reading these two documents, and how they might speak to you today.

As you read, you might like to reflect on what the two letters tell us about how we are to exercise leadership in the Church today. That is an issue that remains very topical indeed, and in recent years we have learnt to see and admire a new way of exercising authority in the See of Peter.

1 Peter is a joy to read, from its very beginning. The author is given his title (just as Paul claims for himself) of 'apostle of Jesus Christ', and his addressees are placed in what we should call Asia Minor (modern-day Turkey), carefully organised to make a circle along the Roman roads in that area: look at a map to see how it works out. Most important is that they are addressed as: 'chosen strangers/sojourners' (that is, people who do not belong). We should notice too the Trinitarian formula that he puts into the second verse: 'the foreknowledge of God the Father; in the sanctification of the Spirit, leading to obedience and the sprinkling of the blood of Jesus Christ'. Then, in a phrase similar to what we often find in Paul (who often writes, 'Grace and peace to you', which is not quite the same), he writes, 'Grace and peace be increased to you.'

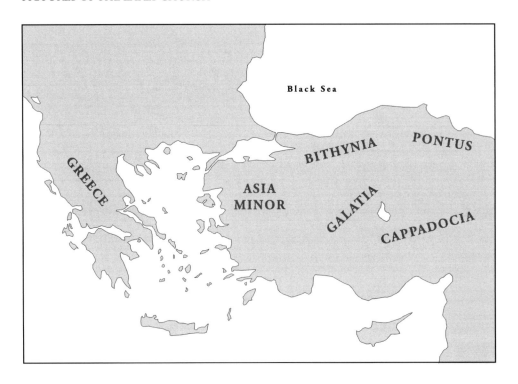

There are instructions here on how to live in the present situation, which seems to be one of persecution, or at any rate unpopularity (not unlike the situation of being Catholic and Christian today). Peter's basic themes are slightly contradictory, but they speak to our day:

- the great joy of being Christian (1:6; 4:13);

- the necessity (and honour!) of sharing in the passion of Christ (combined at 1:11: 'the sufferings directed at Christ, and the glories that follow them'). You should read the lovely hymn to that effect at 2:21-25, and the similar material at 3:18-22, which can help you to revel in your Christian calling, however tough things may seem to be.

Then there is a beautiful blessing (1:3-16), which sings of the author's gratitude to God (the Father of our Lord Jesus Christ). Couched in lovely biblical language, it speaks of the imperishable inheritance (verse 4), of the salvation ready to be revealed (verse 5), of the invitation to rejoice in suffering (verse 6) and the efforts of the prophets to find meaning in suffering (verse 10).

Next you might read 1:17-21 and enjoy the centrality of the Father, Christ in Peter's understanding, and the reference in verse 17 to being a sojourner (and compare 2:11): where do you really belong?

Notice, too, as always in the New Testament, how naturally Peter expresses himself in Old Testament language, including the all-important command to be holy (verse 16), and the contrast with idolatry (18-20). But this is a Christian document, so notice above all the centrality of God, and the importance of resurrection (verse 21).

Go on then to 2:4-10, Peter's meditation on the idea of 'stone', which is a lovely series of pictures. First there is Christ as the 'living stone rejected by human beings, but chosen and precious for God'; then there is the vision of the people of God, the building of living stones into a 'spiritual house', despite having also been 'a stone of stumbling and a rock to trip over (scandal)'. Next listen to the lovely picture of what has happened to the readers:

> You are a chosen race, a royal priesthood, a holy nation, a people for God's acquisition . . . the One who called you into his wonderful light, you who once were not a people, but are now God's people, who were not mercied, but now have been mercied.

It is a beautiful vision.

There is much more to read here; for example, the long section (2:11–3:7) on how to live in the hostile world: how to deal with outsiders and the political authorities, and how to operate within the household. The letter continues with some exhortation about imitating Christ in his suffering, and therefore not worrying too much about persecution. So he writes, 'If you suffer for good reason, then congratulations; but don't be afraid with the fear of them, and don't be disturbed' (3:14). In chapter 4 the suffering is placed in context: 'the end of everything has drawn near' (4:7), 'so be serious and sober, so that you pray for everyone with an intense love for each other'. And they are told (we may feel a bit uncomfortable at this), 'If you are insulted for Christ's name, congratulations, because the Spirit of Glory, the Spirit of God, is resting upon you' (4:14). There is a coherent understanding here of the place of suffering in the Christian life: it is not the worst thing that can happen to us.

Then there is a section (5:1-6) on how to manage relationships in the Church. Peter presents himself as fellow elder and witness, co-sharer in the glory to be revealed (5:1), and uses the happy metaphor of shepherding and chief shepherd (verses 2, 4). As we listen we remember the conversation between Peter and his Lord by the Sea of Galilee after the Resurrection in John 21. And best of all, there is to be no 'lording it' (verse 3) over one another. That is of a piece with the readiness they must have to put up with suffering as a part of what it means to be Christian.

And so, after a final and well-known exhortation (5:8-11), this encouraging letter comes to its conclusion (5:12-14), where we find the mention of Peter's secretary Silvanus and a reference to 'the elect lady in Babylon'. 'Babylon' is often code for Rome in the New Testament, so this may denote the Roman church. There is also a mention of 'Mark, my son', which may be either the cause or the effect of the ancient legend that Mark's Gospel was a report of the preaching of Peter, and may provide evidence for the suggestion that Mark's Gospel was written in Rome (though it has to be said that Mark is a very common name in the Graeco-Roman world). Lastly there are the accustomed greetings, such as you always find in the Pauline letters, which give a sense of the intimacy of those early Christians one with another.

2 Peter breathes a very different atmosphere from that of its predecessor; it does not really read like a letter, but more like a 'Last Will and Testament'. It is odd in some ways. For one thing, in the address (1:1, 2), Symeon, rather than Simon, is a Semitic name. For another, although it follows the opening of 1 Peter, it is all a bit vague, with the reference to the 'equal value faith', which sounds a bit like a modern advertisement.

The big issue that the author is dealing with is approached at 1:16-21, where we have Peter's teaching on the return of Christ. This was a major issue in the New Testament world. It was a common view among those early Christians that Jesus would come back soon and bring it all to an end. The author seems to offer a warning (1:20) that 'no scripture prophecy comes with its own interpretation', which may be an indicator of what they had been getting up to on this issue. There is a hint that there may have been, or the author has been accused of uttering, fictitious stories. In that connection, there is a clear reference to the Transfiguration (1:17, 18), and that worries some people. For if the author is writing in Peter's name and pretending to be him, when in fact it is not, is this not a lie, and how does that coincide with it being 'inspired truth'? For the moment, I suggest that you read the letter as it is and let it speak to you, without worrying unduly about the question of authenticity.

And then, rather than concentrating on that difficult and unrewarding question, I suggest looking ahead to the poetic passage of high quality that immediately follows (1:19):

We have the prophetic message that is more solid.
You do well to pay careful attention to it
as to a light shining in a dark place
until the day dawns, and the morning star rises in your hearts.

The letter is worth reading for that verse alone.

The next thing to notice is that there is some kind of link between 2 Peter and the letter of Jude. Notice how it works: 2:1 = Jude 4; 2:10, 11 = Jude 8, 9; 2:17 = Jude 12, 13; 2:18 = Jude 16. How are we to explain this? I am afraid that there are three possible explanations, each of which can be defended: first, that 2 Peter used Jude; second, that Jude used 2 Peter; and third (yes, you have guessed it), they are both indebted to a common source.

It is only in chapter 3 that we come to the real problem with which the letter is dealing. The chapter starts with a suggestion that this is a second letter (3:1), but it does not feel like a successor to 1 Peter, and we have to say that we cannot be sure what the author means here. Then we learn that mockers were predicted in Scripture (3:2, 3), and that (as in our age) there were plenty of them around in the time when this work was written. We are even given a hint of the form their mockery took: What about this idea of yours that Jesus is coming again? 'Where is the promised second coming?' they clamour. 'For ever since the fathers fell asleep ['fathers' here may be the first generation of Christians], everything remains just the same as it was in the beginning of creation' (3:4). You might hear just such an objection today. And the answer is as valid now as it was then: first, God has certainly prophesied destruction (3:5-7); and secondly, to speak of 'delay' is a misreading of God's time (3:9, 10).

Then the letter comes almost to its end with a reference to the collected letters of St Paul: the point here is not about Paul, but about remaining spotless to the end (3:14). Salvation is a matter of patience, which the mockers are lacking (3:15). The author refers to Paul, rather than quoting him (though the line generally thought to be in his mind is at Romans 2:4, where the Romans are warned not to despise 'the riches of his kindliness, and his patience and endurance . . . knowing that God's kindliness is leading you to repentance'). Then we are given a perfectly sensible reminder that Paul is difficult to interpret (3:16). It is not really part of the argument, but may be of some interest to us in that it suggests that Paul's collected letters may have been circulating by now.

So the letter ends with a warning not to be unstable and, as always in our New Testament, to grow in the grace and knowledge of our Lord and Saviour Jesus Christ. That may be a good place at which to leave this remarkable letter.

Questions

1. Does it matter whether or not these two letters have the same author?

2. Do these two letters both speak to you today?

3. What do you think is their central message?

CHAPTER 27

The letter of James: sharp social satire?

Welcome to this interesting and unusual document. We call it a letter, but it is really nothing of the kind, once you get past the first verse, which sounds a little like one; some scholars call it a 'synagogue homily'. The author describes himself as James (or 'Jacob'), and the assumption is that he is, or is claiming to be, James the brother of the Lord, who was a witness of the Resurrection (he is one of those mentioned at 1 Corinthians 15:7) and a leader of the Jerusalem church. James is mentioned at Acts 15, the story of that decidedly tricky council where the church decided what to demand of Gentiles who wanted to become Christians: should they be forced to be circumcised and to observe the Jewish law, for example, about eating kosher food and keeping Jewish festivals? At the end of the debate, evidently having listened carefully to the arguments, James weighs in with a very balanced, moderate solution. Now we cannot be sure whether Luke was right about this, but the episode, along with the existence of our letter, testifies to James' importance in the early Church. It is the same James whom Paul mentions at Galatians 1:19, and 2:9, 12, and who recognised Paul's mission to the Gentiles.

Is it the same James? We saw with the letters ascribed to Peter that the standard of their Greek posed a problem for his being a Galilean fisherman, and the same would be true for the son of a carpenter from Nazareth. There is always the possibility, as with the letters of Peter, that he handed his material over to an educated Greek scribe and said, 'This is what I want to say; put it into respectable Greek and let me have it back when you have finished it.'

What I suggest we do, therefore, is to read it through together and see what you make of it at the end, and whether you can find any reason for studying it. It must be said that this letter was not immediately accepted into the canon; it is not mentioned before the time of Origen (in the third century), who definitely regarded it as Scripture (which means, presumably, that he was not the only one to value it). A century later, Bishop Eusebius of Caesarea regards it as 'disputed', though he was inclined to accept it. Since then there have been no disputes other than in the sixteenth century, when Martin Luther was disposed to regard it as 'a letter of straw', a verdict he subsequently moderated. However, it must be said that Luther only adopted that severe position because his Catholic opponents made a good deal of what they understood to be James' attitude to 'justification by faith', an idea of immense importance to Luther. And, as we shall see, there were one or two other features of the letter which to both Luther and those who disagreed with him looked like what came to be called, disparagingly, of course, 'early Catholicism'.

Bearing all that in mind, let us simply go through this document, which I shall occasionally call a 'letter' even though it is not. Let us be aware as we do so that the structure of the text is less clear than I might imply. James starts by warning his audience not to get too worried if temptations beset them; indeed, surprisingly enough, they are to greet them with 'joy'. At verse 9 he starts on the theme of 'social justice', which is one of the reasons, I think, why the letter of James has over the last couple of decades become more widely admired. At 1:9-11 he insists on the fundamental equality of those Christians who are of lower social status with those who are higher up. They are to boast of exactly what you would not expect – the lower classes of their 'high status' (as Christians) and the other ones of their 'low standing', with a quotation from Isaiah thrown in to make the point that status is 'as the flower of the field'. Then at verse 12 we go back to the idea of 'testing' or 'temptation', which is not to be regarded as coming from God, since God can only give us what is good.

After that, at verse 19 he introduces another theme, about being 'quick to listen, slow to speak', which later he will exploit in what he says about the tongue, which is one of the more attractive ideas that we find in this letter. James is particularly warning here against anger, which does not, he says, 'accomplish God's righteousness'.

Next he starts another theme, one that Luther found unacceptable in his own context – that of righteousness. It is nowadays quite generally accepted that the author is not making a point against what Paul wrote in Galatians and Romans about the inadequacy of 'deeds' or 'works' to bring about our good standing before God. James is simply making the point (self-evident once you think about it) that if you are in good standing before God, that ought to be obvious from the way you live and the things you do.

And so to chapter 2, and some very sharp social satire, which should still make us feel uncomfortable today. In a very lively illustration about the snobbery of church people, James imagines someone joining the assembly 'with gold rings and a smart suit' and someone else, a destitute person 'with shabby clothes' (2:2, 3), and the very different treatment each is likely to receive from us. We should laugh, ruefully and at ourselves, as we listen. And we should notice how what James says echoes the gospel: God has chosen 'the destitute of the world, who are rich in faith, and are heirs of the kingdom he has promised to those who love him' (2:5). We are supposed to 'love our neighbour as ourselves' (2:8).

Like Paul (Galatians 3:10), James insists that if you want to operate on the basis of the Law, you must keep the whole lot (2:10-13); and, as in the Sermon on the Mount, we have to show mercy, or we shall not receive mercy.

The social justice theme does not go away. We have once more to grin shamefacedly as we hear the voice of the do-gooder that we are all capable of being, who says to a fellow Christian who has nothing to wear or to eat or drink, '"Go in peace; keep warm, and have a good meal" – and then you don't give them what the body needs, what's the use of that?' (2:15, 16).

Then, once again, he comes back to the question of faith and works. Look at 2:18:

> Someone will say, 'You have faith, and I have works': show me your faith, apart from works, and I shall show you my faith precisely by my works. You may well say that 'God is one'; well done – even the demons believe that; and they shudder.

Then, like St Paul, James continues the argument on the basis of what Abraham did, referring to his willingness to sacrifice his beloved son Isaac in that chilling story in Genesis 22. He uses the same quotation from Genesis 15:6 to make the point that Abraham's faith meant not just believing but also doing things. Is James specifically targeting Paul's teaching here? Or that of some of Paul's successors? You must make up your own mind, but be aware that Paul was quite as clear as James about the importance of faith actually leading to particular ways of behaviour, and was deeply critical of Christians who behaved in ways contrary to the gospel. What Paul is opposed to is anything that says all you need to do is fulfil the commands of the Law. James produces the very striking example of 'the prostitute Rahab' (2:25) as someone who was 'justified by works'. The real point is the distinction between life and death: religious faith that makes no difference to the way we operate, especially with regard to the poor, is a faith that is dead, and both Paul and James want a faith that is visibly alive.

Then the author goes on to the question of the tongue, with some lively exhortation on the damage that the uncontrolled tongue can do: it is difficult to tame (3:7, 8) and can have poisonous effects; we can choose either to bless the Father or to curse human beings born in the likeness of God. Once again we find ourselves challenged, to our embarrassment, and this continues as the writer speaks of those (most of us?) who think that they are wise or learned (3:13-18).

Then, with no particularly discernible structure, James goes on to diagnose the fighting to which human beings are especially prone, and how the desires that underlie them lead to all the evils of contemporary society: killing and jealousy and quarrels and wars, all from not being properly in touch with God. This part of the argument reaches an impressive climax at 4:7, 8, when we hear:

> Subordinate yourselves to God, resist the devil, and he'll run away from you.
> Draw near to God, and God will draw near to you.

This is a piece of wisdom that we should recite to ourselves several times a day, and the author follows it up by warning us against slandering one another (4:11) and against making extravagant plans to make money in the future (4:13-17).

The final chapter begins with some more emphasis on the theme of social justice, at 5:1-6. This has lost none of its power.

Then we hear the exhortation to patience, that great and essential Christian virtue, at 5:7-11. After that there is another echo of the Sermon on the Mount (5:12), and an encouragement to pray over the sick and anoint them, which is the start of an ancient tradition in the Church (5:13-15); to confession of sins, which is another (5:16); to prayer, without which Christianity is no good at all (5:16-18); and an encouragement to look after those who drift away (5:19, 20), with which the letter ends, rather abruptly.

So that is this lively and neglected letter. There are just two further points that I should like to draw to your attention. I have mentioned them both already, but you will draw closer to our author if you take good note of them.

The first is the lively illustrations that he uses: the waves of the sea (1:6); the heat of the sun (1:11); the power of light (1:17); how to use a mirror (1:23); the comical contrast of our attitudes to rich and poor (2:2, 3); the tongue compared to the horse's bit and to the helmsman's rudder (3:3, 4) and to the power of even a tiny fire (3:5).

The second is the very sharp critique of the social status quo that I mentioned earlier. You will do well to look carefully at 2:2, 3 and 2:6 (the rich who oppress you). Most of all, read and reflect on the tirade against the rich at 5:1-6, and ask what the Lord may be saying to you here.

Questions

1. Do you think that the 'letter of James' is worth reading today?

2. What are the best parts of the letter for you?

3. Is his teaching on the tongue relevant in our time?

CHAPTER 28

Acts of the Apostles: the Gospel of the Holy Spirit

The next volume in our library that we shall be looking at is called Acts of the Apostles. It has been known by this name since at least the second century, but it is a rather misleading title, since basically it is the Acts of Peter in the first half and of Paul in the second half, with cameo appearances from Stephen, Philip and Barnabas. More accurately, though, we should call it the 'Acts of the Holy Spirit'. It is the story of the triumphant onrushing of the powerful force whom the early Church well knew under the title of 'Holy Spirit' – that force which simply cannot be stopped, whatever obstacles human beings may throw in its way. Indeed, the very last word of Acts is, typically, a Greek word that means 'without being stopped', and that is the picture that we see unfolding in Acts.

The best way to observe this, I think, will be to look at some of the texts of Acts, but before we do that I want to give a kind of overview of the whole book, so that you will know what to look for as you read or listen. Here I want to make four points about Acts in general.

The first is that 'Luke' makes a deliberate link with volume 1, the Gospel of Luke. He does this by making a kind of 'bridge' by giving another dedication to his patron 'Theophilus' (1:1). Then he links the two volumes in that each of them has an account, albeit slightly different in each case, of Jesus' ascension into heaven. After that, another link is provided by the fact that the disciples in both cases return to Jerusalem after the ascension. Finally there is a link in the position of the Temple. As we saw in a previous chapter, Luke's Gospel started in the Temple and ended there. Acts also starts in the Temple, and the story keeps coming back to it (the Temple functions virtually as a character in the two-volume work), until finally at 21:30 the Temple doors are slammed shut behind Paul at the moment of his arrest, as they make an attempt on his life.

That is the first point. The second point is closely linked to it, and is that Acts continues the story of the life of Jesus. In both volumes, the Spirit is at work (though, as we saw, it goes underground from quite early in the Gospel until it resurfaces in Acts). In both volumes, the Spirit is unmistakably at work; in both, the upshot is a journey, which is evident in Luke, and in Acts is even more powerfully expressed as a progression that is absolutely Spirit-driven. In both volumes, the heroes (Jesus and his successors in the early Church) are imprisoned and flogged, and they perform miraculous healings; in both, their innocence is declared by Roman imperial authorities (Pontius Pilate at Luke 23:4, and by Agrippa at Acts 26:31). In both volumes there is a great role for prayer: early on in both we witness the descent of the Holy Spirit in bodily form, at Jesus' baptism in Luke 3:22 and at Pentecost at Acts 2:2-4. In both cases, the representatives of the force for good find themselves doing battle with the Jewish religious leaders; and also, of course, there is the parallel drawn between the imprisonment of John the Baptist (Luke 3:19, 20), and the arrest and murder of Stephen (Acts 6:8-15; 7:54–8:1).

The third point for us to observe is that there are many speeches in Acts. Something like one-third of the book is taken up with speeches, 24 of them, depending on how you count them. And, as is often the case in ancient history, the speeches seem to function as the author's commentary on the action that is happening. That is to say, it does not so much matter to Luke whether the speeches were actually delivered in the way that he suggests; it is more a matter of ancient historians being allowed a certain freedom. An important example of such a speech would be the Pentecost speech by Peter and others, at Acts 2:14-36: a heroic production, if he did indeed deliver it as advertised. Others would include Stephen's thoroughly subversive presentation of his position (Acts 7:2-53). Then there are the speeches, including one uttered by Peter, on the coming of the Spirit upon the house of Cornelius (10:30-33, 34-43, 47). And, of course, we may never forget Paul's frequent speeches in chapters 16 onwards to both Jews and Gentiles.

Then the fourth linking point to notice is that both works are rewritten as journeys. The Gospel starts with several mini-journeys, as we saw, between Judea and Galilee, and then at 9:52 it starts in the full and proper sense, as the pilgrimage to Jerusalem. In the Gospel, the journey takes them from Galilee to Jerusalem via Samaria. At the beginning of Acts, as the journey starts up once more, Jesus tells his disciples that they are to be ready to go 'to the very ends of the earth' (1:8), and once again the Gospel plays out with further references to that power of the Holy Spirit. For here we are talking about Jesus going to the ends of the earth: 'You will be my witnesses in Jerusalem, throughout Judea and Samaria, and to the ends of the earth.'

This story, then, is nothing else than the story of God. It is the same story that is told in both volumes, except that in Acts it has become that much clearer that the journey is driven by the Holy Spirit 'to Judea and Samaria', which we shall reach in chapter 8, and then to 'the ends of the earth', which we reach in one sense at chapter 17, in Athens, the intellectual centre of the Mediterranean world. In another sense, the journey reaches its end in Rome, where Paul arrives under arrest but free to hold conversation with all who visit him about the kingdom of God, and 'without being stopped'.

With all that in mind, what I now propose to do is to take you through the broad outline of Acts of the Apostles, as I have a sense that this remarkable document is not as well known as it deserves to be. It is also such a good story that the narrative carries the reader along. In what remains of this chapter I want to give you a feel of what we might call the Jerusalem part of the story, which is the first seven chapters and a tiny bit of chapter 8.

Absolutely central to a proper understanding of the text is that it works itself out precisely in the absence of Jesus and under the driving presence of the Holy Spirit, so it is the story of the Church as it is today. Included in that story is the fact that the disciples are not all that bright. So, for example, we listen in some astonishment to them asking Jesus if it is now that he is going to restore the kingdom to Israel (1:6), proving that they have really not understood anything that he has taught them. And it is no good our sneering at them, for the story of these dumb disciples is also our story. What they have to learn to do, and what we have to learn to do, is to listen prayerfully in order to compensate for our dumbness.

That indeed is what we find them doing. Before anything else can happen in the narrative, they have to give themselves over to prayer, along with the women, and especially with Mary the mother of Jesus, and with Jesus' brothers, who are now at last on board in the Jesus enterprise.

The first task of the little group is to restore the number 12, which has been reduced to 11 with the suicide of Judas. The moral here is that they have now learned to trust in God, and so after prayer they cast lots (there are those who suggest that this might be a good way of choosing bishops today), and Matthias is counted with the Eleven (1:15-26). One element to notice here, by the way, is that Matthias is never heard of again: the main point is that after prayer the number should be restored, for (and this will be the keynote throughout our reading of Acts) God is in charge.

That becomes clearer in the next and highly dramatic episode – the story of Pentecost and the coming of the Spirit in noisy and burning mode. The effect of the Spirit is a kind of foreshadowing of the history of the Church, the speaking of the 'great things of God' in every known language and to all the regions under the sun. In the list of territories that is given here we go from Iran in the Far East to Rome in the West and Africa in the South, as well as a good part of Asia Minor. For Luke's readers that would have covered the known world, so continents that he did not know about would readily be included in his compass, under 'Parthians, Medes and Elamites' (2:9).

After Peter's powerful speech on the day, explaining what is happening to the stunned inhabitants of Jerusalem (2:14-36), Luke starts to paint a picture of what life was like in this newly Spirit-filled Church. He manages this by way of what are known as 'Lucan summaries', where with a broad brush he deftly paints a picture of what it was like to be Church in those early days: listening to the teaching of the apostles, praying and sharing the Eucharist together. In addition, they held everything in common, met regularly in the Temple and in private houses. It is a wonderful vision, even if it is not precisely a portrait of the Church as it was at any particular time in its history (2:42-47).

Now at last the Church starts to act. Do you often find yourself clamouring, 'Why doesn't the Church *do* something?' If so, just have a glance at Acts and recognise that the Church cannot simply *do* something until it has prayed and reflected before the Lord. What happens now is actually quite complex. For a beggar is looking to the Church, in the shape of Peter and John, for alms, but he doesn't receive any. Instead what happens is that he is healed, and goes jumping around the Temple (3:3-10). That needs some explanation, of course, and explanation duly comes in the shape of yet another speech from Peter. The answer is, first, that this miracle had nothing to do with Peter and John but came through faith in the name of Jesus (3:16), and, second, that this is all part of the old story of God and was what the prophets had predicted.

We are not, however, to expect that things are going to be easy for the infant Church (or in our contemporary life as church persons). So Peter and John are arrested, mainly, it seems, because they have been preaching the Resurrection of Jesus. Once again Peter makes a speech, and once again the miracle is placed where it belongs – not with the apostles, but (4:10) 'in the name of Jesus Christ the Nazorean, whom you people crucified, whom God raised from the dead'. That is the heart of the matter in Acts: it is the story of what God did in Jesus. The authorities can think of nothing better to do by way of riposte than warn them and let them go. Living as Church is uncomfortable at times, but it is the way to go.

The response of the community at large (4:23-31) is to pray, and the effect is an earthquake, the sign of the presence of the Spirit: 'they were all filled with the Spirit, and they were speaking God's word with confidence'. That is the Church as it is supposed to be.

Then, once again, Luke offers us one of his summaries, and we are given this spectacular picture of the Church as it should be: 'of one heart and soul, and no one claimed that any of their possessions belonged to them alone; they held everything in common'. At the same time, 'the Apostles were offering the witness about the Lord Jesus' resurrection, and there was great grace upon all of them'. That is what the Church is for (4:32-37).

This is a radiantly attractive picture, and its charm comes down to us through the ages. But just in case you were starting to think that it was all different then, Luke now gives us the scandalous story of Ananias and his wife Sapphira, a scene of dark comedy, which ends up with capital punishment for these two, for the sin of 'lying to the Holy Spirit'. Read the story, which you will find at 5:1-11, and ask yourself why it is never read in church.

Then, in case we should be too depressed by this tale of falsehood and death, Luke offers another of his charming summaries (5:12-16), which, inevitably, is only the prelude to the apostles being arrested again. But you cannot stop the Holy Spirit, and so the angel of the Lord effortlessly opens the prison doors, and the apostles go and teach in the Temple. Once again they are arrested and interrogated, and once again the authorities are blamed for Jesus' death, but, once again, the apostles insist on the central fact that 'God has raised Jesus from the dead' (5:30). This has the effect of making the authorities want to kill the apostles, until Gamaliel, an eminent rabbi and father of a rabbinic dynasty, warns them that God may be at work here. So the not very satisfactory upshot is that the authorities flog the apostles and send them away, after warning them not to 'speak in the name of Jesus', a highly improbable suggestion, especially since the apostles rejoice (5:41) 'that they were worthy to be dishonoured for the Name'. That is something we might ask for today.

And now to a complex series of events that could have destroyed the infant Church, but actually (this is the story of the Holy Spirit, after all) led to its growth. It starts with racial and religious tension in the early Church, with Greek-speaking widows being neglected at the food bank. To cope with the tension, the apostles decide to appoint seven 'deacons', each with impeccably Greek names, to 'wait at table'. That seems to solve the problem, since Luke tells us that 'the word of God was continuing to grow'. But the odd thing is that we only hear of two of them ever again, namely Stephen and Philip, and neither of them is waiting at table. Stephen turns out to be a brilliant preacher, presumably in Greek, and in consequence is accused of agitating against Moses and against God and against the Temple and the Torah, which sounds highly unlikely (you can read the charges at 6:8-15). Then Stephen embarks on what turns out to be his final speech; it is thoroughly subversive and does not pull its punches. You can read it from 7:1-53.

The effect of the speech is to enrage his hearers, mainly, it seems, because they could not think of an answer. He is therefore stoned to death, having been granted a vision of Jesus 'standing at the right hand of God' (7:55, 56). As he dies he prays, as the Church must always pray, 'Lord Jesus, receive my Spirit' (7:59).

What next? It could have been a catastrophe, but it was not, because God is in charge. At the end we learn that 'Saul', whom we have not hitherto met, is looking after the clothes of those who stoned Stephen, and that he consented to the killing. Then we discover that persecution breaks out, scattering the Church throughout Judea and Samaria. It sounds like disaster, but the reader remembers what Jesus had said, about us being 'my witnesses in Judea and Samaria and to the ends of the earth', and perhaps breathes a sigh of relief. There is more to come.

Questions

1. Do you agree that Acts of the Apostles is insufficiently known? Why might this be?

2. What is the picture of the Holy Spirit that emerges from the early chapters of Acts?

3. Is there a parallel drawn in Acts between the life of Jesus and the life of the early Church? How might that relate to us today?

CHAPTER 29

Acts part 2:
the word spreads to the Gentiles

In the previous chapter, we left the story of Acts at a critical moment. Stephen is dead, someone called Saul helped in the killing, and the Church is scattered to Judea and Samaria. Can God cope?

Well, yes, of course, because this is the Gospel of the Holy Spirit. We leave Saul endeavouring to destroy the Church, Christians piously burying Stephen, and the gospel scattered into Samaria (8:1-4). We should not be surprised, but the disaster turns into triumph, for in Samaria (of all unlikely places) Philip finds a fertile place for preaching the gospel of Christ, with the characteristically Lucan result that 'there was great joy in that city'. If we were starting to worry about what might happen to the future of the Church, we should recall that the Holy Spirit is in charge.

Then there comes a crisis of an unexpected sort, though it is one that we should be alert to today: the idea that God's gifts can be bought and sold. For there is a professional magician called Simon who thinks he can buy the power that the apostles have in the laying-on of their hands (8:18-24). This is the kind of problem that arises as the gospel goes out to a world that does not really understand it, and it is a problem for our world today.

This is followed by a remarkable episode. We have already mentioned in the previous chapter the story of the seven Greek speakers who were appointed to wait at table, and how Stephen turned out to be a brilliant speaker and died by being stoned to death. Now Philip, whom we last saw preaching in Samaria, is given a mission: to go down on the desert road to Gaza from Jerusalem, and the gospel is as a result spread even further, this time in a southerly direction. For at the angel's bidding (you will find the story at 8:26-40), Philip catches up with a eunuch, a high official of the Kandake, the queen of Ethiopia. Philip hears him reading a passage from Isaiah and asks him if he knows the meaning of the passage (it is the one about a 'sheep led to the slaughter', from Isaiah 53:7, 8). The Ethiopian more or less invites him to explain the text, and Philip 'proclaimed Jesus to him'. At the end of that the eunuch spots some water and asks to be baptised, then disappears into history, while Philip turns up in Caesarea. What is going on here is simply that the gospel is expanding beyond the boundaries of traditional Judaism. And God's project is advanced.

In the next chapter it takes another big step forward, for Saul, whom we last saw doing his best to destroy the Church, turns out to be still on the job. He is off to Damascus, armed with the rabbinical equivalent of a papal bull and a commission to bring back any Christians, of either gender, in fetters. It does not work out quite that way, however, for instead he encounters Jesus. You will remember the story, frequently painted by famous artists, and not least because Luke thinks it such an important moment in his tale that he tells it three times, each time in slightly different circumstances (see 9:1-19; 22:6-16; 26:12-18). Here he suffers a 'light from the sky' and a voice that utters the challenge, 'Saul, Saul – why are you persecuting me?'

Not unreasonably he responds, 'Who are you, Lord?'

He is told (and this is a really important moment in the development of Acts), 'I am Jesus, whom you are persecuting.' That is to say that Jesus and his Church are in some sense identical. Saul's companions see nothing, but they hear the voice. As for Saul, he is blinded; he goes fasting to Damascus and his life is forever changed.

Then Saul is brought to another Christian, Ananias, who has been forewarned of what is coming (and is not all that enthusiastic about Saul because of what he has already done against the Church). Ananias overcomes his reluctance (it is what Jesus wants that counts), and lays his hands on Saul, for him to regain his sight and be filled with the Holy Spirit (we are never to forget that Acts is the Gospel of the Holy Spirit).

It is not, however, an uninterruptedly triumphant progress, for we already know that Saul will have to suffer for the name of Jesus, but he does start proclaiming that Jesus is 'the Son of God'. And his argumentation is so good that he confounds all his opponents. They don't like that, of course, so Saul has to make an undignified escape from Damascus, in a basket from a window, of all things (9:25, and see also 2 Corinthians 11:32, 33). However, the gospel continues to be preached, over an ever wider range of territory. The Holy Spirit is in charge.

Then, however, if Saul is to go any further, he has to face those in Jerusalem whom he used to persecute. Not surprisingly, they are far from enthusiastic about him, but once Barnabas intervenes, Saul is accepted, and he preaches the gospel with the best of them, 'in the name of the Lord'. However, as we saw with Stephen, successful preaching can be a death sentence, and when the Greek-speaking Jews debate with him, it all ends in attempted murder.

So once again the gospel is on the move, for Saul goes first to the port city of Caesarea, and then back home to Tarsus. When the Holy Spirit is driving the narrative, setbacks turn into successes. Now we have another of Luke's charming summaries: 'The Church throughout the whole of Judea and Galilee and Samaria had peace, being built up and journeying in the fear of the Lord, and was filling up, by the power of the Holy Spirit' (9:31).

With Saul now offstage, the attention turns back to Peter, who heals a man and a woman at Lydda and at nearby Joppa (9:32-35 and 9:36-43; it is a thing that Luke often does, to have a pairing like this across the genders).

Do you see what is happening now? The gospel is spreading further and further afield, and at last something happens that changes the story fundamentally, for Peter is brought face to face with a Gentile, and a centurion to boot! This man, Cornelius, meets an angel, who persuades him to send for Simon Peter. Meanwhile Peter has a powerful vision to teach him that he does not need to worry any longer about the Levitical rules for purity. This vision takes the form of a sheet lowered to the ground, containing all kinds of animals, not just those it was permissible to eat. Peter is persuaded three times in this vision, and then the centurion's emissaries arrive. Peter, significantly, gives them hospitality, so the vision has taught him something, and he returns with the emissaries to Cornelius in Caesarea. Cornelius (a Roman centurion, remember: the Holy Spirit is in charge of this scene) tells Simon, 'Now we are all in God's presence, ready to hear everything that has been commanded you by the Lord.' This marks an extraordinary turn in the narrative, for it is Peter, of all people, who is opening the gospel to non-Jews and declaring that 'God is not a snob' (10:34). So he preaches a little sermon about Jesus and his gospel, and how 'all the prophets bear witness to him, for everyone who believes in him to receive forgiveness of sins through his name'. And notice that word 'everyone'. The Holy Spirit is turning the gospel outwards to the whole of humanity.

That insight is then dramatically proved by the fact that the same Holy Spirit comes upon the assembled Gentiles. Peter baptises them and (this is important) accepts their hospitality.

Meanwhile (we are now in chapter 11), the news has reached Jerusalem, and the Jewish Christians are not at all pleased at this turn of events, so Peter tells the story of his vision (it is always significant when Luke tells a story twice, so listen carefully), and how he remembered what Jesus had said to them. The point is that God and his Holy Spirit are at work here, and are not to be contradicted. This convinces his Jewish colleagues, and we know that the gospel is going to spread wider.

So indeed it proves. For nothing can stop the gospel. And Luke reminds us of this in the next episode. Do you remember how with the death of Stephen the whole gospel enterprise seemed to have been brought to an end, but in fact expanded? Because the Holy Spirit is in charge, that process is still continuing, as Luke reminds us (11:19): 'Those who had been scattered as a result of the trouble that arose because of Stephen got through as far as Phoenicia and

Cyprus and Antioch.' Now at this stage, and despite Peter's example, Luke tells us that they 'were giving the message to nobody except Jews'. But you cannot stop the Holy Spirit, for in the very next verse we hear that some of them were Cypriots and people from Cyrene, so the gospel has now moved way beyond its origins in Galilee and Judea, down to the fertile plain and to the islands of the Mediterranean, and even as far as North Africa. Anyway, these strangers from foreign parts start speaking about Jesus to Greeks in Antioch, and Luke comments that 'the hand of the Lord was on them, and a great number that believed turned to the Lord'.

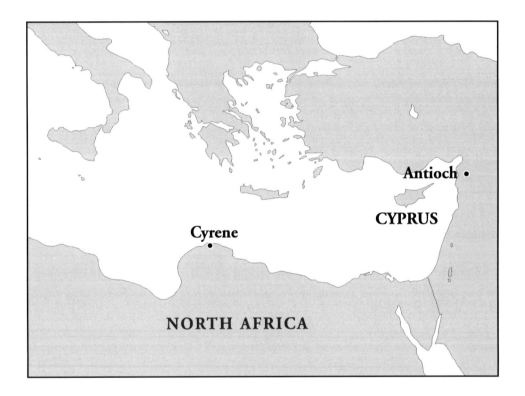

So Jerusalem has to get involved (they keep an eye on things, you see, back in Jerusalem), and Barnabas is sent as a delegation to check that all is in order in Antioch. Everything is just fine, thank you very much, and 'when Barnabas got there, and saw the grace of God, he rejoiced, and encouraged them all to remain in firmness of heart for the Lord' (11:23). Then Barnabas goes on to Tarsus, where (you may remember) we last saw Saul, and brings him to Antioch. Now Antioch is a thoroughly cosmopolitan city, and inevitably, under the guidance of the Holy Spirit, the gospel will be preached much more widely there.

In the meantime, however, all is not well in Jerusalem, for Herod has had James the son of Zebedee executed, and tries something of the same on Peter, putting him in prison. It is Passover time, which might have given Herod pause (for there was always a high state of tension around the feast), but despite the state-of-the-art technology with which he is incarcerated, Peter is set free by an angel (12:7-10) and rejoins his fellow Christians, who are praying for him. This leads to a comical episode when the maid Rhoda fails to open the gate, and Peter practically has to batter the door down. The Spirit, you see, is still at work.

This comes out in another way when at the end of the same chapter Herod is struck down and eaten by worms, and dies. Luke makes no comment except to invoke a striking contrast in the very next verse after reporting the tyrant's demise: 'And the word of God was growing and multiplying.' Do you see how the Spirit cannot be stopped?

So we are not surprised at this stage to find that the infant Church is positively catholic in its range of nationalities. We are given a report of the prophets and teachers at Antioch: Barnabas (who is Aramaic), Symeon (Hebrew or Aramaic) with a Latin nickname (Niger), and Lucius (a Greek name) from Cyrene (so he is African), and Menahem (a Hebrew name), who grew up with Herod the tetrarch, so someone from the upper end of society. And Saul; we know a bit about him, of course (and we shall come to know a good deal more).

Then Saul and Barnabas set off on a mission across the Mediterranean to Cyprus, where Saul, who is suddenly also named 'Paul', which is the way we think of him, wins a battle of magic with the sorcerer Elymas. Then it is off to the other Antioch, the one in Pisidia, where (and you will find this to be a frequent pattern in the rest of Acts) they enter the synagogue on the Sabbath. Paul (we shall not henceforth know him by that other name) is invited to speak, and we listen attentively to this first performance. He gives a (slightly selective) account of the history of Israel and seeks to demonstrate that Jesus is the fulfilment of that history, after the Jerusalemites and their leaders put him to death, and God had raised him from the dead. This first speech is a spectacular success, and Paul is invited back the following week. In the meantime he makes a good many converts among Jews and proselytes.

As you might expect, however, the next Saturday is less successful, for Paul's Jewish opponents shout him down and expel him and Barnabas.

This is only the beginning of the fun, for the pair then go on to Iconium (chapter 14), where once again they speak in the synagogue, with mixed results, in consequence of which they go on to Lystra. There they heal a crippled man, and suddenly the gospel is being preached to non-Jews, who decide that the two missionaries are in fact pagan deities. But the theme of resistance continues (14:19), and Jews from other cities stone them for blasphemy. But the Holy

Spirit is in charge, and so we are hardly surprised that they are not killed, but stand up and get on with the mission. They go through several cities of Asia Minor, and finally get back to Antioch, where they give their report: 'and when they got there, they gathered the whole assembly/church, and announced to them what great things God had done with them, and that he had opened a door of faith to the Gentiles' (14:27).

That sounds very good, and indeed it is, for the Holy Spirit is clearly at work. But you will not be surprised to learn that the triumphs of the Church do not mean, in either our day or Paul's, that we all live happily ever afterwards. For there is trouble brewing in Jerusalem: someone has been saying in Antioch that Christians have to be circumcised. It is not, of course, an unreasonable position, for that is what it says in the Bible. This issue is one that could have torn the Church apart in its infancy (and you might like to think of other issues that could have this effect in our day), and we watch with some interest to see how it will be resolved. We are now in Acts chapter 15, and what is sometimes called the 'Council of Jerusalem'. For after a good deal of ruction, the Antioch church decides to appeal to Jerusalem, and to send Paul and Barnabas and others to plead their case.

In Jerusalem, Luke gives us a rough outline of the debate, and we must never forget that it was an important question that might have prevented the gospel spreading. We start with the report, 'There arose from the party of the Pharisees who had come to faith' (15:5), and we know what they are going to say: 'They have to be circumcised.' Then we listen and watch for the movement of the Spirit.

Peter makes a speech, describing his conversion to the Gentile mission and arguing against creating obstacles for new converts. Paul and Barnabas then say their piece, though oddly Luke does not tell us what they actually said. Finally, James makes his utterance. He is the leader of the Jerusalem church, and we rather expect him to take a conservative line. We listen nervously and are delighted when he gives his verdict: 'Stop troubling the Gentiles who are turning to God.'

So there it is: a letter is written to that effect, and unless you have by now got the message, you probably think that all will now be well. For that we shall have to wait and see what happens in the rest of this extraordinary fifth Gospel.

Questions

1. How do you think the Holy Spirit works in driving the narrative on?

2. Why do you think the gospel spread so powerfully?

3. What is the most striking episode for you in chapters 8–15? What is striking about it?

CHAPTER 30

Acts part 3:
'To the ends of the earth'

What have we seen so far in Acts? The first seven chapters gave us a powerful picture of the situation in Jerusalem, with the Holy Spirit encouraging the apostles to keep going, despite all obstacles and persecution, and even through death and corporal punishment. Then from chapter 8 to 15 we saw how the story took a new turn, unexpectedly, but clearly under the guidance of the Holy Spirit, going out to the Gentiles and with an ever-wider geographical sweep. It is the drama of the early Church (and of our contemporary Church, for that matter), painfully victorious over all obstacles.

Now we watch the drama continue. We have followed the outlines of Jesus' manifesto: Judea and Samaria have been left behind and we are on the way to the 'ends of the earth'. After the Council of Jerusalem, Paul and Barnabas are now cleared to continue their policy of not asking too much of their Gentile converts. But alas, there is a quarrel, and Paul refuses to have John-Mark with them, and now Paul is going to work with Silas and Timothy. There is nothing new about quarrels in the Church, you see.

At this point the Spirit takes a hand again, for Paul is of the view that they should continue preaching in Asia Minor, but the Spirit stops them (16:6, 7) and directs them across the water to Greece, by way of Troas. So for the first time the gospel comes to Europe, by way of Samothrace, Neapolis and finally Philippi, where they meet with some success, principally among the womenfolk. The powerful and well-to-do Lydia more or less forces them to set up the church in her house. But, as often enough before, the triumph does not last long, and Paul and Silas are put in prison because they have exorcised a slave girl who had a spirit of divination, and who accurately stated who they were.

But, as by now you will expect, prison cannot long detain them, and God sends an earthquake as Paul and Silas keep the other prisoners awake by singing hymns. None of them escapes, and the prison commandant is prevented from committing suicide, with the result that he and his entire family join the Jesus movement. Paul then has a minor triumph over the Philippi magistrates by insisting, when he is offered his freedom, that they, who have submitted a Roman citizen to corporal punishment, should come in person to set him and Silas free (16:25-40).

Then the journey continues westward, down the Via Egnatia to Thessalonica. There, once again, Paul preaches in the synagogue over a period of three weeks. However, the familiar pattern reappears, and there is reaction against him, which continues as far as Beroea, the next stop on the road (17:1-16).

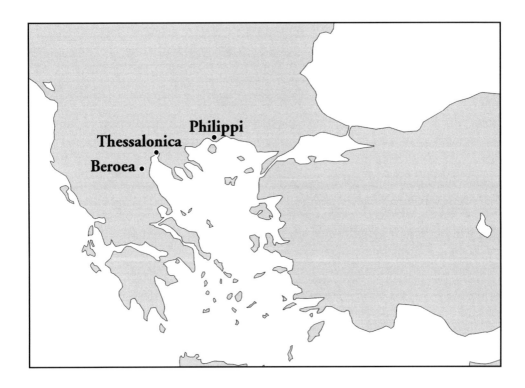

You will not be surprised to learn, however, that this negative reaction leads to another major step on the way, for as a result of the opposition Paul arrives in Athens, the intellectual centre of the ancient world. There, after ecumenical dialogue with Epicurean and Stoic philosophers, he is invited to preach in the Areopagus. Now here we may feel that we are near to fulfilling Jesus' programme, way back at 1:8, of being his witnesses 'to the ends of the earth'. If you can deliver the message to the best minds in the world, then you are halfway there. Paul, according to Luke, now delivers a carefully crafted speech, which is intended to flatter the Athenians ('I see that you are very religious minded') and to engage their culture by referring to a particular altar erected 'To the Unknown God' and by quoting Greek philosophers. Then he gets down to business by talking about God and about Jesus, described as 'a man whom God set apart'. All goes well until Paul makes the further claim that

'God gave grounds for faith by raising this man from the dead'. At that point, they roar with laughter, though a few are impressed, and Paul leaves Athens with his tail between his legs (18:16-34).

Do you see once more the familiar story? What looks like success turns out not to be, but the Spirit is at work, and so we are probably not going to be surprised at what happens next. Paul trudges miserably south to Corinth. Later he was to tell the Corinthians that he arrived 'in weakness and fear and much trembling' (1 Corinthians 2:3). You could sympathise with Paul if that was indeed the case, for Corinth could not be called a promising city for the preaching of the gospel, with a lively sex life, immense social divisions and far too much money for its own good. Against all his expectations, however, it turned out to be one of his success stories, at least for a while, until they all started fighting. For there he met two Jewish Christians, Priscilla and Aquila, of whom we know from Paul's own letters, and who were tent-makers like himself, and who formed the basis of the lively Christian community there.

As we have seen in previous cities on the journey, Paul starts by preaching in the synagogue, arguing that the Messiah has come, and that the Messiah is Jesus. Then he is rejected and goes to preach to the Gentiles (we have seen this coming, of course). There he meets with some considerable success, and even, according to Acts, has a conversation with Gallio, the proconsul of Achaea. Now this Gallio was the brother of the famous Roman philosopher Seneca, who would eventually become tutor to the future Emperor Nero (and how much we may wish that Nero had listened to his old pedagogue, instead of ordering him to commit suicide!) (18:1-17). So the gospel is spreading wider and wider, even to Gentiles, and even to upper-class Romans.

Then Paul sets off east again, through Ephesus, where he does not stay long, and arrives back in the Holy Land at Caesarea. Then he sets off on another tour of preaching, through Antioch and Galatia and Phrygia (you'll have to look at the maps for that, but it is roughly Asia Minor).

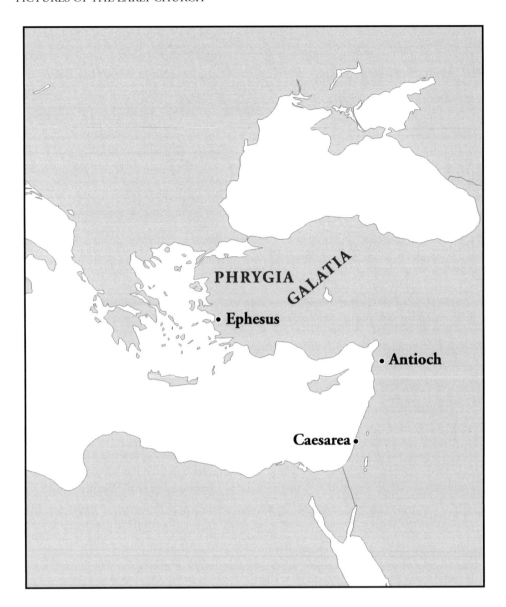

Then he arrives back in Ephesus, and now we are in chapter 19 of Acts. Here Paul is very active, converting some disciples of John the Baptist (19:2-6) and giving them the baptism, not of water but of the Holy Spirit. He also debates in the synagogue, with more success than hitherto, for three whole months, until a failure to convince them persuades him to go into a Gentile philosophical school. There follows a battle with some Jewish exorcists and, more seriously, with the local commercial interests, because Paul has denounced the making of idols. A riot starts, with the slogan, 'Great is Diana of the Ephesians', which endangers Paul's life, but in the end comes to nothing very much.

Then (and we are now in chapter 20) Paul moves on to Greece once more, but has, yet again, to escape a plot against his life, and starts a journey back to Jerusalem. This means sailing to Troas, the principal port for such a journey. There he offers an object lesson to all lengthy preachers when a young man called Eutychus is nearly killed, having been overcome by sleep during a too-long homily. Once that little difficulty has been sorted out, the little group moves south and east to Miletus. Paul summons the leaders of the church at Ephesus, obviously a favourite place of his, and delivers a long farewell address (20:18-35), in which he tells them that they will never see his face again, and exhorts them to keep the church going. All he knows, and this is familiar to us now from our reading of the text, is that 'the Holy Spirit testifies to me, in each city, that imprisonment and tribulation await me'. So the journey is not to be triumphant, except when we get to the very end.

Nothing, however, is going to stop Paul, and he goes on with the journey, eventually reaching Tyre, the ancient city on the Mediterranean coast, and then the Holy Land, at Caesarea. Here we encounter Philip once more, now equipped with four prophetic daughters. Another prophet, called Agabus, warns Paul against going to Jerusalem, but you will not be surprised to learn that Paul remains unstoppable: 'I am ready, not only to be imprisoned, but even to die in Jerusalem, for the name of the Lord Jesus Christ.'

On with the journey, then, up to Jerusalem, accompanied by something of a bodyguard. On arrival there, they are greeted with surprising enthusiasm by the brothers, and there is a meeting with James. This goes quite well, except that Paul and his party are warned that there is a problem, for some Jewish Christians have been told that 'you are teaching rebellion against Moses, saying that all those who are Jewish by race are not to circumcise their sons, nor walk in the ways of Moses'. So they suggest a device to make it clear that Paul is still following the ancestral ways, of taking four men into the Temple to do the right thing and make it clear where Paul stands. This group does not want to revoke the generous allowance for Gentiles, but they do regard it as important to insist on proper observance on the part of those who are born as Jews (they do not, of course, say what they want Paul to do, as one who was born a Jew).

The stratagem works for a while, but after seven days some Jews from Asia, possibly the very people who had brought about Stephen's death (6:9), recognise Paul's presence in the Temple. In a piece of religious hysteria, familiar even in our day, they allege that Paul is trying to defile the Temple. A riot follows, the Temple doors are slammed shut and (since the Holy Spirit is driving the action) Paul is rescued by the Roman army.

Then Paul establishes something of a relationship with the Roman 'chiliarch', something like a military tribune, by establishing that he speaks Greek. As a result he is permitted to address his fellow Jews in Aramaic (21:40).

The speech goes very well, with Paul telling the story of his encounter with Jesus, until he comes to the crunch and indicates that the risen Jesus has sent him to preach to the Gentiles (22:21). That causes chaos, and once again the Romans rescue Paul. 'Rescue' may be too strong a word, since they are on the point of flogging him in order to find out the truth, when Paul reveals to the centurion that he is a Roman citizen and therefore should not be flogged. At that point our friend the chiliarch comes back into play and we discover that he bought his citizenship, while Paul was actually born into it. You can hear the pride in Paul's voice when he makes that claim (22:27).

So Paul is set free once more, and a meeting with the Sanhedrin is arranged. We remember, of course, what happened to Jesus in this very city, and when the high priest orders Paul to be struck on the mouth and Paul calls him a 'whitewashed wall', it seems to be happening again. But cleverly Paul exploits the division between Sadducees and Pharisees on the question of Resurrection, and makes it clear that he is on the Pharisee side. So, once again, Paul has to be rescued by the Romans (this may have been rather encouraging for his readers, worried about whether Rome was against them). This happens twice, in fact, because some radical hotheads make an oath to kill Paul, and so he is escorted, with a huge bodyguard, to Caesarea by night, since that is where the procurator lives (23:24).

The adventure continues, and it must be said that now it has something of the breathless haste of a *Boys' Own* story. The chiliarch writes a letter to Felix, the procurator and a man who was close to Nero. Paul is then imprisoned to await trial, and his Jewish opponents, led by the high priest, come down to Caesarea some days later. We are allowed to listen to the trial, in which Paul handles the charges with some skill and wit, so much so that he is invited to perform before Felix and his wife Drusilla, who is Jewish. It turns out that Felix is hoping for a bribe from Paul, but as Paul does not do that sort of thing he is returned to prison for two years.

Suddenly the action is slowed down, and we wonder what the Holy Spirit is up to. That is resolved when Felix is replaced by a new governor, Festus, and Paul's Jewish opponents once more press charges against him. Paul defends himself quite successfully and refuses the offer of a trial in Jerusalem by appealing to Caesar.

So the journey towards Rome is resumed, with a brief pause for an encounter with King Agrippa, the grandson of Herod the Great, and his wife Bernice, who was Drusilla's sister and would later be mistress to the Emperor Titus. So we are on the shady edges of the Roman establishment.

Agrippa in effect finds Paul 'Not Guilty', as for a third time we are given the account of Paul's meeting with Jesus (26:2-23). This descendant of Herod, at home in both Jewish and Roman culture, points out that since he has appealed to

Caesar, that is where he must go. And the reader of Acts knows that this is where the Holy Spirit has been driving the narrative all this time. So that is where we are going, and that furnishes us with an adventurous couple of chapters, which I recommend that you read on your own. It includes the following events: a variety of boats that get them as far as Crete, then a warning from Paul that the boat is not going to make it. No one takes any notice, but he is proved right, and they are completely lost when hit by a storm, and Paul tells them what to do. After two weeks of helpless drifting they run aground on the island of Malta, as Paul had predicted, as the result of an encounter with the angel of the Lord (27:22-26).

The natives welcome them, and Paul has a narrow escape from a poisonous snake, which makes the Maltese think that he must be a god. Paul cures the father of the Number One person of the island, whose name is the admirably Roman one of Publius. Then they are on the final lap of the journey, when finally the Holy Spirit lands them up in Italy and in Rome. There Paul debates with his fellow Jews (the Holy Spirit still at work, you see), but finally the mission to the Gentiles is vindicated (28:28).

Then we come to the final words of Acts of the Apostles, which I should like to read with you:

[Paul] remained for two whole years at his own expense, and he gave hospitality to all those who journeyed in to him, announcing the kingdom of God, and teaching the things about the Lord Jesus Christ, with all confidence – and without being stopped.
(28:30, 31)

Questions

1. What is Luke's attitude to Judaism and to Roman culture?

2. Is it true to say that the Holy Spirit is driving the narrative of Acts?

3. Does Acts have anything to say to us today?

CHAPTER 31

The Book of Revelation: introduction

The book of Revelation, the last document in our New Testament and therefore in our Bible, is a most extraordinary piece of work. It is dramatic and mind-boggling, and has a vivid power of description, even when the reader is not quite sure what might be going on.

Readers are very often simply put off by the extravagant imagery and what they regard as savage predictions about the end of the world. My task, it seems, is to encourage you to read this extraordinary document (and indeed all the other 26 documents of the New Testament), and what I am proposing to do is to take you through the text to see what we can make of it, and why you might find it appropriate to read it today, without becoming too alarmed by it all.

The first thing to do is to see what kind of thing it might be, otherwise we can't possibly say anything sensible about it. So we consult the opening verse, and there we read what looks like the title of the work: 'an apocalypse'. Now that word means simply 'uncovering' in Greek, and its Latin equivalent is 'Revelation' (and this work is *never* to be called 'Revelations', in the plural, for there is just *one* revelation here). This is a technical term for a Jewish style of writing that often emerges in times of persecution, often written under a false name, though here the author is named as 'John', and there is no particular reason to doubt that attribution, since no particular John is named. Such documents, often called 'apocalyptic' (presumably because they sound a bit like this work) generally report visions of the heavenly world; sometimes with a heavenly guide to assist, they go in for quite extraordinary imagery and give the reader a glimpse of that other world. All that and more is going on here, but that does not mean we know what it is about.

Besides 'revelation' or 'apocalypse', another word that this document uses of itself, several times as a matter of fact, is 'prophecy' (you will find that it so describes itself at 1:3; 19:10; 22:7, 10, 18, 19). Now it is important to get the meaning of this word properly understood: prophecy is not prediction, foretelling the future, but speaking on behalf of God. So if you are looking for a timetable for the last days of the world, you are not going to find it here. Instead, you will do better to see it as a vision of God's view of the world, God's comment on what believers are suffering.

Another word often used by this text of itself is the word 'scroll'. This word is used five times, all of them in chapter 22, at the very end, so possibly we should not make too much of this. However, it might be good to recall that in the ancient world the ability to write and read was not as common as it is said to be in our world today, and for that reason alone there is power in the ability to make and to decipher intelligible marks on paper, the ability to make a 'scroll' into a medium for the propagation or exchange of knowledge. In this document that power may be said to offer encouragement to the persecuted Christians of Asia Minor, to whom it seems to be addressed.

There is another way in which this document understands itself, and that is as a kind of letter. Listen to this, from 1:1-8, which is clearly meant to sound like the kind of letter that would go round the ancient world:

> The revelation of Jesus Christ, which God gave him, to show his slaves what must speedily happen; and he signalled, sending through his messenger, to his slave John, who bore witness to the word of God and the witness of Jesus Christ the things that he saw. Congratulations to the one who reads and to those who hear the words of the prophecy, and who keep the things that are written in it – for the time is near.
>
> John: to the seven churches which are in Asia, grace to you and peace from The Is and The Was and the Coming One, and from the seven spirits which are before his throne, and from Jesus Christ, the witness, the reliable one, the firstborn from the dead, and the ruler of the kingdom of earth.
>
> To the one who loves us and freed us from our sins by his blood. And he made a kingdom for us, priests for his God and Father, to him be glory for ever and ever. Amen.
>
> Look! He is coming with the clouds
> and every eye shall see him
> including those who pierced him,
> and all the tribes of the earth shall mourn over him.
> Yes! Amen!
> I am the Alpha and the Omega, says the Lord God,
> The Is and the Was and the Coming One, the Almighty.
> (1:1-8)

In addition, as we shall shortly see, the text goes on in chapters 2 and 3 to produce no fewer than seven letters, to seven churches in Asia Minor (modern Turkey). They go to the following cities, and if you look at a map, you will see that they make a perfectly logical journey by good Roman roads; so we are to imagine the carrier of this letter going round by way of, in order: Ephesus, Smyrna, Pergamum, Thyatira, Sardis, Philadelphia, and Laodicea.

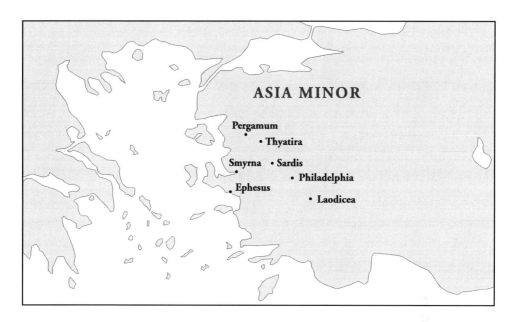

Now you may already know that the number seven, the number of perfection, is very important in Revelation, where we shall find, as well as our seven letters, seven stars, seven golden lampstands, seven seals, seven trumpets, seven thunders and seven plagues. So you may find yourself thinking that the seven cities to which the letters are sent are purely fictional, vehicles of the author's vision. But this is not the case. For one thing, as I have already indicated, the seven cities are real cities, linked by genuine Roman roads; and for another, the various snippets of information about the seven cities fit well enough with what we know about them from other sources.

What else can we say about the book before we start on our journey through it? Sometimes people like to deduce a good deal from its structure, but the difficulty with that is that no two scholars can be persuaded to agree on what the shape of it is. So perhaps we had better leave that question and simply go through the book, in the order that was presumably intended by the author, to see what we can make of it together.

We have already seen how it begins, and we looked at some of the implications of this for how we are supposed to read it. It is, we saw, from John; and now (1:9) we gather that he is in exile on the tiny island of Patmos 'because of the word of God and the witness of Jesus'. Then our attention is focused sharply, with a trumpet blast and a divine figure ('one like a son of man'), who describes himself (1:17, 18) as 'the first and the last and the Living One. And I was a corpse – and look! I am living for ages of ages.' It is clearly Jesus, but quite different from the Jesus who preached and taught in Galilee in the Gospels.

Then this apparition instructs John to convey the vision, which he now starts to do in the shape of the seven letters. They all have the same basic form: an address 'to the angel of the church in . . .'; then there is a series of possible titles of Jesus (for example, 'the one who holds the seven stars in his right hand', or 'the first and the last, who died but came to life'). This is then followed by an account of what that church has been up to, for weal and woe. Then comes a rebuke for what they have got wrong, and also some encouragement. Finally they are warned to hear what the Spirit says to the churches, and a promise is made about the reward for anyone who is victorious.

It is probably worth giving you an example of at least one of these letters, so here is the last one, that to Laodicea:

And to the angel of the church in Laodicea, write:
Thus says the Amen, the Reliable and True Witness,
the Beginning of God's creation:
I know your works, that you are neither cold nor hot;
I wish you were cold or hot;
and so, because you are lukewarm and neither hot nor cold,
I am about to vomit you out of my mouth, because you say,
'I am affluent and have become affluent, and I have no need',
and you do not realise that you are wretched and pitiable and destitute
and blind and naked, I am advising you to buy from me
gold that has been burnt in the fire that you may be affluent,
and white garments for you to wear,
so that the embarrassment of your nakedness should not appear,
and ointment to smear on your eyes that you may see.
I reprove and punish anyone whom I love;
so be committed and repent.
Look! I am standing at the door and knocking:
if anyone hears my voice and opens the door, then I shall come into them
and have supper with them, and they with me.
The one who conquers I shall allow to sit with me on my throne,
as I also have conquered and taken my seat with my Father on his throne.
Let the one who has ears listen to what the Spirit is saying to the churches.
(3:14-22)

So we are living in the real world, but we are permitted to hear God's comment on the situation.

Now we move into chapters 4 and 5, and here something remarkable happens, for we are invited to join the heavenly liturgy. The point of good liturgy is to enable us to plod on with a sense of where God is inviting us. Look at chapter 4, which starts with 'a door opened in heaven', and the visionary is invited, 'Come up here,' which causes him to 'be in the Spirit', sometimes translated as 'in a trance', and then we are offered a vision: 'Look! A throne in heaven, and on the throne One Sitting. And the One Sitting was like a vision, jasper and carnelian; and a rainbow around the throne like a vision of emerald.'

Clearly this is the throne of God, and 24 other thrones surround it, each with an elder in white garments and a gold crown. We allow our eyes to become accustomed to the brightness of the vision, and then we hear the singing that is going on:

'Holy, holy, holy is the Lord God the Almighty,
the Was and the Is and the Coming One.'

What is happening here is nothing less than the heavenly liturgy, worshipping the 'One who lives for ever and ever'.

Then, still as part of the liturgy, we are invited to look at the right hand of the Sitting One, and we see that it holds a scroll sealed with seven seals, and written on both sides (inside and on the back). Now the visionary looks to see who might open this sealed scroll, and his attention is directed to 'a Lamb standing as though slaughtered, with seven heads and seven eyes', who comes and takes the scroll 'from the right hand of the One Sitting on the throne'. This is the cue for more liturgical hymn-singing by massed choirs (ten thousand times ten thousand and a thousand times a thousand).

Now we follow the action, and we watch as the Lamb opens the first of the seven seals. The tension rises as he opens them, one after another, each one producing all kinds of highly symbolic effects. After this, we are made to wait for the seventh seal, and we are granted a vision of the people of God, 144,000 from the tribes of Israel and a number beyond counting for the rest of the world. All the time, the heavenly chorus continues its liturgical chant:

And they cry out in a loud voice, saying,
'Salvation to our God who sits on the throne,
and to the Lamb.'
And all the angels stood around the throne and the elders and the four
living creatures, and they fell down before the throne on their faces and
worshipped God, saying,
'Amen: blessing and glory and wisdom and thanksgiving
and honour and power and strength to our God for ever and ever. Amen.'
(7:10-12)

Then one of the elders gives the clue:

> These are those who come from the great tribulation,
> and have washed their robes and made them white in the Lamb's blood.
> Because of this they are before the Throne of God,
> and they worship him day and night in his Temple,
> and the One sitting on the Throne will pitch his tent upon them.
> They shall not be hungry any more, nor be thirsty any more,
> nor shall the sun fall upon them, nor any scorching,
> for the Lamb that is in the middle of the Throne shall shepherd them,
> and shall guide them to the springs of the waters of life,
> and God shall wipe every tear from their eyes.
> (7:14b-17)

And now at last we start to get the message: these are the persecuted, and the Lamb, who will now open the seventh seal, is going to shepherd them. The liturgy continues, with incense, the prayers of all the saints and a golden altar before the Throne.

Our vision is not ended, however, for after the seven seals there are to be seven trumpet blasts, heralding destruction (although we realise that it cannot be complete destruction, because God is in charge). Six of the trumpets are blown, and then we turn to seven thunders, but as our author hastens to write them down, he is told not to: 'Seal it up; do not write it down.' So we are not going to find out absolutely everything that is going on.

The vision rages on, and now we are suddenly in Jerusalem, where the 'two witnesses' (also known as the two olive trees and the two lampstands) are going to be killed by the beast who comes up from the abyss. Then, we learn,

> And their corpse shall be on the square of the Great City,
> which is called (spiritually) Sodom and Egypt,
> where their Lord was crucified.
> And they look where also their Lord was crucified,
> and some of the peoples and tribes and languages and nations
> look upon their corpse for three and a half days,
> and they do not allow their corpses to be placed in a tomb.
> And those who live on the earth rejoice over them and celebrate, and they
> shall send presents to each other,
> because these two prophets tormented those who dwell on the earth.
> And after the three and a half days,
> the spirit of life from God entered in them,
> and they stood on their feet and great fear fell upon those who saw them,
> and they heard a great voice from heaven saying to them, 'Come up here.'

And they went up to heaven on the cloud,
and their enemies saw them.
And at that hour there came a great earthquake,
and a tenth of the city fell, and there were killed by the earthquake
7000 names of human beings, and the rest became afraid,
and they gave glory to the God of heaven.
(11:8-13)

It would be idle to pretend that we know what is going on, but the point is that the liturgy shows us that God is in charge; everything that happens is known in advance, and that means that, somehow or other, all will be well.

Finally the seventh trumpet is blown, and we are given a glimpse of the Ark of the Covenant.

The drama continues, and we are introduced to a 'great sign in heaven' (12:1). The sign is one of conflict between a pregnant woman and a dragon:

And a great sign appeared in heaven,
a woman clothed with the sun, and the moon beneath her feet,
and on her head a crown of twelve stars,
and she was pregnant, and she cried out in her labour pains,
and she was in the agony of giving birth.
Then there appeared another sign in heaven,
and look! A dragon, great and fiery-red,
with seven heads and ten horns, and on these heads seven crowns.
And his tail wipes a third of the stars of heaven and flung them onto the earth.
Then the dragon stood in front of the woman who was about to give birth,
to devour her child when she should give birth.
And she gave birth to a male son,
who is going to shepherd all the nations with an iron rod.
And her child was snatched up to God, and to his throne.
And the woman fled into the desert,
where she has a place prepared by God,
to look after her for one thousand two hundred and sixty days.
(12:1-6)

What all of this means is that we are in the midst of a battle, but our liturgical glimpse of the truth is a guarantee that all will be well, and that Satan (whom we have not yet properly identified, other than as 'the great dragon, the Ancient Snake, the one called Devil and Satan') is to be flung down to the earth (12:9).

Then, just when we think we can see God's victory dawning, we notice (12:18) that the dragon is standing on the sand of the sea. Not only that, but in the very next verse there is 'a beast coming up out of the sea, with ten horns and seven heads and ten diadems on its head, and on its heads are blasphemous names' (13:1).

What is this beast? Well, it is for one thing a satanic parody of the Lamb, which, back in the liturgy of 5:6, had 'seven horns and seven eyes, which are the seven spirits of God'. So the beast is the Lamb's enemy, and the seven heads stand for the seven hills upon which Rome is built. This is therefore the Roman Empire by which the readers of this story are being persecuted. It also has 'authority', and 'opened its mouth for blasphemies'.

And what else? Well, listen to this:

And the whole earth went admiring after the Beast,
and they worshipped the Dragon, saying,
'Who is like the Beast, and who can make war on it?'
(13: 3b, 4)

And this:
And it was granted him to make war on the holy ones and to conquer them,
and he was granted authority
over every tribe and people and tongue and nation.
And all the dwellers on the earth shall worship him,
whose name is not written in the Book of Life of the Lamb
slaughtered before the creation of the world.
If anyone has an ear, let them pay attention.
(13:7-9)

It is a battle to the death between the followers of the Lamb (that is, those of us who are witnessing the heavenly liturgy) and the followers of the Roman Empire in its decadence, and its attempt to take on the role that is reserved to God alone. As we realise this, the narrator tells us:

This is wisdom. Let the one who has intelligence calculate the number of the beast. For it is the number of a human being – and his number is six hundred and sixty-six.
(13:18)

And here, almost certainly, we are talking of the talented but disappointing Emperor Nero, of whom the legend persisted after his suicide that he was after all still alive.

There is more to come.

Questions

1. Do you think it might, after all, be possible to read the book of Revelation?

2. Does the message that 'God is in charge' speak to us in our day, do you think?

3. Do you find the idea of Revelation as a 'heavenly liturgy' at all helpful?

CHAPTER 32

Revelation part 2

The story so far is that I have been suggesting that if you feel the book of Revelation is too bizarre to cope with, and if you feel that it threatens your sanity or your integrity so that you would be better off not reading it at all, then you should reconsider and think about whether after all it might be a good idea to read this extraordinary, and extraordinarily influential, document. (Have you ever thought why the word 'apocalyptic' has such resonances in our culture today, for example?)

To that end, we made our way through the first half of the Apocalypse, trying to see it for what it really is: a journey into hope, a liturgy, indeed a paying of attention to the heavenly liturgy, which reveals that God is after all in charge. In this chapter, which deepens our enquiry by going through the second half of the story, I am proposing to do more by way of reading from the text of the book, for in the case of the book of Revelation there is no substitute for getting to grips with what it actually says. In my experience, people have very often given up reading by the time that they get to this point of the book.

Just to get you back into the mood, I should like to read with you a key passage at the start of this second half of the document. You will find it at 14:1-5, and it goes like this:

> And I looked, and see! The Lamb standing on Mount Zion, and with him a hundred and forty-four thousand who have his name, and the name of his Father, written on their foreheads. And I heard a voice from heaven, like the voice of many waters, and like the voice of a great thunder. And the voice that I heard was of harpists, playing harp-melodies with their harps. And they sing a new song before the throne and before the four living creatures and the elders. And no one could learn the song except the one hundred and forty-four thousand, who have been purchased from the land. These are they who have not defiled themselves with women, for they are virgins. These are they who follow the Lamb wherever he goes. These ones were purchased from human beings, first fruits for God and for the Lamb. And in their mouth no falsehood is found – they are blameless.
> (14:1-5)

What is happening here, then, is that we are starting to see God's judgement visited on the enemy, who are code-named 'Babylon' (14:8), which is almost certainly Rome. The writer recognises that Christians are going to be martyred (14:13), but if you think that is an eccentric and masochistic view of Christianity, then you have not been reading the Gospels with sufficient attention. We should instead be heartened when we hear the author say, 'Blessed are they who die in the Lord,' for that is a mantra that has given courage to Christians all down the centuries; it is right at the heart of our faith. The point is that we are promised victory.

> And I saw something like a crystal sea mixed with fire, and those who are victorious over the Beast and over his likeness and over the number of his name, standing on the crystal sea, holding the harps of God. And they are singing the song of Moses, God's slave, and the song of the Lamb, as they say,
> 'Great and wonderful are your works,
> Lord God Almighty.
> Just and true are your ways,
> King of the nations.
> And who is not afraid, Lord,
> and [will not] glorify your name?
> For you alone are holy,
> and all the nations shall come and worship before you.
> For your righteous deeds have been made manifest.'
> (15:2-4)

After that we resume our series of sevens, with seven plagues and seven bowls, which you will find in chapter 16. Then we proceed to the picture of Rome as the 'Great Prostitute'. Feminist scholars sometimes profess themselves, understandably enough, a little uneasy at this apparent disparagement of women, but I don't think that is really the name of the game here. What is going on is a disparagement not of the weakest in society, but of the oppressor and the strong, that apparently unassailable Roman Empire under which they are suffering persecution. And how do we know it is Rome? I don't think there is much doubt about this, but you might like to look at the seven hills and ten kings (we shall come to this later on). There is going to be a battle, but the oppressed Christians are not to fear, for the Lamb (a symbol of vulnerability, of course) is going to win in the battle.

This is the truth that we start to hear in 18:2: 'Fallen, fallen is Babylon the Great!' Now you may feel uncomfortable at what is unmistakably gloating over the ancient enemy, but that may be because you have never known what it is like to be bullied by the more powerful. If you have had that experience, you may want to allow the singer some leeway here. Sometimes gloating is all that the oppressed can manage by way of resistance. Listen as the visionary depicts all the commercial and marine interests lamenting the destruction of Rome in chapter 18, and try to feel what it was like for those at the bottom of the heap.

Then, to make them feel stronger, we are offered the vision of Christ fighting the enemy:

> And I saw the heaven opened, and look! A white horse, and the one sitting upon it was called 'Reliable' [or 'Faithful'] and 'True'. And with righteousness he will judge and make war. His eyes are like a flame of fire, and on his head there are many crowns, with a name written which no one but he himself knows. And he is wearing a garment dipped in blood. And his name was called 'The Word of God'. And the armies in heaven followed him on white horses. They were dressed in pure white linen; and out of his mouth comes a sharp sword, in order that he might strike the nations with it. And he shall shepherd them with an iron staff. And he shall tread the winepress of the wine of the anger of the rage of God the Almighty. And he has on his garment and on his thigh a name written: 'King of kings and Lord of lords'.
> (19:11-16)

The enemy is going to be defeated, but it will not be a simple once and for all victory. At first it will be only for a thousand years (you might think that quite long enough to be going along with, but you have not quite grasped what is happening here). After that, Satan will emerge from prison and be finally defeated (20:14). If it seems a long way off, then that is so as not to offer an unrealistic source of hope.

> And I saw thrones, and they sat upon them, and judgement was given them. And the souls of those who had been beheaded because of [their] witness to Jesus, and those who had not worshipped the Beast, nor his likeness, and who had not accepted the mark on their forehead and on their hand.
> And they lived and reigned for a thousand years with the Christ.
> The rest of the dead did not come to life until the thousand years were completed. This is the first Resurrection. Happy and holy is the one who has part in the first Resurrection. Over people like this the second death has no power – they shall be priests of God and of his Christ, and shall reign with him for a thousand years.
> (20:4-6)

We need to be aware, though, that the sigh of relief that we hear at this point is because the readers of this extraordinary text are in a really bad way, and cannot see any hope at all. That is why Apocalypse offers no easy answers. So in 20:7-10, when our visionary speaks of Gog and Magog, and the size of the army that opposes us and attacks the 'camp of the holy ones', we are meant to feel the note of realism, and to recognise our apparently impossible situation. But we are invited to be certain that the victory is coming.

Now we are coming to the end of the story, and we are offered a beautiful vision:

> And I saw a new heaven and a new earth.
> For the first heaven and the first earth had gone away,
> and the sea was no more.
> And I saw the holy city, new Jerusalem, coming down out of heaven,
> made ready like a bride made up for her husband. And I heard a great voice
> from the throne saying,
>> Look! God's tent with human beings,
>> and God will pitch his tent with them, and they shall be God's peoples,
>> and God shall be with them, as their God.
>> And God will wipe away every tear from their eyes,
>> and Death shall be no more,
>> nor shall mourning nor weeping nor suffering be any more,
>> for the first things have gone away.
> (21:1-4)

Notice how this reading is absolutely redolent of Scripture, what we should call the 'Old Testament', even though it is not always possible to be certain which particular bits of Scripture are being cited or alluded to. The message for the persecuted Christians is that we are here speaking the old story of God's people, and their certainty that God is incapable of letting them down, no matter how grim things may seem to be. So when the One Sitting on the Throne despatches 'cowards and faithless people and the defiled and murderers and those who commit sexual immorality and who use drugs and witchcraft and all liars – their portion is in the burning lake of fire and sulphur, which is the second death', when we hear that, it is not, as religious people all too often take biblical statements of that sort to be, an invitation to rejoice in the fate of the ungodly. For Scripture is interested not in punishing the wicked, but in offering hope to the oppressed and marginalised. That is what the book of Revelation is about.

You can see something of this in this next piece, about the 'Bride of the Lamb'. Now the bride is us, those who belong to the Church, and, as you will see, we are not being invited to gloat; instead, we are being encouraged to keep going:

'Come here: I am going to show you the Bride, the wife of the Lamb.' And he took me away in the Spirit, to a great and high mountain, and he showed me the holy city, Jerusalem, coming down out of Heaven from God, with the glory of God. Its radiance was like a most precious stone, like a jasper stone, clear as crystal. It had a great and high wall, with twelve gates, and on the gates twelve angels, and names written, which are the names of the twelve tribes of the children of Israel: three gates on the East and three gates on the North and three gates on the South and three gates on the West. And the wall had twelve foundation-stones, and on them twelve names, of the twelve apostles of the Lamb.
(21:9b-14)

And there you have it – the completeness of the city, and a glimpse of something that the holy city offers: security and illumination. And there is something else – there is no Temple there: a secularist's dream, you may think, a land without churches. But listen to why this is so:

And I saw no Temple in the city.
For the Lord God Almighty is its Temple – and the Lamb.
And the city has no need of sun or moon to shine on it.
For the glory of God gave it light, and its lamp was the Lamb.
And the nations shall walk by its light.
And the kings of the earth bring their glory into it.
And its gates shall not be closed by day, for there shall be no night there.
And they shall bring the glory and honour of the nations into it,
and no profane thing shall ever enter into it,
nor anyone who performs an abomination or falsehood,
but only those who are written in the Lamb's scroll of life.
(21:22-27)

Notice, once again, that the attention is not given to the punishment of the wicked nearly as much as to the radiant vision of hope for the persecuted. That vision is beautifully expressed in an ancient biblical metaphor of 'water of life'. And I have to say that, until you have seen a really dry land and the effect that a little water can have on it, you have not really understood the hope that this image can offer to those who are struggling with life.
Here is the vision:

And he showed me the river of the water of life, bright as crystal,
coming out of the throne of God and of the Lamb,
in the middle of its square and of the river, on this side and that,

the tree of life yields twelve fruits, each one giving its fruit each month, and
the leaves of the tree are for healing the nations.
And there shall no longer be any accursed thing,
and the throne of God and of the Lamb shall be within it,
and his slaves shall worship him.
And they shall see his face, and his name shall be on their foreheads.
That night shall be no more;
and they have no need for the light of a lamp and the light of the sun,
for the Lord God shall shed light upon them,
and they shall reign for ever and ever.
(22:1-5)

What, then, are you and I to do with this prophecy (remembering that it is
not meant to be a prediction)? The author concludes by suggesting no fewer
than four ideas.

First, we are to keep the message of the prophecy (22:7). So we need to read
it and learn from it and give it reality by the way we live.

Second, it is our task to worship God (22:7). It is astonishing how very often
we believers need to be reminded of that essential fact of our existence. It is easily
forgotten, and we drift into overlooking the reality of God. Sometimes we think
to ourselves that we shall be free if only we can do that. We are fooling ourselves,
however, for what happens when we stop worshipping God is not that we can
put ourselves in the centre of our existence, but that we select some other 'god'.
Such a 'god' might be success or fame or power or wealth or that very beautiful
car that we saw in the advertisement last night, or that very beautiful woman
whom we passed in the street, or that high-grade heroin that we have just been
offered. None of these is real, at least not in the sense that they will give us the
freedom and happiness that we think they promise. If we give ourselves over to
any of them, we shall find that they enslave us rather than set us free, whereas if
we become slaves of the Living God, we discover that our slavery is in fact a most
unexpected freedom, that for which we were designed and created.

Then the third thing that we have to do is to recognise Jesus, who comes to
us every day in unexpected guises, and whose only desire is to set us free and
make us genuinely become who we could be. So we hear him say, 'Look – I am
coming soon, and my reward is with me, to pay back each one in accordance
with what they do' (22:12).

Fourth, we may have to recognise that if we follow the road to which Revelation
invites us, there will be suffering ahead. It was true for Jesus, it was true for those
for whom this text was originally written and, as you are probably already aware,
it will be true for you. If that is the case, then you should be encouraged when

you hear Jesus proclaim, 'Congratulations to those who washed their garments, that they may have authority for the tree of life, and that they may enter the city by its gates' (22:14).

And there is one more thing that we are invited to do, to ask for Jesus to come: join in the song of the Spirit and the Bride:

> They say, 'Come!' And let the one who hears say, 'Come!' And let the one who is thirsty come; let the one who wishes accept the water of life for free. (22:17)

Then we are offered the final prayer for those who hear and read this text: 'The grace of the Lord Jesus be with everybody.'

So there you are. That is the end of this remarkable book. I hope that by now you may be seeing that it is neither as bizarre nor as repellent as you may have feared, but in fact it offers a beautiful vision of hope, one that has not lost its relevance in our present darkened age but speaks loud and clear and offers us a beam of radiant light in our darkened world. Read it, and be inspired.

Now I should like to finish by returning to where we started, to the very beginning of this book, and to read its splendid opening, in the hope that you will feel more attuned now to its message:

> The revelation of Jesus Christ, which God gave him, to show his slaves what must speedily happen; and he signalled, sending through his messenger, to his slave John, who bore witness to the word of God and the witness of Jesus Christ the things that he saw. Congratulations to the one who reads and to those who hear the words of the prophecy, and who keep the things that are written in it – for the time is near.
>
> John: to the seven churches which are in Asia, grace to you and peace from The Is and The Was and The Coming One, and from the seven spirits which are before his throne, and from Jesus Christ, the witness, the reliable one, the firstborn from the dead, and the ruler of the kingdom of earth.
>
> To the one who loves us and freed us from our sins by his blood. And he made a kingdom for us, priests for his God and Father, to him be glory for ever and ever. Amen.
>
> Look! He is coming with the clouds
> and every eye shall see him
> including those who pierced him,
> and all the tribes of the earth shall mourn over him.
> Yes! Amen!
> I am the Alpha and the Omega, says the Lord God,
> The Is and the Was and the Coming One, the Almighty.
> (1:1-8)

Questions

1. Do you think it is possible to read the book of Revelation today?

2. Do you find in this text a helpful vision?

3. Does Revelation assist you to see God at work in your life?

CHAPTER 33

Who needs the Old Testament?

Since at least the second century AD there has been a tendency among some
Christians to think that we don't need the Old Testament any more, now that
we have the New Testament. Jewish friends point out, courteously, that it is
neither Old (for it contains the undying freshness of God) nor a Testament,
since it is not the last wishes of a person who is dying.

What is it that causes people to try and give up on the Old Testament? They
will give you all kinds of excuses; they will allege, for example, that it is long
and boring. Long it certainly is, but if you think it is boring, you have not been
paying attention. Others will say that the Old Testament presents a very bad-
tempered God, or one who petulantly demands that his enemies are butchered,
or selfishly insists that he is the only 'god' in town, when everyone knows that
there are really lots of them.

Then there are other people who will tell you that the Old Testament is
against all the discoveries of modern science, and that it is 'all about the world
being created in six, or possibly seven, days'. That, of course, is a sure sign of a
lazy reader; it is certain to be someone who has got as far as page 1 and become
fed up and looked no further.

As a matter of fact, if you really want a sensible place to start, look at the psalms,
the hymnbook of the Temple, and see the wide range of emotions and feelings that
are there, the innermost thoughts of a people utterly in love with its God, and able
to sing songs of anger, joy, praise, gratitude and misery. Or there are hymns to God
the creator, royal songs for the coronation of a king, historical songs that tell the
story of what God has done for Israel's past, and some hymns written especially for
use in the Temple liturgy, as well as one or two written to instruct God's people in
the wisdom that they needed. There is the clue: anything that narrows the scope of
our Scriptures, whether what we call the Old Testament or what we call the New
Testament, is missing the point. All human life is there, and what we have to fear
above all is not the wrath of God but the woodenness of the servants of God, and
sometimes also the woodenness of their opponents.

It is hard to be sure when it started, this sense that the Old Testament is 'not
for us'. There is not a hint of it in the New Testament, for the New Testament
authors are utterly at home in Israel's Scriptures, and they know how much
they matter. Certainly an early example was the second-century radical known
as Marcion. As far as we can learn from those who were his opponents, this

221

wealthy ship-owner rejected the Old Testament God and thought that Jesus revealed a different God, one who was better able to cope with the world, and that Old Testament theology could not be reconciled with that of the New Testament. What is significant for our purposes is that Marcion found himself unable to accept much of the New Testament either: a slimmed-down version of the Gospel of Luke and just ten of the Pauline epistles was all that was left after he had applied the razor.

We have to be grateful to him, of course, since his observations and his stern views on Scripture meant that Catholic Christians were, in that second century, forced to ask themselves the all-important question of which documents were and which were not part of the New Testament canon, and the related question of which documents should be accepted in the Old Testament (for the Greek and the Hebrew canons were different in some ways). One of the things that was undoubtedly going on in Marcion was more than a touch of anti-Jewish feeling, something that has bedevilled Christians down the centuries ever since. It does us little credit, though, for the idea that Jesus' beautiful doctrine replaces the gnarled old religion that had outlived its usefulness actually takes no notice at all of the New Testament and the way it operates.

It was, we have to admit, doctrines of that sort that led to the tragic work of evil known as the Holocaust, and for that reason alone that they must be rejected. But in any case, people who pursue this line of the uselessness of the Old Testament have not paid any attention at all to the New Testament.

So, what about the Old Testament? To start our enquiry, I should like to make four important points. The first is this: all those first characters whom we encounter in the New Testament and who follow Jesus are Jews, including, of course, Jesus himself. Jesus appears as harbinger of a reform movement within Judaism, asserting, in good biblical fashion, the fatherhood of the one and only one God. Those whom he gathered round him were all good Jews, who owned and loved the Hebrew Scriptures as part of their heritage, though they may not have been able to read.

Secondly, it is important to say that every one of our New Testament authors, like Jesus, leans heavily on the Old Testament for their landmarks on the journey to God, and depends on it in order to find their bearings in talking about Jesus.

Thirdly, if you feel that the Old Testament is perhaps a bit daunting for you, it may be best to start with those parts of it that Jesus clearly relished. The Psalms would be good, and that wide-ranging and multifarious scroll to which we give the umbrella title of the 'Prophet Isaiah'.

Fourthly, once you start playing Marcion's game and cutting out the Old Testament, you very soon find that you have absolutely nothing left. And it is not just a matter of obvious Old Testament quotations, nor even of just allusions; it is, rather, that the Old Testament (and I wish we had a better term for it) creates a whole world in which Jesus and his disciples (then and now) operate, a backcloth against which the drama is played out, a source for all their efforts to try and make sense of life.

The first thing to grasp is that we cannot even begin to understand Jesus except against the background of the story of God and of the people of God, as we have frequently remarked in the course of this book. Jesus will certainly have been circumcised within a week of his birth; Jesus is often seen in the synagogue on the Sabbath day; indeed, it would not cross his mind to be anywhere else.

So from the very beginning Jesus reveals himself as a faithful son of Israel. Jesus knows the Scriptures by heart, like all good Jews. That is how he is able to make that devastating response to the Sadducees which is recorded at Mark 12:18-27. You remember the story: this group, which more or less represented the Temple aristocracy and the priests, and who believed only in the five books of Moses, the Torah or the first five books in the Old Testament, tried to prove that Jesus was wrong about the resurrection by asking a very silly trick question about a woman who was married to a series of brothers under the rules of the levirate. Triumphantly, after setting up the narrative and telling the story at immense length, they ask him (12:23), 'In the "resurrection", whose wife is she going to be?' and remind him that in terms of the story she had been wife to no fewer than seven of them.

Jesus' response is admirably biblical, and decidedly brisk: 'Is not this the reason that you go wandering off? That you do not know the Scriptures or the power of God?' Jesus himself was enormously aware of God's power and profoundly acquainted with Scripture. Briefly and dismissively he answers the trick question: 'After the resurrection they don't marry or get married; instead, they are like the angels in heaven.' Then, having left their argument threadbare, he goes right to the heart of the matter with a brilliant and original argument from Scripture: 'With regard to the dead getting raised, did you never read' (and no doubt they will have expected him to mention one of the books whose canonicity they will have disputed) 'in the book of Moses' (that is to say, in their precious Torah) 'in the episode of the bush' (which every good Jew will have been able to place at Exodus 3) 'how God spoke to him saying, "I am the God of Abraham and the God of Isaac and the God of Jacob"?' And, triumphantly, Jesus concludes, 'God is not the God of the dead, but of the living.' Then, having wiped the floor with them, he concludes, 'You are very much astray.' Such a response is only conceivable for one who has the Scripture at his fingertips and has reflected on it at length.

If we can judge by what emerges in the Gospels, in particular Jesus was at home in the psalms, which we have already seen to be Israel's hymnbook, and in Isaiah. For a lovely example of his citing Isaiah, you might like to look at the story of what he did in the synagogue in Nazareth (Luke 4:14-21), where he has that splendid text from Isaiah 61:

> 'The Spirit of the Lord is upon me, therefore he has anointed me; he has sent me to preach good news to the poor, to proclaim liberty to captives and sight to the blind . . . to proclaim the acceptable year of the Lord.'

Luke reports that 'the eyes of all in the synagogue were looking intently at him' (as indeed are ours as we contemplate the scene). Then we hear his sermon, the shortest in history: 'Today this Scripture has been fulfilled in your hearing.' Now you might want to argue that this is just Luke's particular angle, but all the Gospels have Jesus preaching in synagogues, and this is just such an example of originality and relevance as you might expect from someone so thoroughly grounded in the Scriptures.

And references to the psalms come pouring from Jesus' lips. For example, in the Sermon on the Mount Jesus effortlessly quotes Psalm 6:8: 'Away from me, all you evil-doers' (Matthew 7:23). Likewise at Matthew 21:16, when the high priests and scribes are shocked at the Palm Sunday cry of 'Hosanna to the Son of David', Jesus instinctively quotes Psalm 8:3: 'out of the mouths of babes and sucklings'.[3] And at Matthew 16:26, when Jesus asks, 'What shall a person give as a ransom for his life?', he is quoting Psalm 49:7-9. For that reason one is not surprised to hear the themes of Psalm 22, 'My God, my God, why have you abandoned me?' as Jesus is on his cross, faithfully approaching death. Even if it did not happen precisely as Mark recounts in his telling of the Passion (15:34), it is clear that this is the world where Jesus belongs.

Nor is it just Jesus. His followers, trying to make sense of his story and to find meaning in it, had to go to the Scriptures in which he and they had been brought up. They had nowhere else to go, not least because the story of Jesus was so clearly the story of God. Those texts, which Luke calls the Law and the Prophets and the Psalms (Luke 24:44), represented the inherited wisdom of their culture, the only place to look if they were going to find out what to say about Jesus and the people of God.

There are many examples of this. Paul, exploring the mystery of Jesus with his converts, can hardly write a sentence without mentioning his beloved Jesus. Equally, he can hardly write a sentence without quoting what I shall continue to call the 'Old Testament'. He even does this when talking to his Corinthians, who seem to have been Gentiles rather than Jews. Trying to stop those Corinthians

---

3. In some versions of the Bible, this may be verse 2 of Psalm 8. Some translations enumerate the psalms rather differently, including the headings (as does the Hebrew versification).

from fighting each other, in the very first chapter of his correspondence with them, and to prevent them boasting, he says, very firmly, 'As it is written, let the one who boasts, boast in the Lord' (1 Corinthians 1:31).

The remarkable thing to notice is that Paul, devout monotheist as he was, and steeped in the Hebrew Scripture, is not afraid to use divine language of Jesus. Possibly the best-known example is the famous hymn to Christ in Philippians 2:9-11, where he says of Jesus:

> God . . . gave him the free gift of the name that is above every name, that at the name of Jesus every knee should bend, of those in heaven and on the earth and under the earth, and every tongue confess that Jesus Christ is Lord, to the glory of God the Father.

Interestingly, the hymn here is quoting Isaiah 45, which, as all good Jews will have known, is a hymn to the one and only one God. It is in that context that Jesus is given this remarkable equality with God. And it is significant that Paul is probably quoting an existing text, which means that he was not the first devout Jew to use divinity language of Jesus.

You will find another, very daring, example of Paul doing the same sort of thing at 1 Corinthians 8:6. In constructing an argument about what to do with food offered to idols, Paul quotes the Shema, the Jewish prayer that asserts that the Lord your God is one and only one God, but he makes a subtle change, so that 'we have one God – the Father' is split from 'and one Lord, Jesus Christ, through whom everything comes, and we are through him'. This is a very daring move, but only a committed Jew brought up in the Old Testament could possibly make it.

Then there is the Gospel of Mark. It starts in a deeply scriptural way, calling Jesus 'Son of God', and then explicitly citing Isaiah. Mark even plays a little joke with his scripturally minded readers because the lines he then quotes (Mark 1:2) are not from Isaiah at all, initially, but from Malachi or Exodus.

Matthew does the same, only more consistently than Mark. We could take many examples, but one of the most striking is the way in which his first two chapters stress the way in which Jesus brings the Hebrew Scriptures to their proper fulfilment. He does this in two ways: first by outlining a possible genealogy of Jesus, divided quite explicitly into three groups of 14 (double the perfect number, as we saw in a previous chapter), and covering the high and low points of the history of Israel down to its climax in Jesus Christ. The second way that he does it, of course, is by emphasising, almost to a fault, the phrase, 'This whole thing happened in order that it might be fulfilled what was spoken by the Lord through the prophet.' This is the fullest version of that particular idea (Matthew 1:22), but you will also find the same idea at 2:5, 15, 17, 23.

Indeed, the whole atmosphere of those first two chapters is redolent of the Hebrew Scriptures: the presence, for example, of a dreamer called Joseph, or the references in 2:13-15 to Israel's Exodus. There is no real way to understand the opening of the first Gospel except against an Old Testament background. And it is not just in the Infancy Narratives: if you can get hold of one of those Bibles with scriptural cross references on the side of the page, see how many allusions and quotations there are in Matthew. Look particularly at the Sermon on the Mount (chapters 5–7) for its setting in the Hebrew Scriptures, especially at 5:17, where we read, 'Do not think that I came to destroy the Law or the Prophets; I did not come to destroy but to fulfil.'

For Matthew, it is of immense importance that Jesus is the high point of what God has been doing with the people, and that is why we hear a hint of autobiography at 13:52, when at the end of the parable discourse Matthew's Jesus is heard to say that 'every scribe discipled in the kingdom of the heavens is like a man, a householder, who brings out of his treasure chest new things and old'.

Luke's Gospel is a different sort of thing and has a different feel to it, but just look at how it begins. Luke, for example, deliberately uses the language of the Greek Old Testament (phrases that come into English, for example, as something like 'it came to pass', which give the narrative a biblical flavour). Why does he do this if not to locate Jesus firmly in the background provided by the story of God's people? Examples abound in Luke, but you might think of those couples who come straight from the pages of the Old Testament, like Zachary and Elisabeth, or Simeon and Hanna, or indeed Mary and Joseph themselves. Mary deals obediently with the angel Gabriel, who also belongs in the setting of the Hebrew Scriptures, as does the story of Lazarus in Abraham's bosom that we find at Luke 16. And when Luke mentions Caesar Augustus in chapter 2, or Tiberius and Pontius Pilate and the various tetrarchs who took over the power from Herod at the beginning of chapter 3, it is only so that the reader can be brought smartly to attention by the fact that 'the word of God came' to none of these, but 'to John the son of Zachary in the desert', which is then underpinned with an explicit quotation from Isaiah.

So even Luke sees Jesus against his Old Testament background, and never pretends that anything else is conceivable.

For John's Gospel, this claim hardly needs proving. That majestic prologue presents us with a Jesus who is in a profound relationship with the One who is obviously the Old Testament God. There is only one God, it says, and that is the God of life, which is a very Jewish thing to say. Like Paul, it is into that context that John sets Jesus, as someone who is intimately related to God and yet different from God. But the way he does this bears no relationship at all to the way in which pagan authors would deal with their deities. This is the

God of the Old Testament, and Jesus' mysterious identity is set out in precisely that context. So when at John 8:58 Jesus annoys his Jewish interlocutors by claiming that 'before Abraham was, I AM', and they pick up stones to kill him, we understand why they do it, because both sides of this debate are Jews, having a very Jewish, if also very irascible, debate about the nature of God.

Only Jews could understand what Jesus is talking about when he calls God his 'Father' and claims a certain identity with God (if also a certain difference). We cannot really understand the fourth Gospel except against the background offered by the Scriptures. Jesus, for John, is what the Old Testament God would look like in the unlikely event of our being able to see him. And there we are, straight back in the world of Exodus 33:18-20, where Moses was not permitted to see God's glory but was permitted to see the divine back. Contrast that with the last words of the prologue of John's Gospel: 'God – no one has ever seen; the one and only God who is in the bosom of the Father, that one has explained him.'

One other example among many will have to do: the extraordinary letter to the Hebrews trying to find the right way to talk about Jesus. We cannot possibly make sense of this elevated theological treatise (it is not really a letter) unless we are prepared to accept all the Old Testament background and the scriptural allusions that it employs in its attempt to get Jesus right, and to demonstrate that Jesus is indeed the Real Thing. Only a great Jewish thinker could have written this document, and it is an extraordinary way of doing justice to the thoroughly Jewish identity of Jesus. All the arguments about the Levitical priesthood, that intricate exegesis of Psalm 95 and the role of Melchizedek are impossible except for someone utterly at home in the Old Testament.

And, of course, there is the book of Revelation. We have not here the space to go through it, but let me simply point out that it has been calculated that there are more citations, allusions or references to the Old Testament than there are verses in the book. It is unimaginable except in a Jewish setting.

Questions

1. Do you agree that the New Testament is unthinkable without the Old Testament?

2. Is it possible to have a non-Jewish Jesus?

3. Why do you think people try to get rid of the Old Testament?

CHAPTER 34

What about inspiration, then?

Sometimes people are a little worried by the line of thinking that we have been taking in the course of this book – that, for example, the divine authors of the New Testament can make mistakes, or that they think (incorrectly, of course) that the sun goes round the world, or that we might not be able to get back to what Jesus originally said or did. Do different accounts of, for example, the Sermon on the Mount, or the feeding of the multitudes, or the Resurrection appearances, mean that it is all a pack of lies?

Probably the difficulty here runs something like this: if the texts are inspired, does that not mean that they are the word of God, and if they are the word of God, how can their authors possibly make mistakes and be proven fallible? Well, of course, it depends what we mean by 'inspiration'. It has to be said that there are many different things that we might mean by 'inspiration'. One particular understanding of the term is almost a matter of dictation, so that we have to imagine the Holy Spirit whispering in the ear of the Gospel writers, who obediently write down everything that they have been told. If we think about it, that is not a very probable way for God to proceed, even though when we were young we likely thought that inspiration was something very much like that.

Press it a bit, however, and we start to see some difficulties. For example, when you were young, you probably thought that St Paul or the Gospel writers probably wrote in English (or whatever was the language you heard in church or in which you had Bible stories read to you at home). Think about it and you will realise that that was not the case, so if you read the Bible in any language other than Greek for the New Testament or Greek, Aramaic or Hebrew for the Old Testament, you are dependent on a translator. And, if we are thinking about the doctrine of inspiration, are we to suppose that Bible translators are inspired?

There is a serious danger here of a rather magical view of Bible inspiration. I remember a student of mine trying to tell me why he could no longer attend services in a particular church. The reason was, he said, 'I have been reading my Bible, and I realise that God is opposed to . . .' I can't now remember what God was opposed to, but it may have been something like homosexuality or women priests, and he felt that the particular church was peddling non-biblical attitudes to that issue. But do you see what he understood by inspiration? It was that there is a proposition, X, of which it is true to say, 'The Bible says X', and the Bible is inspired and therefore X is true. In this particular case, I suspect that what had happened was that my student had an existing view on the issue in question, and that enabled him to find just the right sort of passage to defend his view and triumphantly to proclaim that 'the Bible says . . .'. In my experience, on most occasions when people claim that 'the Bible says', it turns out to do nothing of the kind, or at least not in any unnuanced way.

The fact is that this attitude cannot easily deal with an important but perhaps rather surprising fact – namely, that we do not necessarily know as much about 'what the Bible says' as we think we do. For, obviously, most of us are dependent on translators, and sometimes (the Old Testament scholars estimate as much as 30 per cent of the time) it is impossible to be sure of the translation. Equally obviously, we are dependent on manuscripts: we have more than 5000 for the New Testament, and each of them is different. So we cannot be sure of the 'original version'.

Inspiration, you see, simply cannot be a matter of magic, if it is to be of any use to us. So perhaps we might look at another possibility for what we might mean by this difficult word 'inspiration'. Perhaps we might understand it in terms of 'commitment'. By that I mean not that the readers or hearers of the word are committed, important though that is, but that the Word is committed, that in the pages of the Bible the Divine and Loving Mystery, whom we call by the deceptively simple name of God, is reaching out to God's beloved humanity. In ways we cannot quite understand, the mystery reveals itself to us, and (of course) leaves us free to accept or reject what it reveals.

In what we call the Bible, this Loving Mystery tells its story, in all sorts of different ways, in songs and in narratives (especially narratives) and in regulations for eating. But in all these millions of words which make up the Bible that you have on your desk, or by your bed, there is, we must always remember, only one Word, and that is the single word that God unceasingly and faithfully addresses to his beloved humanity, and to those portions of humanity who are singled out to be the people of God.

This means that perhaps the word 'Bible' is not after all a very helpful term, since using that word makes it sound as though all the many texts of which the Bible is composed are all the same sort of thing, and to be understood in each case in exactly the same way. Yet the mystery reveals itself in many different ways. However, I think it may be important to continue using the word 'Bible', and the reason is this: there is something special about the many different texts that make up our Bible, and we need to be clear about what that 'something' is. My claim is that in the lines of the text that we hear or read there is a privileged means of access to the unending mystery of God, and that therefore the Bible is different from any other text that we might ever read.

So there is only one Word, but fallible human beings write down this word, and each of these authors has their own set of limitations and their own particular viewpoint, which scholars can, as we have seen, fairly easily detect in the different books that compose our Bible. What happens, though, is that in these many different approaches to God, God's word gradually makes itself heard. This does not happen all at once but over many different centuries, in the richness of the joint vision of many different human beings, brought together by God, as a great conductor brings together an orchestra that is in constant danger of sinking into dissonance. And that single self-revealing word of God gradually reveals the mystery, though the mystery can never be exhausted, never fully revealed, and we must always be ready, thanks to the undying freshness of God, to apprehend the mystery from a different perspective.

Does that mean that doctrine changes in the course of time? Well, yes and no. What does not change is that the mystery of love is right at the heart of existence. But then human beings, with their God-given intellect, start to question earlier solutions. Consider the mystery of what happens when life comes to an end, as it will at some point for all of us. The most obvious answer is nothing: look at dead bodies and we see that once the life has left them, they rapidly start to decompose, more rapidly in the heat of the Middle East than in colder countries. So one solution, the earliest in the Bible, to what happens after death is that your memory lives on in your children and grandchildren. That is not a bad solution.

But then the problem arises, in the minds of questioning authors like Ecclesiastes[4] about whether this solution really works. Some people, it seems, die absurdly young, and you can't say that they 'deserved it', because very often that is not in fact the case. One option is to abandon faith in the divine mystery, but those of questing intellect who feel unable to accept that solution, because they live so close to that mystery, are driven to find another solution.

So we see, over the course of the Old Testament, an evolution of beliefs. Job says (though we may not know exactly what he means by it), 'I know that my Redeemer liveth', and we applaud the insight: that God is God, however difficult things may seem to be. The psalmists lament the inevitability of death and feel permitted to complain against God. Then things evolve, and later in the history of Judaism they move towards the idea of life beyond death. This is already clear in 2 Maccabees, which means that it was in the wind earlier, and it becomes crystal clear in a work like the book of Wisdom, which was being composed perhaps at about the time when Jesus was exercising his mission, and which offers a full-blown account of life continuing in a deeper way after our present bodies die.

---

4. Or *Qoheleth*, as it is known in Hebrew. Both words mean 'Preacher', which is not a bad name for this author.

Once we come to the New Testament, of course, the Resurrection of Jesus makes all the difference, as we shall see in the next chapter, even though we still may not fully understand the nature of this post-death existence of his (or of ours).

Do you see what is going on? The unfailing inspiration of God's one Word speaks into our situation and encourages us to reflect on doctrines and beliefs that we have held as certain, and to undo the woodenness and rigidity that we sometimes bring to our beliefs. Can you think of apparently unchanging religious beliefs that the divine mystery may be today asking us to rephrase and understand afresh? And if that is the invitation of God, does this inspiration mean that we are being unfaithful if we contemplate new ways of expressing the mystery (for example, of love in domestic life) under the guidance of God's undying freshness? I raise these questions not to shake your faith, but simply to raise the possibility that inspiration may be something far deeper and wider than we sometimes imagine.

So a truly respectful understanding of inspiration means that we have to recognise the wide range of documents in which the mystery presents itself in our Bible. It is not respectful to read the stories of the book of Genesis in the same way as we read the multifarious songs in the book of Psalms, or the regulations about eating and drinking and dealing with lepers and widows and orphans that we find throughout the biblical texts. Each different document has its own way of being read, and in each of them the inspiration of God means that they can speak to us in a number of different ways, not all of them being precisely what the original human author might have expected.

Inspiration, that is to say, means that God's view of our world becomes slowly, and in each generation freshly, accessible to human beings, ever clearer as time goes on. And that means that the doctrine of the Holy Spirit, so closely linked to our word 'inspiration', is of immense importance. The 'Spirit of God' is already there in the Hebrew Scriptures, but something happens to that in the New Testament, where the Holy Spirit becomes a potent force. In the book of Revelation, John the Elder is 'in the Spirit'. In Matthew and Luke the Spirit is the Father of Jesus. In John's Gospel the Spirit is described, in a brilliant and powerful innovation, as the 'Paraclete', which means something like 'Counsel for the Defence', the attorney who stands at your side in court, and it may also be understood as the 'Comforter'. What we are talking about here, you see, is the undying and fresh presence of the God who is Loving Mystery, guiding our steps on the journey. And because God is God, we cannot make any progress into the mystery unless God is beside us and within us and ahead of us; and that is 'inspiration'.

But wait a minute, you cry! Surely God can self-reveal in all circumstances? Isn't it possible for people to come into a glimpse of the mystery of God through a beautiful sunset, a snowstorm or the love of another person? Are these not all ways of coming to terms with the mystery of life? That is true, of course, but it can only go so far, for the real God is beyond our human resources, and will always remain so. A friend of mine, who has been on a long and painful journey with God, put it recently to me, 'I am fairly sure that when we die, we shall discover that God is still a mystery – and that it is all right.' So a uniquely Catholic position is, as Catholic positions tend to be, the 'both-and', rather than the 'either/or'. So, yes, you can indeed see the mystery of God in a raindrop shining on a leaf, and you can call that inspiration, but the mystery of God (both-and, you see) also deliberately reveals itself in the pages penned or dictated by eminently fallible and sinful human beings, the children of their own age and culture, that we call the Bible.

This is to say that what our scriptural texts, both Old and New Testament, do is to put us more deeply in touch with the ultimate Mystery, because we can only draw anywhere near it if it reveals itself to us. This is what the Old Testament does: Abraham is called in Genesis 12 to 'Go – to a land that I shall show you,' and because the mystery is so powerful, he does, and it turns out to be the right move.

Earlier in Genesis we learn that the Mystery is deeply involved with human beings, even worried about them: 'It is not good for the man to be alone,' we hear it say in 2:18, and we watch in astonishment as God comes looking for Eve and Adam after they have eaten the forbidden fruit. 'Where are you?' God cries at Genesis 3:9, not because God does not know, but because God wants the relationship with his beloved human race.

In Genesis 3:21, even though they have to be exiled from the Garden because of what they have done, God sits down and makes leather garments for them. This is a vulnerable God that puts itself at the service of human beings, and that is not the kind of God that you and I would invent for ourselves.

But the biblical texts are also very much aware that this God is way beyond anything that they can grasp. It is a God that powerfully liberates the people (look at the Exodus story), and a God that cares about the poor and marginalised. Yet it is also a God that is utterly remote, an idea that is conveyed by the word 'holy', as in Exodus 3:5 when Moses learns that he must take off his sandals because he is standing on 'holy ground'; or in Isaiah 6:3, when the prophet is given his vocation, he hears the seraphim cry, 'Holy, Holy, Holy,' and he knows that he is too unclean to be there. Inspiration also needs to teach us that we do not begin, ever, to be 'worthy' of this loving Mystery that we call God.

And yet this God is faithful, even when human beings are not. Look at the way the Mystery puts up with human sinfulness, with the people demanding a king, or the children of Israel accusing God and Moses of genocide in their weary march through the desert. See the gentle way in which he deals with David's appalling behaviour with Bathsheba – both adultery and murder – and the abuse of his kingly power. Or see how God stays close to the northern kingdom in its gradual decline from the old high standards, and how God never abandons the southern kingdom either, even when their disobedience lands them in the horror of Exile.

The God revealed to us in the inspired pages of the Bible is one who will come to judgement and demand accounts of us, treating us as responsible, and of course beloved, adults. It is the God of the Psalms to whom the poets can sing in love and gratitude and intimacy, but to whom they know that they can also express anger and complaint. That Old Testament God, to go back to a previous chapter, is the God of the New Testament, and both these libraries of texts are inspired and reveal the mystery to us.

That is why contemporaries of Jesus, such as those Pharisees, who were much better men than Christians tend to realise, or the monastic-looking group who preserved and probably wrote the Dead Sea Scrolls discovered at Qumran, kept coming back to what they called the 'Scriptures' to make sense of their situation. The Pharisees were seeking to build a community into which the Messiah might come, and so they applied to themselves as laymen the purity rules of the books of Exodus and Leviticus. Their contemporaries at Qumran read through the scrolls about building the Temple and the prophecies of Habakkuk and Nahum and Isaiah, to name but three, in order to read off their story in God's undying inspired word.

So, to end with, here is my suggestion about the doctrine of inspiration. Think about it in this way: the Bible may be said to be inspired if and only if as you read or hear the text, or see it engraved in stained glass or performed on stage, you encounter the God of Abraham, Isaac and Jacob. Likewise the New Testament is inspired if and only if as you turn its pages or listen to it speaking to you, it turns out that you encounter there the Jesus who spoke to his grieving disciples on the road to Emmaus:

> And look! Two of them on that day were journeying to a village that was sixty stades (seven or eight miles) distant from Jerusalem. And they were talking to each other about all these things that had happened. And as they talked, Jesus himself actually drew near and was journeying with them. Their eyes were prevented from recognising him. He said to them, 'What words are these which you are exchanging with each other as you walk?' And they stopped dead, looking sullen.
>
> One of them, called Cleopas, answered him, 'Are you the only one visiting Jerusalem, and you don't know the things that have taken place in Jerusalem during these days?'

And he said to them, 'What sort of things?' They told him, 'Things about Jesus the Nazarene, who appeared as a man, a prophet, powerful in word and deed before God and before the entire populace? How they handed him over, our Chief Priests and rulers, to a death-sentence, and they crucified him? We had been hoping that he was going to be the one to ransom [or 'liberate'] Israel. And now, some women from our lot have astonished us; they got to the tomb at dawn and didn't find his body, and they came saying that they'd seen a vision of angels, who said he was alive. And some of those with us went off to the tomb; and they found it just as the women had said – but they did not see him.'

And he said to them, 'What *fools* you are! [So] lacking in imagination, [not] to believe all that the prophets had said! Wasn't it *essential* for the Messiah to suffer this and [so] enter into his glory?' And he started with Moses and with all the prophets, and explained the stuff about himself in all the Scriptures.

And they drew near to the village to which they were journeying – and he pretended to be journeying further. But they pressed him, saying, 'Stay with us, because it is towards evening, and the day has already declined.' And he went in to stay with them. And it turned out, as he lay down [to eat] with them, he took the loaf, and blessed [it] and broke [it] and handed [it] over to them – and their eyes were opened wide, and they recognised him! And he vanished from them.

And they said to each other, 'Wasn't our heart burning within as he was talking to us on the journey? As he was opening up the Scriptures to us?'

And they got up at that moment and returned to Jerusalem, and found the Eleven gathered, and their companions, who were [all] saying, 'The Lord really is risen, and he's appeared to Simon.' And they in their turn related the things that had happened on the way, and how he'd been recognised by them in the breaking of the bread.
(Luke 24:13-32)

To conclude then, who do you think is inspired? Is it, in the case of our New Testament, those who originally saw the events as narrated? Is it the first oral reporter of them? Or is it the first person to put them down on papyrus? Or the person who edited the patchwork together? Or those who combined sources like Q in the Gospels of Matthew and Luke?[5] Or what about the final redactors of the Gospels? And then, since most people do not know the original languages,

---

5. The explanation for why Matthew and Luke run so close to each other when they are not following Mark is called *Quelle*, the German word for 'source', often abbreviated as 'Q'.

are the translators of your version inspired? Or what about the scholars who can piece together the original events, who can use their brains and skills to interpret a cuneiform tablet that transforms our understanding of the biblical text or to excavate an ancient Israelite tell? Or is it the community for which the texts were written and in which they are read today? We are dealing with mystery here, for we are dealing with the undying freshness of God.

Questions

1. What does 'inspiration' mean?

2. Can the biblical authors make mistakes?

3. Does it matter if we are given different and contradictory accounts of the same event, do you think?

CHAPTER 35

Did the Resurrection really happen?

And so we come to the question of Resurrection, which in some ways is the hardest to cope with, and the most important. It is hard because in our secular age the normal assumption is that anything that looks 'supernatural', or that seems to break the rules that science has laid down for our guidance, cannot possibly be true. And this is particularly so in the case of death. When someone has recently died, the person is no longer there and their body soon starts to decay. How, then, can Christians possibly maintain that there is 'life after death'?

In our arrogance we tend to assume that we know more than the ancients, that they were a pretty credulous lot, ready to believe almost anything if they could simply avoid facing the yawning chasm of certain death. But that is a mistake; they knew far more than we about what death meant, for they were face to face with it in a way that we are not in our clinically hygienic society. So they knew better than we do what death is like, and about what happens with death, and perhaps they hoped for life after death; after all, they knew the teachings of that eminently Jewish work, the book of Wisdom. Moreover, the Pharisees, who were very close to Jesus in certain respects, for all the tensions between them, believed that if God were indeed to be the God they knew from the experience of the community, then death could not be the end of the story, or God would be an unjust God.

But that is not quite what the documents of our New Testament mean by resurrection. Consider the situation: the disciples had been with Jesus for a good long time, and it looks as though they thought something significant would happen when they went up to Jerusalem, for all Jesus' predictions of arrest and death. Then they all ran away.

It is important to recognise that important fact, because all the Gospels agree on it, and it means that the disciples, both men and women, were not expecting Jesus' Resurrection. The men had disappeared in a panic, and although the brave women stayed to the bitter end, the fact that they eventually ended up bringing spices to the tomb to anoint his empty body means that resurrection was very far from what they were expecting. So those scholars who say that all this talk of Resurrection appearances is just wishful thinking are missing the point: those sad and fearful disciples were simply not in a place where they could possibly expect Jesus' return.

Other scholars say that the Resurrection stories are just a dramatised form of a feeling that 'wouldn't it be nice if Jesus were still with us?' This is likewise to miss the point: none of them was expecting Jesus' Resurrection; all of them were either terrified or depressed. For the most part, they did not even recognise the risen Lord when he appeared to them. And yet, within a very few days of the disgusting and brutal death that he had endured, there they were proclaiming with absolute certainty that Jesus was still alive and that, in the terms of the earliest form of the Easter proclamation, 'God raised him from the dead.' So God was vindicated, and their original belief in him was vindicated. But make no mistake about it: they were not expecting it, and yet from somewhere they found the courage to proclaim widely that Jesus was after all alive and with God, and that they had a mission to perform.

The unassailable fact is that with the Resurrection something very new, very different and very unexpected had taken place that now affected their theology, their thinking about God, in a very permanent way. This had three elements to it. First, it meant that their understanding of God had to change; it was not just that God had vindicated Jesus, but also that God could actually intervene even in the disgusting and brutally painful situation of crucifixion. Second, it meant that their understanding of who Jesus was had to change; very soon indeed they realised that, if they were to do justice to their experience of him, they had to use language of him that had hitherto been used only of God, and so their understanding of God became far richer. Third, it meant that they had a job to do (you will see that in each of the Easter stories), of proclaiming this very new state of affairs.

The result is that every single one of our 27 New Testament documents pays tribute, each in their own different way, to the Resurrection of Jesus, and to the permanence of Jesus and his Holy Spirit with them. Because the authors are only human, they present this account of what God has done in their own unique way. We have not space here to read all the accounts in which they describe it, but the following will give you the flavour.

The first account that we have of the Resurrection comes, you may not be surprised to learn, from the pen, or at least the dictation, of the apostle Paul:

> Fellow Christians, I am making known to you [again!] the gospel which I gospelled to you, which you received, on which you stand secure, through which you are being saved, the terms in which I gospelled you, if you still hold it fast (unless, of course, you came thoughtlessly to faith).

So, in the first place [you will recall], I passed on to you what I had also received,

- that Christ died for our sins according to the Scriptures
- that he was buried
- that he was raised on the third day according to the Scriptures
- and that he appeared to Kephas, then to the Twelve.

Then he appeared to more than five hundred brothers and sisters at once, of whom the majority still remain [alive], although some have fallen asleep. Then he appeared to James, and then to all the apostles. Last of all, as though to an abortion, he appeared also to me. I am, you see, the least of the apostles; I'm not fit to be called an 'apostle', because I persecuted God's church. By God's grace, I am what I am, and God's grace towards me hasn't turned out unprofitably. Actually, I worked harder than all of them – not really me, though, so much as God's grace [working] with me. So whoever, they or I, that's how we preach, and that's how you came to faith.
(1 Corinthians 15:1-11)

You can see the decisive impact of Paul's encounter with Jesus, so important to Luke that, as we have said, he describes it no fewer than three times in Acts. What Luke does not quite express, though, possibly because it was altogether too intimate a matter, was the important point of what had happened to Paul. It was not just that he came to realise that Jesus was unmistakably alive, and that therefore these crazy Christians were right, after all, in their insistence that God had raised their Messiah from his disgusting death. It was also, and we should not be shy to admit this, that Paul had fallen head over heels in love with him, to a point where he could hardly write a sentence without mentioning the name of his beloved Jesus. This brought Paul to a place where (and you can see this happening in his letters) any problem that he encounters has hereinafter to be solved in terms of the unfailing presence of the risen Jesus.

See what he says, writing from prison, about Christ:

You see, for me, to live is Christ, and to die is a gain; but if continuing to live in the body means that my work will bear fruit, then I do not know which I shall choose. I am torn between the two: I have a desire to depart and be with Christ (for that is far better).
(Philippians 1:21-23)

And remember his firm statement in Philippians 1:21 that 'for me, to live is Christ' (and compare what he says in Galatians 2:20: 'I live, no longer I, but Christ lives in me: the life that I am now living in the flesh, I live with the life of the Son of God, who loved me and handed himself over for me.') You should also look out, all the way through Paul, for that phrase 'in Christ', which is where Christians belong. Sit with it (he uses it again and again) and ask Paul what he means by it.

But for a real encounter with that love, what about this, from the very difficult letter to the Romans, at the end of a long passage where Paul is trying to give the Roman church reasons for confidence in what God has done in Christ.

> So what shall we say to this? If God is on our side, who is against us? God [you remember] did not spare his own Son, but handed him over on behalf of all of us – how can he help but give us everything as a free gift, along with him [the greatest of God's gifts]? Who shall bring charges against God's chosen ones? God is the One who Reckons-as-Righteous – who is the Condemner? Christ Jesus is the one who died, and – more than that – was raised!
>
> He is the one who is at God's right hand.
>
> He is the one who intercedes for us.
>
> What shall separate us from Christ's love? Affliction? Anguish? Persecution? Famine? Nakedness? Danger? Execution? As it is written,
>
> 'For your sake we are done to death all day [long].
>
> We are reckoned as sheep for the slaughter.'[6]
>
> No – in these matters we are winning a most glorious victory through the one who loved us. I am persuaded, you see, that neither Death nor Life, nor Angelic nor Demonic Rulers, nor Present nor Future Events, nor Powers, nor Height nor Depth, nor any other created thing, will be able to separate us from the love of God, which is in Christ Jesus our Lord.
>
> (Romans 8:31-39)

Now I hope you notice that none of these excerpts from Paul's writings says exactly the same thing about the Resurrection. That is not what it is about. The important point is Paul's certainty that God has raised Jesus from the dead. And when you meet Paul, just try telling him that he was fooling himself and it was all wishful thinking on his part. But stand back a bit as you do so, for he has a short fuse.

So we should not be too alarmed when we look at the Gospel accounts. I am going to read with you some of the Gospel stories, just to give you a feel of the range of approaches that these very different authors adopt towards the Resurrection. Does it matter that they all tell a different story?

---

6. Psalm 44:22

Not in my view. What I think they have in common is not a uniformity, like the reports of last night's football match, but a joint certainty, first that God raised Jesus from the dead, and second that this means that they have a job to do.

We start with the ending of Mark's Gospel:

And when the Sabbath was at last over, Mary the Magdalene and Mary of James, and Salome bought spices in order to come and anoint him. And extremely early on the first of the Sabbaths they come to the tomb. The sun had already risen. And they said to themselves, 'Who will roll away the stone for us from the door of the tomb?' And looking up [or 'recovering their sight'] they see that the stone has been rolled away. For it was very big. And going into the tomb they saw a young man sitting on the right wearing a white robe. And they were alarmed. But he said to the women, 'Do not be alarmed. You seek Jesus the Nazarene, the one who was crucified. He is risen; he is not here. See the place where they put him. But go, tell his disciples, and Peter, that "he is going before you [or "leading you"] into Galilee. There you will see him, as he said to you."' And going out they fled from the tomb, for quivering and astonishment had hold of them. And they said nothing to nobody. For they were afraid . . .
(Mark 16:1-8)

Then, for a different angle on the story, what about this, from Matthew:

The next day, which was after the Preparation Day, the Chief Priests and Pharisees gathered together [literally, 'synagogued'] to Pilate, and said, 'Lord, we have remembered that this impostor said, while he was still alive, "I am being raised after three days." So order the grave to be made secure until the third day; [we don't want] his disciples to come and steal him and tell the people "he's been raised from the dead", [because then] the last imposture will be worse than the first.' Pilate told them, 'You have a guard; go and secure it as you know [how].' They went off and secured the tomb, with the guard.

As they went, look! Some of the guard came to the city and reported to the chief priests everything that had happened. And they gathered together ['synagogued'] with the elders, and took counsel, and gave the soldiers plenty of silver pieces, telling them, 'Say that his disciples came by night and stole him while we were asleep. And if the report gets to the governor, we'll reassure him and see you right.' They took the silver pieces and did as they had been taught. And this story has spread about among the Jews until the present day.
(Matthew 27:62-66; 28:11-15)

Do you see the point? Incredulity: then, as now, it seems impossible that death should not be the end.

Luke deals with this incredulity (which is in all the Gospel narratives, by the way) in his own way:

> As they were saying these things, he himself stood in the middle of them, and he says to them, 'Peace [be] with you.' They were panic-stricken and terrified – they thought they were seeing a spirit! And he said to them, 'Why are you so disturbed, and for what reason do doubts arise in your mind? See my hands and my feet: it is me, in person. Feel me, and see that a spirit does not have flesh and bones, as you see that I have.' Saying this, he showed them his hands and feet. As they still didn't believe (it was too good to be true), and were [just] marvelling, he said to them, 'Do you have anything edible here?' They gave him a piece of grilled fish, and he took it, in front of them, and ate it!
> (Luke 24:36-43)

And then there is, as there always must be, the Gospel of John. Here is a story that does not appear in any of the other Gospels:

> But Mary stood outside by the tomb, weeping. And so, as she wept, she stooped down [to look] into the tomb; and she sees two angels in white [garments] sitting [there], one at the head and one at the feet, where Jesus' body had lain. And they say to her, 'Woman, why are you weeping?' She says to them, 'They took my Lord away, and I don't know where they have put him.' Saying this, she turned around backwards and sees Jesus standing there – and she did not know that it was Jesus. Jesus says to her, 'Woman, why are you weeping? Whom are you looking for?' She, thinking that it was the gardener, says to him, 'Sir' [or 'Lord'] 'if you have taken him, tell me where you have put him, and I shall move him.' Jesus says to her, 'Mary.' She turns round and says to him in Aramaic, 'Rabbouni' (which means 'Teacher'). Jesus says to her, 'Don't touch me – for I have not yet gone up to the Father. But go to my brethren, and tell them, "I am going up to my Father and your Father, and my God and your God."' Mary the Magdalene comes announcing to the disciples, 'I have seen the Lord,' and [that] he had said these things to her.
> (John 20:11-18)

The name of what is going on here, between the weeping lady longing for the body of her beloved and the seeming gardener who actually is that Beloved, is none other than the victory of love.

And that victory of love is, make no mistake about it, what is going on in the New Testament's insistence on Jesus' Resurrection. It is not a belief that you can take or leave: as Paul told us at the beginning, if there is no such thing as resurrection, as some of his Corinthians were inclined to believe, then there is no such thing as Christianity. It is not magic; it does not mean that we do not suffer or grieve, or that serious illnesses are miraculously cured. It does mean that at the heart of our faith, God is indeed in charge.

You could check this out in any one of the other documents of the New Testament, each in their very different way, but what about these passages, from the last book of all? What do they tell us of the author's faith in the Resurrection of Jesus?

'Do not be afraid; I am the First and the Last, and the Living One. And I was dead, and look! I am alive for ever and ever. And I possess the keys of Death and [the keys] of Hell.

'Therefore write down what you saw: both the things that are and the things that are about to happen after this, the mystery of the seven stars which you saw at my right, and the seven golden lampstands.'
(Revelation 1:17b-20a)

'Worthy is the slaughtered Lamb
to receive power and wealth and wisdom and strength and honour and glory and blessing.'
And every creature in heaven and on earth and under the earth and in the sea, and I heard everything in them saying,
'To the One Sitting on the Throne and to the Lamb
blessing and honour and glory and power for ever and ever.'
(Revelation 5:12-13)

And I saw no Temple in her, for the Lord God Almighty is her Temple – and the Lamb. And the City has no need of the sun or of the moon to give her light, for the Glory of God illuminated her; and the Lamb is her lamp.
(Revelation 21:22, 23)

And he showed me the River of the Water of Life, bright as crystal, coming from the throne of God and of the Lamb. In the middle of the City's street, and its river, on both sides is the Tree of Life, yielding twelve fruits, every month each one yielding its fruit; and the leaves of the Tree [serve] for the healing of the nations. And no longer will there be any cursed thing there. And the Throne of God and of the Lamb shall be in her; and his slaves shall worship him, and they shall see his face, and his name shall be on their foreheads. And night shall be no more, and they have no need of the light of a lamp or the light of the sun, because the Lord God shall shine upon them; and they shall reign forever and ever.

(Revelation 22:1-5)

Questions

1. Does it matter that there are different accounts of the Resurrection in the New Testament?

2. Did God indeed raise Jesus from the dead, do you think?

3. Does the Resurrection make a difference to us?